श्रीकालिदासविरचितं

मालविकाग्निमित्रम्

MĀLAVIKĀGNIMITRAM OF KĀLIDĀSA

श्रीकालिदासविरचितं

मालविकाग्निमित्रम्

MĀLAVIKĀGNIMITRAM OF KĀLIDĀSA

Critically edited with introduction, translation, notes and useful appendices

by

C. R. DEVADHAR

MOTILAL BANARSIDASS PUBLISHERS
PRIVATE LIMITED • DELHI

10th Reprint : Delhi, 2018
Third Edition : Delhi, 1966

ISBN : 978-81-208-0221-6

MOTILAL BANARSIDASS
41 U.A. Bungalow Road, Jawahar Nagar, Delhi 110 007
1 B, Jyoti Studio Compound, Kennedy Bridge, Nana Chowk, Mumbai 400 007
203 Royapettah High Road, Mylapore, Chennai 600 004
236, 9th Main III Block, Jayanagar, Bengaluru 560 011
8 Camac Street, Kolkata 700 017
Ashok Rajpath, Patna 800 004
Chowk, Varanasi 221 001

Printed in India

by RP Jain at NAB Printing Unit,
A-44, Naraina Industrial Area, Phase I, New Delhi–110028
and published by JP Jain for Motilal Banarsidass Publishers (P) Ltd,
41 U.A. Bungalow Road, Jawahar Nagar, Delhi-110007

PREFACE

It will be readily admitted that in spite of the many critical editions of the plays of Kālidāsa, editions of the plays on the lines of the up-to-date editions of the classics in the West have not so far been published. This edition is, to our knowledge, the first which is infinitely more useful and handy than either having the translation on the same page just below the text, or at the end of the text. Further it has been our endeavour to make the work as critical and useful for the students as possible, without either encumbering it with tiresome discussions of technical and scholastic points, or skipping over difficult and necessary details about *Variae Lectiones* or rhetorical or grammatical points. Special care has been taken to give a correct orthography of the Prakrit words, after a careful and critical comparison of the various editions of the play before us.

In preparing this edition, we have fully availed ourselves of the already numerous published editions of the play and critical articles and books on the subject; and we gratefully make our acknowledgements to them.

We are very thankful to our publishers for their readiness in undertaking to bring out this edition.

C. R. Devadhar

PREFACE TO THE THIRD EDITION

This third edition is virtually a reprint of the second, and we take this opportunity of expressing our gratitude to our publishers, M/s Motilal Banarsidass, who have so kindly and so readily undertaken to bring out the present volume.

Poona
Sept. 9, 1966

C. R. Devadhar

INTRODUCTION.

Kalidasa—the Poet.

What De Quincy says of Shakespeare meets the case of Kālidāsa far more appropriately than that of the English poet. "That he lived and that he died and that he was a little lower than the angels," this pretty nearly makes up the amount of our undisputed report of the great poet. Tradition has given us numerous legends, but they are no more than a mere farrago of absurd anachronisms. Modern research has done a good deal indeed to lift the veil from India's past, and yet an exact and authentic account of the author is yet to be given. Of the numerous theories advanced by scholars regarding his age, only two seem now to have the support of indefeasible evidence both internal and external. There is the strong testimony of the quotations in the Mahābhāṣya of Patañjali which goes to prove that Sanskrit court epic dated from before the time of the Christian Era, and the same is now amply corroborated by the recent epigraphic researches of modern scholars. This lends feasibility to the traditional legend of a king Vikrama the founder of the Saṁvat Era—57 B. C. who had at his court a circle of nine gems including Kālidāsa, Varāhamihira and Ghaṭakarpara.

It is on the other hand contended that a comparison of the inscriptions which are mostly panegyrics of kings and which employ the Gupta Era which was first used by Candragupta Vikramāditya II, with the classical poems proves that the poetical style of the inscriptions prevailing in the fourth and fifth centuries did not much differ from the style of the Kāvyas; and on the strength of this and similar epigraphic evidence it has been sought to prove that Kālidāsa must have flourished under Candragupta II who assumed the title of Vikramāditya and succeeded his father Samudragapta in 375 A. D. and made Ujjain his capital. Vincent Smith in his early history of India (p. 304, footnote) expresses the view that the earlier works of Kālidāsa were composed before 413 A. D. during the regime of Candragupta, and his later works were written under Kumāragupta I (413 A. D. to 455 A. D.) and that possibly his literary career extended even into the reign of Skandagupta (455 A. D. 480 A. D.).

This is the sum of our knowledge of the external details of the poet's life; and yet it may be asked: Are the few broad bare facts of life the only thing one should prize? Is not the poet known to us in the far richer world of his imaginative creations? He neighbours us on every side, rouses our intellect, moves our passions, and stimulates our activity. It is well said, "The magnitude of life is not as to its external displacements but as to its subjective experiences."

The impression that one gathers of the poet from his works is that of a man, deeply learned in literature and philosophy and other traditional lore of the times, and more deeply learned in the book of natare. A charming trait of his personality is his modesty which Coleridge recognises as a sure sign of great genius. He was a widely-travelled man and was a keen observer of nature. Not only did the sublime and wild aspects of nature stir his imagination, but the milder and minuter manifestations also caught his fancy, and he is very fond of describing to us how the garden-plants bend to catch the beauty of spring, or how the march of seasons affects them.

But above all he is a student of the human heart and is rarely excelled in his "delicate appreciation of its most refined and tender emotions and his familiarity with the workings and counter-workings of its conflicting feelings." Particularly he excels in depicting love "from the first suggestion in an innocent mind to the perfection of passion." All the three plays sing of love happy at the last and 'havened after tempest.'

Of his three plays, Mālavikāgnimitra was the earliest written and Śākuntala came last, while the Vikramorvaśīya belongs to his middle period. We have merely to compare the prologues of the three plays to be convinced of this; for in our play the author deems it necessary to explain away what would seem presumption in a contemporary poet to have offered his play for exhibition before the elite to the exclusion of the plays of renowned writers. There is no such diffidence in the next two plays; moreover it will be observed from a comparison of the three plays that "his ethical outlook on life was becoming progressively deeper and more spiritual." And lastly in spite of the frequent *curiosa felicitas* of his diction, we do not come across that smoothness and rounded perfection and inevitable grace that mark the mature style of the poet.

The political background of the play.

The Mālavikāgnimitra is a drama of court intrigue. King Agnimitra is a historical character of the second century before Christ; he was the son of Puṣpamitra—,

The commander-in-chief—who killed his master Bṛhadratha Maurya and established himself as a sovereign of the Maurya dominions, thus founding a dynasty known to history as that of the Śungas (183 B. C.). As the seat of empire was in Pātaliputra, and as Agnimitra's capital is Vidiśā—the modern Bhilsa–it is possible that he was appointed as regent of certain provinces during his father's lifetime. In the later years of his reign, Puṣpamitra was threatened by serious danger. Menander, the Greek king of Kabul and the Punjab wanted to emulate the exploits of Alexander and at the head of a formidable force annexed the Indus delta, the peninsula of Saurāṣṭra (Kāthiawar), Mathurā and besieged Madhyamikā (Nāgari near Chitore) and Sāketam in southern Oudh, and threatened even Pātaliputra, the capital. This invasion (155-153 B. C.) was repelled by Puṣpamitra after a severe struggle and Menander was obliged to retire to his own country. The fight with the Greek cavalry force in our play seems to be an echo of the struggle with Menander from whose repulse in 153 B. C. until the bombardment of Calicut by Vascodagama in A. D. 1502, India enjoyed immunity from attack under European leadership.

The war with the king of Vidarbha also seems to be a historical occurrence, in which Yajñasena was worsted by king Agnimitra, as a result of which Vidarbha was divided between two provinces, separated by the river Varadā (Wardha) which is now the boundary between Berar aud the central Provinces. Agnimitra appointed Mādhavasena to the southern and Yajñasena to the northern principality.

The poet has very skilfully utilised these historical events for the purposes of his play. In the last act we get a report of the victory won by Agnimitra's army over the king of Vidarbha; among those who came with the good news were two girls who recognized Mālavikā as the Vidarbha princess; and this served to remove all objections, if indeed there were any, to Agnimitra's marrying below his rank. Secondlv the communication by Puspamitra of the victory won by Vasumitra (his grandson, and son of Agnimitra and Dhāriṇī) over the cavalry of the Yavanas who had captured the sacrificial horse let loose by Puṣpamitra is an event of great joy to Dhāriṇī and to the ladies of the king's household, and in the moment of her elation, the queen unites Mālavikā with her royal lover.

Analysis of the plot.

Act I. After the invocation, the manager tells his assistant how he has received from the spectators the order to act the play 'Mālavikāgnimitra' at that spring festival; and when the latter wonders how the spectators could have passed over the compositions of famous poets and done such great honour to the work of a modern, the poet Kālidāsa, the former tells him that it is all right. 'For a poem is not good because it is old; nor is every new poem to be blamed because it is new;' he then bids him make haste and help him to carry out the order of the spectators.

Then enter Kaumudikā and Bakulāvalikā and we learn from their conversation that king Agnimitra has seen in the picture-gallery a new painting of queen Dhāriṇī and her attendants. Among them is Mālavikā, who is so beautiful that the king is smitten with love, but the jealous queen takes especial care to guard the original from the sight of the king. Then enters Gaṇadāsa, the dancing-master from whom Bakulāvalikā learns that Mālavikā has proved to be an exceedingly clever and intelligent pupil; and on his asking whence such a choice attendant is secured by the queen she informs him that the queen's brother of inferior caste, Vīrasena by name, in command of a frontier fortress, sent this girl as a present to his sister.

In the main scene of the act, the king is discovered listening to a dispatch from the king of Vidarbha, who had imprisoned the king's cousin Mādhavasena together with his wife and sister and in response to Agnimitra's demand that they should be liberated, he declares that the sister had disappeared in the confusion of the capture, and that Mādhavasena would be released only if Agnimitra set at liberty his brother-in-law, the Maurya minister. This letter so angers Agnimitra that he orders his army under the command of Vīrasena to march against the king of Vidarbha.

At this point, Gautama enters and informs the king that he has devised a plan for bringing Mālavikā into the king's presence. He has set the two dancing-masters by the ears, who soon appear on the stage, each abusing the other vigorously, and claiming for himself pre-eminence in his art. It is agreed that each shall exhibit his best pupil before the king, the queen, and the learned Parivrājikā, Kauśikī. The queen raises a number of difficulties and disfavours the whole proceeding, but her jealous opposition is overborne. The sound of the drum now is heard which was a signal for them to proceed to the concert-hall of the palace where the orchestral arrangements are by now made ready.

Act II. The scene is laid in the concert-hall. The Parivrājikā, the mistress of the ceremony, directs that

Gaṇadāsa shall exhibit his pupil first; upon which Mālavikā enters in thin stage-costume and she dances and sings a song which pretty clearly expresses her own passion for the king. The king is almost transported to find that she is lovelier than the picture; the Vidūṣaka manages to detain her for a little while by pretending that he has observed a serious flaw in her performance and when she is finally permitted to depart, both she and the king are deeply in love. The hour of noon is now announced, whereupon the exhibition of the other dancing-master is postponed.

Act. III. The scene is laid in the Pramadavana garden. From the conversation of two maids we learn that although both the teachers are thoroughly acquainted with the science of dancing, yet the teaching power of Ganadāsa was ranked the higher of the two on account of the admirable qualities of his pupil, Mālavikā. The king is now desperately in love with her but in order to spare the feelings of Dhāriṇī, he makes no use of his power to behold the object of his desire. We are further informed that a favourite Aśoka tree is late to blossom, and requires, so the belief runs, to be touched by the foot of a handsome woman to be induced to burst into blossom.

After this introductory scene, the king and the Vidūṣaka enter. The former describes how desperately he is in love with Mālavikā, whereupon the Vidūṣaka his confidant asks him to possess his soul in patience because as a matter of fact he has devised an expedient for ensuring the end that he wished to attain. He then reminds the King of his promise to join Irāvatī and pass the day enjoying a ride in the swing with her in the garden. Both now enter the garden, but before Irāvatī's arrival,

Mālavikā enters, as she is commissioned by Dhārinī to touch the Asoka-tree with her foot and thus induce it to blossom for the queen herself is disabled to perform the ceremony, as owing to Gautama's carelessness she has had a fall from a swing and is not able to move her feet in consequence The King and his confidant now hide in a thicket. Presently Bakulāvalikā appears on the scene and while she adorns Mālavikā for the ceremony she engages her in conversation about the King. A third pair, Irāvatī somewhat flushed with wine, and her maid Nipunikā, now enter, and they also conceal themselves to spy upon the two girls; the two girls believe themselves to be alone, and Mālavikā talks freely of her love and Bakulāvalikā tells her how the king also is pining for her. The King now starts forward and expresses his love for Mālavikā, whereupon Irāvatī, mad with jealousy joins the group, dismisses the two girls and rudely snapping at the king and not accepting his excuses, such as they are, leaves him with words of stinging jealousy to inform Dhārinī of what is going forward.

Act IV. The Vidūsaka informs the king that Mālavikā and her friend with fetters on them are locked in the cellar by queen Dhārinī who has given orders to the door-keeper that they shall be let out only on presentations of her signet-ring bearing the seal of a serpent. He, however, has a plan in his head, which he will presently employ to release them. The king then pays a visit to the queen to inquire how she is doing, when the Vidūsaka rushes into their presence, pretending that he has been bitten by a venomous snake on the finger, and shows them the two marks of the teeth. Then imploring the king to take care of his helpless mother he awakens genuine sympathy in the queen who readily parts with her signet-ring bearing a serpent-seal, as it was required by the poison-doctor to effect a magical cure. He thus procures the freedom of Mālavikā and her friend and leading them to the summer-house brings about a meeting between the King and Mālavikā. The love-scene is again interrupted by Irāvatī; but the timely news that princess Vasulakṣmī has been terribly frightened by a brown ape and would be comforted only by him, extricates the King from a very embarrassing situation indeed. The act ends with the announcement that even before five nights have elapsed from the time of the ceremony, the Asoka tree is covered all over with blossoms.

Act V. The queen has sent word to the King that she desires him to go with her to behold the beauty of the Aśoka in blossoms; the maids announce that the avenging forces of the King have subdued the King of Vidarbha. The King and the Vidūsaka now proceed to the garden where they find the queen and her attendants including Mālavikā waiting for him under the Aśoka tree. At this point the chamberlain comes with a message from the minister that the present sent by the king of Vidarbha included two accomplished maidens who were till now not introduced because they represented themselves to be fatigued with the journey. They are now brought before the group gathered under the tree, and give considerable surprise to everyone by falling prostrate before Mālavikā whom they address "Our princess". They inform the King that Mālavikā was the younger sister of prince Mādhavasena and that when he came into the power of his kinsman, the king of Vidarbha, Mālavikā was secretly carried off by Sumati, the minister of the captive prince, while attendants like them were left behind. At this point, the Parivrājikā takes up the tale and declares how her brother who was the minister of Mādhavasena, had rescued her and Mālavikā from the king of Vidarbha, and had started for Agnimitra's court ; but they were set upon and overpowered by bandits; her brother was killed and she herself separated from Mālavikā who came from the power of the foresters into that of Vīrasena and was sent by him to the queen. She, for her own part, assumed the red robes and made her way to Agnimitra's court where she found Mālavikā again. She, however, forbore to speak of this, because of a prophecy that Mālavikā would have to endure for one year only the position of a slave before she obtained a husband of equal rank. Agnimitra now issues orders regarding the terms to be granted to the king of Vidarbha, half of whose territory he now assigns to Mādhavasena the brother of Mālavikā, their dominions to lie respectively north and south of the Varadā river.

Now a letter arrives from Puṣpamitra announcing that Vasumitra, Agnimitra's son by Dhāriṇī, who was appointed as the defender of the sacrificial horse let loose by Puṣpamitra, his grand-father, has won victory over a cavalry squadron of the Yavanas. Puṣpamitra further invited the court to be present at the sacrifice which he would now offer.

The queen Dhāriṇī, overjoyed by the news of her son's victory, now sends an attendant to the ladies of the harem with the glad news and asks her to tell Irāvatī of the promise she had made to Mālavikā when she deputed her to perform the ceremony of fertilizing the Asoka, and of her birth also. Irāvatī communicates, though somewhat ungraciously, her concurrence in the arrangement and queen Dhāriṇī now presents Mālavikā to the king. The play concludes with the king's expressing the hope that he may ever retain his queen's regard and that his subjects may never suffer any calamity while Agnimitra was king.

Appreciation of the plot.

The plot of the Mālavikāgnimitra is a masterpiece of clever construction, where the interest is chiefly concentrated on the central story of the king's love for the maid, and every incident is subordinated to the main theme. The element of conflict, which is of the very essence of drama is mainly external; we see how the queen almost feebly and pathetically opposes the king's attempts to secure the sight of Mālavikā; but finding that the forces ranged against her were too strong for her, she decides to go along the current and make the better of its course rather than endeavour to stem the tide at the risk of a capsize. She cleverly withdraws from the conflict, realising it was her November to the young rival's May, and hopes forlornly that her chance lies in 'playing one new favourite against another'. The irascible Irāvatī, flushed with wine and with the grapes she has gathered in Cupid's vine-yard, next comes to disturb the noon-day tryst, and succeeds for a while to veil the sky with clouds, but a clever ruse of the Vidūṣaka and the queen's serene though not yet quite frank and open acceptance of Mālavikā combine to lift the cloud and the lovers are finally united to the discomfiture of the irascible Irāvatī, who none too calmly resigns to the inevitable. The final stages of the action are cleverly managed and the anagnorisis is a clever piece of concentrated and brief narrative, where from the maids the thread is cleverly taken up by the Parivrājikā.

It will thus be seen that the plot is essentially coherent and organic; there is no bye-plot, so that our attention is focussed upon the central theme. There is further a clever selection of incidents which are presented on the stage, the remaining being relegated to the entr' acts which are brief narratives put in the form of dialogue linking up incidents of the previous act with those of the succeeding one. These scenes—the 'scenes a faire' the scenes which had to be done, which if shirked would cause dumb disappointment in the spectator if they take place behind closed doors and if they are only narrated—these scenes are chosen with a view to arouse and sustain the interest of the audience, and present to us the spectacle of the contending forces at close grapple. These are the great dramatic moments of the story ; and there are also those scenes which have been chosen from the beauty of the spectacle such as the music-hall scene where the lovely Mālavikā draped in diaphanous garments,a vision of sensuous beauty,bursts upon our sight, or the garden-scene where the clever Bakulāvalikā artfully pours love's sugared delights into the ears of the eager maiden and the romance of the lover's noon-day tryst is rendered with all the tenderness and incisive vigour the poet could command.

Characters.

King Agnimitra is commonly criticised as an unheroic hero. He is an elderly person whose 'yeasting youth' is by now expected to clear itself and 'crystal turn again', when love's little follies are laid on the shelf One has however to remember that the poet is here dealing with a historical person and is only furnishing artistic raiment to traditional material. He has given us studies of men not in life's moments of stress and strain but in its 'secluded pleasances and verdurous wooded ways.' And here is a picture of an oriental monarch, devoting his hours of gilded leisure to the pursuit of love and beauty, for benign providence has preserved his father to pursue his ambitious career of conquest and given him a son who even at that tender age has given a foretaste of his masterful and vigorous manhood. So the king has provided himself with a philosophy of tender frailty. "Women are angels wooing, things won are done, joy's soul lies in the doing." The lovely but irascible Irāvatī is passed over and the handsome Mālavikā who has "a very shower of beauty for her earthly dower" now takes her place. He believes what the English poet has said:—

"Who loves but one lassie, just rides for a fall:
The ladies, God bless them! There is safety in numbers;
Love one, love fifty, I have room for them all."

The king does, however, realise that mere lounging and larking is not enough. Witness the quick decision he takes in dealing with the king of Vidarbha, and his last prayer is quite significant. "There is not a blessing that will not be secured by his subjects, while Agnimitra is their protector."

Mālavikā. By birth, beauty and accomplishments in the fine arts, the triune of perfect starriness, Mālavikā is the most attractive of the young maidens drawn by our poet. Her love for the king is as natural as the breaking out of blossoms, and it is this devotion of an innocent and pure maiden that hallows and elevates the love-story above the sordid pruriency of a vulgar liaison. She is extremely clever and intelligent and shows considerable acuteness when she boldly tells the king how she had reason to be afraid of the queen, considering the great fear in which the king himself stood of her. In Mālavikā the poet has given us a rare vision of sensuous beauty. 'Awake for ever in a sweet unrest' that pretty correctly pictures the temper of her mind almost throughout the play.

With regard to the other female characters of the play it may be remarked that although there is very little scope for the development of character, yet every one of them is very carefully individualised. Dhāriṇī possesses dignity and forgiveness, and Irāvatī the passionate jealousy and virulence of a co-wife. The Parivrājikā is the female counterpart of the scheming Vidūsaka and considering that Mālavikā was her princess, there is nothing vulgar in her joining the plot of the Vidūsaka.

The liveliest character of the play is the Vidūsaka who is not merely invested with the traditional frippery of the conventional confidant, but is a being of flesh and blood, ready-witted, quick of discernment and resourceful. He takes almost the principal part in securing Mālavikā for the king : he sets the dancing masters by the ears, cleverly detains Mālavikā after her performance, causes queen Dhāriṇī to suffer a fall from the swing; and pretending to be bitten by a snake secures the queen's signet-ring in order to liberate Mālavikā and her friend from imprisonment. He is not the conventional Vidūṣaka of the Sanskrit play who is continually to be knocked over and set on his feet again for the cheap delight of the audience ; and yet much of the humour of the play comes from his witty remarks, from his off-hand manner and from the little audacities of address which he affects from time to time.

मालविकाग्निमित्रम् ।

Malavika and Agnimitra.

॥ श्रीः ॥

मालविकाग्निमित्रम् ।

प्रथमोऽङ्कः ।

एकैश्वर्ये स्थितोऽपि प्रणतबहुफले यः स्वयं कृत्तिवासाः
कान्तासंमिश्रदेहोऽप्यविषयमनसां यः पुरस्ताद्यतीनाम् ।
अष्टाभिर्यस्य कृत्स्नं जगदपि तनुभिर्बिभ्रतो नाभिमानः
सन्मार्गालोकनाय व्यपनयतु स वस्तामसीं वृत्तिमीशः ॥१॥

(नान्द्यन्ते ।)

सूत्रधारः (नेपथ्याभिमुखमवलोक्य)—मारिष इतस्तावत् ।

(प्रविश्य ।)

पारिपार्श्विकः—भाव अयमस्मि ।

सूत्रधारः—अभिहितोऽस्मि परिषदा कालिदासग्रथितवस्तु मालविकाग्निमित्रं नाम नाटकमस्मिन् वसन्तोत्सवे प्रयोक्तव्यमिति । तदारभ्यतां सङ्गीतकम् ।

पारिपार्श्विकः—मा तावत् । प्रथितयशसां भाससौमिल्लकविपुत्रादीनां प्रबन्धानतिक्रम्य वर्तमानकवेः कालिदासस्य क्रियामिमां द्रष्टुं कथं परिषदो बहुमानः ।

सूत्रधारः—अये विवेकविश्रान्तमभिहितम् । पश्य,

पुराणमित्येव न साधु सर्वं
न चापि काव्यं नवमित्यवद्यम् ।

Mālavikā and Agnimitra,

PROLOGUE.

May the Lord who, though enjoying absolute sovereignty from which result many blessings to his votaries, yet himself wears an elephant-hide; who although united in body with his beloved, yet excels the ascetics whose minds are free from (pleasures of) sense; in whom there is no pride, although with his eight-fold forms he sustains the universe—may he remove your state of ignorance that you may behold the right way. (1).

(At the end of the Nāndī)

The stage-manager. (*Looking at the curtain*). Ho! mārisa, just come hither.

(Entering)

Actor. Here am I, sir.

Manager. I have been asked by this assembly to stage the play Mālavikāgnimitra composed by the poet Kālidāsa, at this spring-festival. Therefore let music be begun.

Actor. Nay, not so. How do the spectators pass over the plays of poets of established repute, such as Bhāsa, Saumilla, Kaviputra and others, and do great honour to the work of Kālidāsa, a present-day poet?

Manager. You speak thoughtlessly. See

Every old poem is not good simply because it is old; nor is a poem without charm, because it is new; sound critics favour the one or the

सन्तः परीक्ष्यान्यतरद्भजन्ते
मूढः परप्रत्ययनेयबुद्धिः ॥ २ ॥

पारिपार्श्विकः—आर्यमिश्राः प्रमाणम् ।

सूत्रधारः—तेन हि त्वरतां भवान् ।

**शिरसा प्रथमगृहीतामाज्ञामिच्छामि परिषदः कर्तुम् ।
देव्या इव धारिण्याः सेवादक्षः परिजनोऽयम् ॥ ३ ॥**

(निष्क्रान्तौ ।)

प्रस्तावना ।

(ततः प्रविशति चेटी ।)

चेटी—आणत्तम्हि देवीए धारिणीए अइरप्पउत्तोवदेसं चलिअं णाम णट्टअं अन्दरेण कीरिसी मालविअत्ति णट्टाअरिअं अज्जगणदासं पुच्छिदुं । ता जाव संगीदसालं गच्छेमि । (इति परिक्रामति ।)
[आज्ञप्तास्मि देव्या धारिण्या अचिरप्रयुक्तोपदेशं चलितं नाम नाट्यमन्तरेण कीदृशी मालविकेति नाट्याचार्यमार्यगणदासं प्रष्टुम् । तद्यावत्सङ्गीतशालां गच्छामि ।]

(ततः प्रविशत्याभरणहस्ता द्वितीया चेटी ।)

प्रथमा (द्वितीयां दृष्ट्वा)—हला कोमुदिए कुदो दे इअं धीरदा। जं समीवेण वि मं अदिक्कमंती इदो दिट्ठिं ण देसि ।
[सखि कौमुदिके, कुतस्त इयं धीरता। यत्समीपेनापि मामतिक्रामन्तीतो दृष्टिं न ददासि ।]

द्वितीया—अम्मो बउलावलिआ । सहि इदं देवीए सिप्पिसआसादो आणीदं णाअमुद्दासणाहं अंगुलीअअं सिणिद्धं णिज्झाअन्ती तुह उवालम्भे पडिदम्हि । [अम्मो बकुलावलिका । सखि इदं देव्याः शिल्पिसकाशादानीतं नागमुद्रासनाथमङ्गुलीयकं स्निग्धं निध्यायन्ती तवोपालम्भे पतितास्मि ।]

बकुलावलिका (विलोक्य)—ठाणे खु सज्जदि दिट्ठी । इमिणा

other, after (proper) examination ; while a blockhead is guided by another's judgment. (2)

Actor. You speak the truth, sir.

Manager. Well then, make haste.

I long to carry out the order of the spectators which I have already received with my (bowed) head, even as this attendant of queen Dhāriṇī, intent on serving her. (3)

(Exit).

End of the Prologue

(Enter a maid).

Maid. I am ordered by queen Dhāriṇī to ascertain from the noble Ganadāsa, our dancing master, what degree of proficiency Mālavikā has attained in the Calita at which she is lately taking lessons. So I will proceed to the music hall. *(Walks round).*

(Enter another maid with an ornament in her hand).

First. *(Seeing the other)* Hola, Kaumudikā, what makes you so serious that you do not see me although you pass so close to me ?

Second. Ho, Bakulāvalikā ! Friend, I was intently looking at this ring with its serpent-seal, (just) brought from the jeweller's, and so I fell under your reproof.

Bakulāvalikā. *(Observing)* It is but proper that

अंगुलीअएण उब्भिण्णकिरणकेसरेण कुसुमिदो विअ दे अग्गहत्थो पडिभादि । [स्थाने खलु सज्जति दृष्टिः । अनेनाङ्गुलीयकेनोद्भिन्नकिरणकेसरेण कुसुमित इव तेऽग्रहस्तः प्रतिभाति ।]

कौमुदिका—हला तुमं कहिं पत्थिदासि । [हला त्वं कुत्र प्रस्थितासि ।]

बकुलावलिका—देवीए वअणेण णट्टाअरिअं अज्जगणदासं पुच्छिदुं उवदेसग्गहणे कीरिसी मालविआत्ति । [देव्या वचनेन नाट्याचार्यमार्यगणदासं प्रष्टुमुपदेशग्रहणे कीदृशी मालविकेति ।]

कौमुदिका—हला ईरिसेण वावारेण असण्णिहिदा वि दिट्ठा कहं एसा भट्टिणा । [हला ईदृशेन व्यापारेणासन्निहितापि दृष्टा कथमेषा भर्त्रा ।]

बकुलावलिका—आम् देवीए पस्सगदो सो जणो चित्ते दिट्ठो । [आम् देव्याः पार्श्वगतः स जनश्चित्रे दृष्टः ।]

कौमुदिका—कहं विअ । [कथमिव ।]

बकुलावलिका—सुणाहि । चित्तसालं गदा देवी पच्चग्गवण्णराअं चित्तलेहं आलोअन्ती चिरं चिट्ठदि । तस्सिं अन्तरे उवट्ठिदो भट्टा । [शृणु । चित्रशालां गता देवी प्रत्यग्रवर्णरागां चित्ररेखामालोकयन्ती चिरं तिष्ठति । तस्मिन्नन्तर उपस्थितो भर्ता ।]

कौमुदिका—तदो तदो । [ततस्ततः ।]

बकुलावलिका—उवआराणन्दरं एक्कासणोवविट्ठेण भट्टिणा चित्तगदाए देवीए परिअणमज्झगदं आसण्णपरिआरिणिं देक्खिअ देवी पुच्छिदा । [उपचारानन्तरमेकासनोपविष्टेन भर्त्रा चित्रगताया देव्याः परिजनमध्यगतामासन्नपरिचारिणीं दृष्ट्वा देवी पृष्टा ।]

कौमुदिका—किंत्ति । [किमिति ।]

बकुलावलिका—देवि अपुव्वा इअं दारिआ तुह आसण्णा लिहिदा किंणामहेआत्ति । [देवि अपूर्वेयं दारिका तवासन्ना लिखिता किंनामधेयेति ।]

your eyes were rivetted on it. With this ring, with its filaments of rays upshooting, the palm of your hand appears to have bloomed.

Kaumudikā. Friend, where are you going ?

Bakulāvalikā. I am going by the queen's orders to the dancing-master, the noble Ganadāsa to inquire what sort of pupil Mālavikā has shown herself.

Kaumudikā. Friend, how could she have been seen by his majesty, though she was kept out of the way by such an employment. ?

Bakulāvalikā. Why, she was seen in a picture, painted by the side of the queen.

Kaumudikā. How ?

Bakulāvalikā. Listen, the queen had gone to the painting-hall and stood looking at the picture (shining) with the freshly-laid colours. And at that very moment entered his majesty.

Kaumudikā. well, what happened next ?

Bakulāvalikā. Then after the usual salutations, his majesty sat down in the same seat with the queen, and saw in the picture, among the queen's retinue, a maid ·lose to her, and asked the queen—

Kaumudika. Pray, what ?

Bakulavālikā. 'What is the name of this extraordinary girl painted close to you, my queen '?

कौमुदिका—णं आकिदिविसेसेसु आदरो पदं करेदि। तदो तदो। [नन्वाकृतिविशेषेष्वादरः पदं करोति। ततस्ततः।]

बकुलावलिका—तदो अवहीरिदवअणो भट्टा संकिदो देवीं पुणो पुणो णिब्बन्धिदुं पउत्तो। जाव देवी ण कहेदि दाव कुमारीए वसुलच्छीए आचक्खिदं आउत्त एसा मालविअत्ति। [ततोऽवधीरितवचनो भर्ता शङ्कितो देवीं पुनः पुनर्निर्बन्धुं प्रवृत्तः। यावद्देवी न कथयति तावत्कुमार्या वसुलक्ष्म्याख्यातमावुत्त एषा मालविकेति।]

कौमुदिका (सस्मितम्) सरिसं खु बालभावस्स। अदो वरं कहेहि। [सदृशं खलु बालभावस्य। अतः परं कथय।]

बकुलावलिका—किं अण्णं। सम्पदं मालविआ सविसेसं भट्टिणो दंसणपहादो रक्खीअदि।

[किमन्यत्। साम्प्रतं मालविका सविशेषं भर्तुर्दर्शनपथाद्रक्ष्यते।]

कौमुदिका—हला अणुचिट्ठ अत्तणो णिओअं। अहं वि एदं अङ्गुलीअअं देवीए उवणइस्सं। [हला अनुतिष्ठात्मनो नियोगम्। अहमप्येतदङ्गुलीयकं देव्या उपनेष्यामि।

(इति निष्क्रान्ता।)

बकुलावलिका—(परिक्रम्यावलोक्य च।) एसो णट्टाअरिओ अज्जगणदासो संगीदसालादो दाणिं णिक्कमइ। जाव से अत्ताणं दंसेमि। [एष नाट्याचार्य आर्यगणदासः सङ्गीतशालात इदानीं निष्क्रामति। यावदस्यात्मानं दर्शयामि। (इति परिक्रामति।)

(प्रविश्य) **गणदासः**—कामं खलु सर्वस्यापि कुलविद्या बहुमता। न पुनरस्माकं नाटयं प्रति मिथ्यागौरवम्। कुतः

देवानामिदमामनन्ति मुनयः कान्तं क्रतुं चाक्षुषं
रुद्रेणेदमुमाकृतव्यतिकरे स्वाङ्गे विभक्तं द्विधा।

Kaumudikā. Surely such forms of surpassing loveliness engage one's admiration. Pray, tell me further.

Bakulāvalikā. But finding that his words were not heeded, his majesty grew suspicious and began to importune the queen. And when the queen would not reply, the princess Vasulaksmī made answer : " Brother, this is Mālavikā."

Kaumudikā. (*smilingly*) How like a child ! Tell me what happened next.

Bakulāvalikā. What else, but that now Mālavikā is particularly guarded from the sight of his majesty.

Kaumudikā. Come now, do your errand. I, on my part, will take this ring to the queen.

(*Exit.*)

Bakulāvalikā. (*Walking round and looking.*) Here is the dancing-master, the noble Gaṇadāsa, just stepping out of the music-hall. So I will show myself. (*Walks round.*)

(*Entering.*)

Gaṇadāsa. It is true that everyone regards very highly the science affected by his family ; but then the importance I attach to the dramatic art is not without foundation. For

sages look upon this as a sacrifice that is pleasing to the eyes of the gods ; Rudra has divided it into two parts in his own person which is blended with that of Umā. Herein are to be observed the actions of the people prompted by

त्रैगुण्योद्भवमत्र लोकचरितं नानारसं दृश्यते
नाट्यं भिन्नरुचेर्जनस्य बहुधाप्येकं समाराधनम् ॥४॥

बकुलावलिका—(उपसृत्य) अज्ज वन्दामि । [आर्य वन्दे ।]

गणदासः—भद्रे चिरं जीव ।

बकुलावलिका—अज्ज देवी पुच्छदि अवि उवदेसग्गहणे णादिकिलेसेदि वो सिस्सा मालविअत्ति । [आर्य देवी पृच्छति अप्युपदेशग्रहणे नातिक्लेशयति वः शिष्या मालविकेति ।]

गणदासः—विज्ञाप्यतां देवी परमनिपुणा मेधाविनी चेति । किं बहुना ।

यद्यत्प्रयोगविषये भाविकमुपदिश्यते मया तस्यै ।
तत्तद्विशेषकरणात्प्रत्युपदिशतीव मे बाला ॥५॥

बकुलावलिका (आत्मगतम्)—इरावदिं अदिक्कमन्तिं विअ पेक्खामि । (प्रकाशम्) किदत्था दाणिं वो सिस्सा जस्सिं गुरुअणो एव्वं तुस्सदि । [इरावतीमतिक्रामन्तीमिव पश्यामि । कृतार्थेदानीं वः शिष्या यस्यां गुरुजन एवं तुष्यति ।]

गणदासः—भद्रे तद्विधानामसुलभत्वात्पृच्छामि । कुतो देव्यास्तत्पात्रमानीतम् ।

बकुलावलिका—अत्थि देवीए वण्णावरो भादा वीरसेणो णाम । सो भट्टिणा अन्दवालदुग्गे णम्मदाऊले ठाविदो । तेण सिप्पाहिआरे इअं जोग्गा दारिअत्ति भइणीए उवाअणं पेसिदा । [अस्ति देव्या वर्णावरो भ्राता वीरसेनो नाम । स भर्त्रा अन्तपालदुर्गे नर्मदाकूले स्थापितः । तेन शिल्पाधिकार इयं योग्या दारिकेति भगिन्यै उपायनं प्रेषिता ।]

गणदासः (स्वगतम्)—आकृतिविशेषप्रत्ययादेनामनूनवस्तुकां संभावयामि । (प्रकाशम्) भद्रे मयापि यशस्विना भवितव्यम् । पश्य

the three qualities, and exhibiting various sentiments : the dramatic art is the one chief amusement of the people, albeit they have diverse tastes. (4).

Bakulavālikā. (*approaching*) Noble sir, I salute you.

Ganadāsa. My good girl, may you live long.

Bakulāvalikā. Noble sir, the queen inquires if Mālavikā does not cause great trouble at her lessons.

Ganadāsa. Say to the queen that she is very efficient and clever.

Whatever gesture in the mimetic art is taught by me to her, that the girl, as it were, teaches to me in return by improving upon it. (5)

Bakulāvalikā. (*To herself*) she seems to me to surpass Irāvatī. (*Aloud*) Your pupil may well be looked upon as a success, since her teacher is so well satisfied with her.

Ganadāsa. Good girl, as such people are very difficult to meet with, I ask from where did the queen secure this rare person.

Bakulāvalikā. The queen has a brother of inferior caste, Vīrasena by name. He has been placed, by his majesty in command of a fortress on the frontier of his kingdom on the banks of the Narmadā. He it was who, thinking that the girl was fit to receive instruction in the fine arts, sent her on to his sister as a present.

Ganadāsa. (*To himself*) Assured by her distinguished appearance I judge that she comes of a noble family. (*Aloud*) Good girl, I am sure to succeed (with her). See

पात्रविशेषे न्यस्तं गुणान्तरं व्रजति शिल्पमाधातुः।
जलमिव समुद्रशुक्तौ मुक्ताफलतां पयोदस्य ॥६॥

बकुलावलिका——अज्ज कहिं दाणिं वो सिस्सा। [आर्य कुत्रेदानीं वः शिष्या।]

गणदासः—इदानीमेव पञ्चाङ्गाभिनयमुपदिश्य मया विश्रम्यतामित्यभिहिता दीर्घिकावलोकनगवाक्षगता प्रवातमासेवमाना तिष्ठति।

बकुलावलिका—तेण हि अणुजाणादु मं अज्जो। जाव से अज्जस्स परिदोसणिवेदणेण उच्छाहं वड्ढेमि। [तेन ह्यनुजानातु मामार्यः। यावदस्या आर्यस्य परितोषनिवेदनेनोत्साहं वर्धयामि।

गणदासः—दृश्यतां सखी। अहमपि लब्धक्षणः स्वगृहं गच्छामि।

(इति निष्क्रान्तौ।)

मिश्रविष्कम्भकः।

(ततः प्रविशत्येकान्तस्थितपरिजनो मन्त्रिणा लेखहस्तेनान्वास्यमानो राजा।)

राजा (अनुवाचितलेखममात्यमवलोक्य।)—वाहतक, किं प्रतिपद्यते वैदर्भः।

अमात्यः—देव, आत्मविनाशम्।

राजा—लिखितं निर्देशमिदानीं श्रोतुमिच्छामि।

अमात्यः—इदमिदानीमनेन प्रतिलिखितम्—"पूज्येनाहमादिष्टः 'भवतः पितृव्यपुत्रः कुमारो माधवसेनः प्रतिश्रुतसम्बन्धो ममोपान्तिकमागच्छन्नन्तरा त्वदीयेनान्तपालेनावस्कद्य गृहीतः। स त्वया मदपेक्षया सकलत्रसोदर्यो मोचयितव्य' इति। तन्न वो न विदितं यत्तुल्याभिजनेषु भूमिहरेषु राज्ञां प्रवृत्तिरीदृक्। अतोऽत्र मध्यस्थः पूज्यो भवितु-

The skill of a teacher imparted to a worthy pupil attains greater excellence, as the water of a cloud is turned into a pearl in a sea-shell. (6)

Bakulāvalikā. Noble sir, where is your pupil, now?

Ganadāsa. Only a moment ago, after instructing her in the five-fold ways of acting, I gave her permission to retire, and she is now enjoying the sweet gentle breeze from the window which commands the view of the lake.

Bakulāvalikā. Then, noble sir, give me leave to go, so that I might stimulate her zeal by informing her how well the noble teacher is satisfied with her.

Ganadāsa. Well, then, go and see your friend. Meanwhile, now that I have leisure I will go home. *(exeunt both)*.

End of the Misraviskambhaka.

(Enter king, with his attendants standing apart and his minister, holding a letter in his hand, in attendance.)

King. (*Looking at the minister who has read the letter*) Vāhataka, what does the Vidharbha king think of doing ?

Minister. His own ruin, your majesty.

King. Well, I would like to hear the dispatch.

Minister. This is what he writes in reply. " The revered sire orders me that Prince Mādhavasena, my uncle's son, who has promised alliance with yourself was, while going to you, attacked on the way by my frontier-guards and put into prison ; and that I should, out of regard for you, release him along with his wife and sister." But you know very well that kings act in this way towards their kinsmen of a common extraction. And therefore it behoves you to remain neutral in this

२१ मर्हति । सोदर्या पुनरस्य ग्रहणविप्लवे विनष्टा । तदन्वेषणाय प्रयतिष्ये ।
अथावश्यमेव माधवसेनः पूज्येन मोचयितव्यः, श्रूयतामभिसन्धिः ।

मौर्यसचिवं विमुञ्चति यदि पूज्यः संयतं मम श्यालम् ।
मोक्ता माधवसेनं ततोऽहमपि बन्धनात्सद्यः '' ॥७॥ इति ।

राजा (सरोषम्)—कथं कार्यविनिमयेन मयि व्यवहरत्यनात्मज्ञः । वाहतक, प्रकृत्यमित्रः प्रतिकूलचारी च मे वैदर्भः । तद्यातव्यपक्षे
३ स्थितस्य पूर्वसङ्कल्पितमुन्मूलनाय वीरसेनप्रमुखं दण्डचक्रमाज्ञापय ।

अमात्यः—यदाज्ञापयति देवः ।

राजा—अथवा किं भवान् मन्यते ।

६ **अमात्यः**—शास्त्रदृष्टमाह देवः । कुतः

अचिराधिष्ठितराज्यः शत्रुः प्रकृतिष्वरूढमूलत्वात् ।
नवसंरोहणशिथिलस्तरुरिव सुकरः समुद्धर्तुम् ॥ ८ ॥

राजा—तेन ह्यवितथं तन्त्रकारवचनम् । इदमेव निमित्तमादाय समुद्योज्यतां सेनापतिः ।

३ **अमात्यः**—तथा ।

(इति निष्क्रान्तः । परिजनश्च यथाव्यापारं राजानमभितः स्थितः ।)

(प्रविश्य) **विदूषकः**—आणत्तोम्हि तत्तहोदा रण्णा । गोदम चिन्तेहि
६ दाव उवाअं जह मे जदिच्छादिट्ठपडिकिदी मालविआ पच्चक्खदंसणा होदित्ति । मए वि तं तह किदं । जाव से णिवेदेमि । (इति परिक्रामति।)
आज्ञप्तोऽस्मि तत्रभवता राज्ञा । गौतम चिन्तय तावदुपायं यथा मे

matter. As to his sister, she disappeared in the confusion that ensued at the time of his capture; and I would make every effort to recover her. Now if you desire me to release Mādhavasena, then listen to (my) terms :—

> if you release my brother-in-law the minister of Maurya who suffers imprisonment (at your hands) then would I instantly release Mādhavasena from confinement. (7).

King. (*Furiously*) Would the fool bargain with me by exchange of services? Well, Vāhataka, this king of Vidharbha is my natural enemy and dares to oppose me. So give orders that our army, already kept ready under the command of Vīrasena, should extirpate him, now that he stands in the position of an (open) enemy.

Minister. As your majesty commands.

King. Well, but how do you think (about it)?

Minister. What your majesty says well accords with the teaching of politics; for

> an enemy who has just come to the throne and therefore has not secured the devotion of his subjects is like a freshly planted tree that has not struck its roots deep into the soil : both can with ease be extirpated (8).

King. If that is so, may the dictum of the politicians come true. With this as the cause (of hostilities) let our commander-in-chief get ready to act.

Minister. As your majesty commands. (*Exit.*)

(*The attendants stand round the king, engaged in their respective work.*)

(*Entering*)

Vidūsaka. His Majesty has ordered me: 'Gautama, do you devise means to secure me the sight of Mālavikā in person, whose likeness was just by chance

९ यदृच्छादृष्टप्रतिकृतिर्मालविका प्रत्यक्षदर्शना भवतीति। मयापि तत्तथा कृतम्। यावदस्मै निवेदयामि।]

राजा (विदूषकं दृष्ट्वा)—अयमपरः कार्यान्तरसचिवोऽस्मानुपस्थितः।

१२ **विदूषकः** (उपसृत्य)—वड्ढदु भवं। [वर्धतां भवान्।]

राजा (सशिरःकम्पम्)—इत आस्यताम्। (विदूषक उपविष्टः।)

राजा—वयस्य कच्चिदुपेयोपायदर्शने व्यापृतं ते प्रज्ञाचक्षुः।

१५ **विदूषकः**—पओअसिद्धिं पुच्छ। [प्रयोगसिद्धिं पृच्छ।]

राजा—कथमिव।

विदूषकः (कर्णे)—एव्वं विअ। [एवमिव।]

१८ **राजा**—साधु वयस्य निपुणमुपक्रान्तम्। इदानीं दुरधिगमसिद्धावप्यस्मिन्नारम्भे वयमाशंसामहे। कुतः

अर्थं सप्रतिबन्धं प्रभुरधिगन्तुं सहायवानेव।
दृश्यं तमसि न पश्यति दीपेन विना सचक्षुरपि॥ ९॥

(नेपथ्ये)

अलमलं बहु विकत्थ्य। राज्ञः समक्षमेवावयोरधरोत्तरव्यक्तिर्भविष्यति।

३ **राजा**—सखे त्वत्सुनीतिपादपस्य कुसुममुद्भिन्नम्।

विदूषकः—फलं वि देक्खिस्ससि। [फलमपि द्रक्ष्यसि।]

(ततः प्रविशति कञ्चुकी।)

६ **कञ्चुकी**—देव अमात्यो विज्ञापयति। अनुष्ठिता प्रभोराज्ञा। एतौ पुनर्हरदत्तगणदासौ

seen by me.' And I, on my part, have done it. So I will speak to him. (*Walks about*).

King. (*Seeing Vidūṣaka*) Here comes the minister who looks to another branch of our affairs.

Vidūsaka. (*Approaching*) Prosperity attend your majesty.

King. (*Nodding his head*) Sit here.

(*Vidūṣaka takes a seat.*)

King. Well, friend, is your eye of wisdom engaged in finding out means for the attainment of the desired object?

Vidūsaka. Rather ask about the success of the enterprise.

King. What do you mean?

Vidūsaka. (*Whispers in his ear.*) It is thus.

King. Good, my friend. You have begun wisely. Now I feel inspired with hope for the success of this venture, albeit success in it is so difficult to attain. For

only with the help of some friend can one
attain an object which is beset with obstacles;
no one, even though he has the use of his eyes,
can see an object in the dark without the help
of light. (9).

(*Behind the scenes.*)

Enough of bragging. In the presence of his majesty it will be decided as to which of us is inferior or superior.

King. Friend, here has bloomed a flower on the tree of your fine intrigue.

Vidūsaka. You will see the fruit also.

(*Then enter the chamberlain.*)

Chamberlain. King, the minister begs to inform you that your order is carried out. Now these two gentlemen Haradatta and Gaṇadāsa,

2

उभावभिनयाचार्यौ परस्परजयोद्यतौ ।
त्वां द्रष्टुमिच्छतः साक्षाद्भावाविव शरीरिणौ ॥ १० ॥

राजा—प्रवेशय तौ ।

कञ्चुकी—यदाज्ञापयति देवः । (इति निष्क्रम्य पुनस्ताभ्यां सह
३ प्रविश्य ।) इत इतो भवन्तौ ।

हरदत्तः (राजानमवलोक्य)—अहो दुरासदो राजमहिमा । तथाहि

न च न परिचितो न चाप्यगम्य-
श्चकितमुपैमि तथापि पार्श्वमस्य ।
सलिलनिधिरिव प्रतिक्षणं मे
भवति स एव नवो नवोऽयमक्ष्णोः ॥ ११ ॥

गणदासः—महत् खलु पुरुषाकारमिदं ज्योतिः । तथा हि—

द्वारे नियुक्तपुरुषानुमतप्रवेशः
सिंहासनान्तिकचरेण सहोपसर्पन् ।
तेजोभिरस्य विनिवर्तितदृष्टिपातै-
र्वाक्यादृते पुनरिव प्रतिवारितोऽस्मि ॥ १२ ॥

कञ्चुकी—एष देवः । उपसर्पतां भवन्तौ ।

उभौ (उपसृत्य ।)—विजयतां देवः ।

३ **राजा**—स्वागतं भवद्भ्याम् । (परिजनं विलोक्य ।) आसने
तावदत्रभवतोः । [उभौ परिजनोपनीतयोरासनयोरुपविष्टौ ।]•

राजा—किमिदं शिष्योपदेशकाले युगपदाचार्ययोरुपस्थानम् ।

६ **गणदासः**—देव श्रूयताम् । मया तीर्थादभिनयविद्या शिक्षिता ।
दत्तप्रयोगश्चास्मि । देवेन देव्या च परिगृहीतः ।

both teachers of acting, each eager to gain
victory over the other, desire to see you—as if
they are two dramatic sentiments embodied. (10)

King. Usher them in.

Chamberlain. As the king commands. *(Goes out and then again enters with them.)* This way, gentlemen, this way.

Haradatta. *(Looking at the king)* How awe-inspiring the majesty of the king! For

not that he is not familiar to me, nor is he
not accessible, and yet I am all in a flutter as
I advance towards him; though the same, he
seems to change every moment before my eyes,
like the mighty ocean. (11)

Gaṇadāsa. This is a great luminary masquerading in human form. Thus

although the door-guards allowed my entrance
and I am advancing towards him with the atten-
dant that moves about his throne, yet without
words of prohibition, I feel forbidden by his
splendour that repels my gaze. (12)

Chamberlain. Here is his majesty; advance, gentlemen.

Both. *(Advancing)* Victory to his majesty.

King. You are welcome, sirs. *(Looking at the attendant)* Bring seats for the honoured gentlemen.

(Both occupy the seats brought by the attendants.)

King. How comes it, that both of you come here together, at a time when you should be instructing your pupils?

Gaṇadāsa. Listen, your majesty; I have learnt the art of acting from a noble teacher and I have given lesson in that art and your majesty and the queen have favoured me.

राजा—दृढं जाने । ततः किम् ।

गणदासः—सोऽहममुना हरदत्तेन प्रधानपुरुषसमक्षमयं न मे पादरजसापि तुल्य इत्यधिक्षिप्तः ।

हरदत्तः—देव अयमेव मयि प्रथमं परिवादकरः । अत्रभवतः किल मम च समुद्रपल्वलयोरिवान्तरमिति । तदत्रभवानिमं मां च शास्त्रे प्रयोगे च विमृशतु । देव एव नौ विशेषज्ञः प्राश्निकः ।

विदूषकः—समत्थं पडिण्णादं । [समर्थं प्रतिज्ञातम् ।]

गणदासः—प्रथमः कल्पः । अवहितो देवः श्रोतुमर्हति ।

राजा—तिष्ठतु तावत् । पक्षपातमत्र देवी मन्यते । तत्तस्याः पण्डितकौशिक्या सहितायाः समक्षमेव न्याय्यो व्यवहारः ।

विदूषकः—सुट्ठु भवं भणादि । [सुष्ठु भवान् भणति ।]

आचार्यौ—यद्देवाय रोचते ।

राजा—मौद्गल्य, अमुं प्रस्तावं निवेद्य पण्डितकौशिक्या सार्धमाहूयतां देवी ।

कञ्चुकी—यदाज्ञापयति देवः । (इति निष्क्रम्य सपरिव्राजिकया देव्या सह प्रविश्य ।) इत इतो देवी ।

देवी (परिव्राजिकां विलोक्य)—भअवदि, हरदत्तस्स गणदासस्स अ संरम्भे कहं पेक्खसि ।

[भगवति हरदत्तस्य गणदासस्य च संरम्भे कथं पश्यसि ।]

परिव्राजिका—अलं स्वपक्षावसादशङ्कया । न परिहीयते प्रतिद्वन्द्विनो गणदासः ।

देवी—जइ वि एव्वं तह वि राअपरिग्गहो से पहाणत्तणं उवहरदि । [यद्यप्येवं तथापि राजपरिग्रहोऽस्य प्रधानत्वमुपहरति ।]

King. That I know full well. What of that?

Ganadāsa. And yet I was grossly insulted in the presence of prominent courtiers by Haradatta with the words: 'You are not the equal of the dust on my feet.'

Haradatta. King, it was he who started abusing me saying 'Your reverence is to me what a puddle is to the ocean!' So your highness should examine us both in the theory and practice of the art; for your highness is the only discerning judge of us both.

Vidūṣaka. A fair proposal that.

Gaṇadāsa. A capital idea! Let your highness listen to us attentively.

King. Better wait. The queen may suspect partiality in the case. So it would be only just to decide the matter in her presence and in that of the learned Kauśikī.

Vidūṣaka. You speak proper.

The teachers. Just as it pleases your highness.

King. Maudgalya, speak to the queen of this matter and call her along with the learned Kauśikī.

Chamberlain. As your majesty commands. (*Goes out and then enters along with the queen and the Parivrājikā*). This way, this way, queen.

Queen. (*Looking at the Parivrajikā.*) Revered lady, what do you think of this contest between Haradatta and Gaṇadāsa?

Parivrājikā. Have no apprehensions regarding the success of your side. For Ganadāsa is not inferior to his rival.

Queen. Even if that is so, yet the king's favour gives him the advantage.

परिव्राजिका—अयि राज्ञीशब्दभाजनमात्मानमपि तावच्चिन्तयतु भवती । पश्य

अतिमात्रभासुरत्वं पुष्यति भानोः परिग्रहादनलः ।
अधिगच्छति महिमानं चन्द्रोऽपि निशापरिगृहीतः॥१३॥

विदूषकः—अविहा अविहा उवट्ठिदा पीठमद्दिअं पण्डिदकोसिअं पुरोकदुअ देवी । [अविहा अविहा उपस्थिता पीठमर्दिकां पण्डित-
३ कौशिकीं पुरस्कृत्य देवी ।]

राजा—पश्याम्येनाम् । यैषा

मङ्गलालङ्कृता भाति कौशिक्या यतिवेषया ।
त्रयी विग्रहवत्येव सममध्यात्मविद्यया ॥ १४ ॥

परिव्राजिका (उपसृत्य)—विजयतां देवः ।

राजा—भगवति अभिवादये ।

३ **परिव्राजिका**—

महासारप्रसवयोः सदृशक्षमयोर्द्वयोः ।
धारिणीभूतधारिण्योर्भव भर्ता शरच्छतम् ॥ १५ ॥

देवी—जेदु अज्जउत्तो । [जयत्वार्यपुत्रः ।]

राजा—स्वागतं देव्यै । (परिव्राजिकां विलोक्य ।) भगवति
३ क्रियतामासनपरिग्रहः । (सर्वे यथार्हमुपविशन्ति ।)

राजा—भगवति अत्रभवतोर्हरदत्तगणदासयोः परस्परविज्ञानसङ्घर्षो जातः । तदत्र भगवत्या प्राश्निकपदमध्यासितव्यम् ।

६ **परिव्राजिका** (सस्मितम्)—अलमुपालम्भेन । पत्तने विद्यमानेऽपि ग्रामे रत्नपरीक्षा ।

Parivrājikā. Ah, bethink yourself that you have a right to the title of 'Queen.' Don't you see

that if fire attains its extreme refulgence through the Sun's favour, the Moon too acquires greatness when favoured by the night. (13)

Vidūsaka. Holla, holla, here comes the queen along with her confidant, the learned Kauśikī.

King. I see her, who

being decked with auspicious ornaments, and accompanied by Kauśikī in the garb of an ascetic, looks like the sacred triad embodied, accompanied by the science of metaphysics. (14).

Parivrājikā. (*Advancing*) Victory attend your highness.

King. Revered lady, I salute thee.

Parivrājikā.

May you be, for hundred years, the husband of queen Dhāriṇī and of the Earth,—the one who has given birth to a heroic son and is possessed of great forgiveness, and the other that yields abundant crops owing to plenty of showers and is equally forgiving. (15)

Queen. Victory to my lord!

King. Welcome, queen. (*Looking at the Parivrājikā*) Revered lady, please to take a seat.

(*All take seats in due order.*)

King. Revered lady, there is a dispute between the noble Haradatta and Gaṇadāsa as to which of them is superior in point of learning. So the revered lady should act as their judge.

Parivrājikā. (*Smiling*) Enough of your taunts. When a town is near, would you have a jewel tested in a village?

राजा—मा मैवम् । पण्डितकौशिकी खलु भगवती । पक्षपातिना-
९ वनयोरहं च देवी च ।

आचार्यौ—सम्यगाह देवः । मध्यस्था भगवती गुणदोषौ नः परिच्छेत्तुमर्हति ।

१२**राजा**—तेन हि प्रस्तूयतां विवादः ।

परिव्राजिका—देव प्रयोगप्रधानं हि नाट्यशास्त्रम् । किमत्र वाग्व्यवहारेण ।

२५**राजा**—कथं वा देवी मन्यते ।

देवी—जइ मं पुच्छसि एदाणं विवादो एव्व ण मे रोअदि ।
[यदि मां पृच्छसि, एतयोर्विवाद एव न मे रोचते ।]

१८**गणदासः**—न मां देवी समानविद्यतः परिभवनीयमनुमन्तुमर्हति ।

विदूषकः—होदु देक्खामो उरब्भसंवादं । किं मुहा वेअणदाणेण ।
[भवतु द्रक्ष्याम उरभ्रसम्पातम् । किं मुधा वेतनदानेन ।]

२१**देवी**—णं कलहप्पिओसि । [ननु कलहप्रियोऽसि ।]

विदूषकः—मा दाव । अण्णोण्णकलहिदाणं मत्तहत्थीणं एक्कदरस्सि अणिज्जिदे कदो उवसमो । [मा तावत् । अन्योन्यकलहितयोर्मत्तह-
२४स्तिनोरेकतरस्मिन्ननिर्जिते कुत उपशमः ।]

राजा—ननु स्वाङ्गसौष्ठवाभिनयमुभयोर्दृष्टवती भगवती ।

परिव्राजिका—अथ किम् ।

२७**राजा**—तदिदानीमतः परं किमाभ्यां प्रत्याययितव्यम् ।

परिव्राजिका—तदेव वक्तुकामास्मि ।

श्लिष्टा क्रिया कस्यचिदात्मसंस्था
सङ्क्रान्तिरन्यस्य विशेषयुक्ता ।

King. Do not say so. For the revered lady should not forget that she is the learned Kauśikī. We two, the queen and myself, are not free from bias towards them.

The teachers. His majesty speaks the truth. The revered lady being impartial deserves to gauge our merits and demerits.

King. Well then, why not start the disputation?

Parivrājikā. Your majesty, the dramatic art is pre-eminently a practical art. What use is a mere verbal disputation?

King. But what is the view of our queen?

Queen. If you ask me, I do not relish an argument itself between them.

Gaṇadāsa. The queen should not consider me as one who is likely to suffer defeat from one who is only my equal in learning.

Vidūṣaka. Well, then let us see the fight of the two rams. What is the use of giving them wages for nothing?

Queen. You are ever fond of squabbles!

Vidūṣaka. No, not that. But where can there be peace until one of two wild elephants that have been quarrelling, is completely vanquished?

King. But I believe the revered lady has witnessed the graceful acting exhibited by them in their own person.

Parivrājikā. Well, what of that?

King. What more have they to bring forward by way of proof?

Parivrājikā. That is exactly what I desire to point out.

Some exhibit acting very well in their own
person; while others show greater skill in im-

यस्योभयं साधु स शिक्षकाणां
धुरि प्रतिष्ठापयितव्य एव ॥ १६ ॥

विदूषकः—सुदं भअवदीए वअणं अज्जेहिं । एसो पिण्डिदत्थो उवदेसदंसणेण णिण्णओत्ति । [श्रुतं भगवत्या वचनमार्याभ्याम् । एष पिण्डितार्थः उपदेशदर्शनेन निर्णय इति ।]

हरदत्तः—परमुचितं नः ।

गणदासः—देवि एवं स्थितम् ।

देवी—जदा उण मन्दमेहा सिस्सा उवदेसं मलिणेदि तदा आअरिअस्स दोसो णं । [यदा पुनर्मन्दमेधा शिष्योपदेशं मलिनयति तदाचार्यस्य दोषो नु ।]

राजा—देवि एवमुपपद्यते ।

गणदासः—विनेतुरद्रव्यपरिग्रहोऽपि बुद्धिलाघवं प्रकाशयति ।

देवी (स्वगतम्)—कहं दाणिं । (गणदासं विलोक्य जनान्तिकम् ।) अलं अज्जउत्तस्स उच्छाहकारणं मणोरहं पूरिअ । (प्रकाशं ।) विरम णिरत्थआदो आरम्भादो ।

[कथमिदानीम् । अलमार्यपुत्रस्योत्साहकारणं मनोरथं पूरयित्वा । विरम निरर्थकादारम्भात् ।]

विदूषकः—सुट्ठु होदी भणादि । भो गणदास सङ्गीदावदेसेण सरस्सईउवाअणमोदआइं खादमाणस्स किं दे सुलहणिग्गहेण विवादेण ।

[सुष्ठु भवती भणाति । भो गणदास सङ्गीतापदेशेन सरस्वत्युपायनमोदकानि खादतः किं ते सुलभनिग्रहेण विवादेन ।]

गणदासः—सत्यमयमेवार्थो देवीवचनस्य । श्रूयतामत्रसरप्राप्तमिदम् ।

parting (that art) to another ; he who excels in both these qualities deserves a pre-eminent place among teachers. (16).

Vidūsaka. My noble friends have heard the revered lady. So then, this is the sum (of what she says): the decision will be given after judging of your teaching through its exhibition (in a performance).

Haradatta. That is quite proper to us.

Ganadāsa. Queen, so it comes to that.

Queen. But if a dull-witted pupil brings disgrace on the teaching, will it be accounted as the fault of the teacher ?

King. Yes, that is how it is, my queen.

Ganadāsa. But the acceptance of a bad pupil shows the dullness of the teacher's intelligence.

Queen. (*To herself*) How now ? (*Looking at Gaṇadāsa, aside*) Do not fulfil the desire of my noble lord which will only inflame his passion. (*Aloud*) Desist from these vain proceedings.

Vidūṣaka. The queen speaks well. Ho, Gaṇadāsa, why should you trouble yourself with this disputation where you will easily suffer defeat, when under the pretext of your music, you well enjoy the presents of sweets offered to Saraswatī ?

Gaṇadāsa. This is exactly what her highness means. Now listen to this which is proper to say on the occasion :—

लब्धास्पदोऽस्मीति विवादभीरो-
स्तितिक्षमाणस्य परेण निन्दाम् ।
यस्यागमः केवलजीविकैव
तं ज्ञानपण्यं वणिजं वदन्ति ॥ १७ ॥

देवी—अइरोवणीदा दे सिस्सा । ता अवरिणिट्ठिदस्स उवदेसस्स अण्णाअं पदंसणं ।

[अचिरोपनीता ते शिष्या । तदपरिनिष्ठितस्योपदेशस्यान्याय्यं प्रदर्शनम् ।]

गणदासः—अत एव मे निर्बन्धः ।

देवी—तेण हि दुवे वि भअवदीए उवदेसं दंसह ।

[तेन हि द्वावपि भगवत्या उपदेशं दर्शयतम् ।]

परिव्राजिका—देवि नैतन्न्याय्यम् । सर्वज्ञस्याप्येकाकिनो निर्णयाभ्युपगमो दोषाय ।

देवी—(आत्मगतम् ।) मुद्धे किं मं जग्गदिं वि सुत्तं विअ करेसि । (इति सासूयं परावर्तते ।)

[मुग्धे किं मां जाग्रतीमपि सुप्तामिव करोषि ।]

(राजा देवीं परिव्राजिकायै दर्शयति ।)

परिव्राजिका—(विलोक्य ।)

अनिमित्तमिन्दुवदने किमत्रभवतः पराङ्मुखी भवसि ।
प्रभवन्त्योऽपि हि भर्तृषु कारणकोपाः कुटुम्बिन्यः ॥१८॥

विदूषकः—णं कारणादो एव्व अत्तणो पक्खो रक्खिदव्वो त्ति । (गणदासं विलोक्य ।) दिट्ठिआ कोवव्वाएण देवीए परित्तादो भवं । सुसिक्खिदो वि सव्वो उवदेसदंसणे ण णिउणो होदि ।

[ननु कारणादेव आत्मनः पक्षो रक्षितव्य इति । दिष्टया कोपव्याजेन देव्या परित्रातो भवान् । सुशिक्षितोऽपि सर्व उपदेशदर्शने न निपुणो भवति ।]

a man who shrinks from contest on the ground that his position is secure, and (calmly) suffers insults by others, whose learning only serves as a means of livelihood, is called a mere huckster that traffics in knowledge. (17)

Queen. Your pupil has but lately been put under your charge. It would, therefore, be unjust to exhibit knowledge which is not yet well assimilated.

Gaṇadāsa. That is why I insist.

Queen. Well then, show your skill to the learned Kauśikī alone.

Parivrājikā. That is hardly fair, your highness. Even an omniscient judge may deliver a wrong judgment if he delivers it alone.

Queen. (*To herself*) You simpleton, how do you take me to be asleep when I am wide awake ? (*Turns away in a pet.*)

(*The king draws the attention of the Parivrājikā to the queen.)*

Parivrājikā. *(Looking)* How without cause do you, O moon-faced lady, turn yourself away from the king ? For although wives may have power over their husbands, yet they require some cause before they fall out with them. (18).

Vidūsaka. Why, the cause is plain : she wants to uphold her side. (*Looking at Gaṇadāsa.*) Fortunately for you, you have been saved by her majesty, under this pretence of resentment. For although one is very learned, yet one may not possess skill in imparting knowledge.

गणदासः—देवि श्रूयताम् । एवं जनो गृह्णाति । तदिदानीं

विवादे दर्शयिष्यन्तं क्रियासङ्क्रान्तिमात्मनः ।
यदि मां नानुजानासि परित्यक्तोऽस्म्यहं त्वया ॥१९॥

(आसनादुत्तिष्ठति ।)

देवी—(स्वगतम् ।) का गई । (प्रकाशम् ।) पहवदि आअरिओ सिस्सअणस्स ।

[का गतिः । प्रभवत्याचार्यः शिष्यजनस्य ।]

गणदासः—चिरमपदे शङ्कितोऽस्मि ।(राजानमवलोक्य) अनुज्ञातं देव्या । तदाज्ञापयतु देवः । कस्मिन्नभिनेयवस्तुन्युपदेशं दर्शयिष्यामि ।

राजा—यदादिशति भगवती ।

परिव्राजिका—किमपि देव्या मनसि वर्तते । तच्छङ्कितास्मि ।

देवी—भण विस्सद्धं । णं पहविस्सं अत्तणो परिअणस्स ।

[भणं विस्रब्धम् । ननु प्रभविष्याम्यात्मनः परिजनस्य ।]

राजा—मम चेति ब्रूहि ।

देवी —भअवदि भण दाणिं । [भगवति भणेदानीम् ।]

परिव्राजिका—चतुष्पदोद्भवं छलितं दुष्प्रयोजमुदाहरन्ति । तत्रैकार्थसंश्रयमुभयोः प्रयोगं पश्यामः । तावता ज्ञायत एवात्रभवतोरुपदेशान्तरम् ।

उभौ—यदाज्ञापयति भगवती ।

विदूषकः—तेण हि दुवे वि वग्गा पेक्खाघरए सङ्गीदरअणं कदुअ अत्तहोदो दूदं पेसअन्तु । अहवा मिअङ्गसद्दो एव्व णो उट्ठावइस्सदि ।

[तेन हि द्वावपि वर्गौ प्रेक्षागृहे सङ्गीतरचनां कृत्वात्रभवतो दूतं प्रेषयताम् । अथवा मृदङ्गशब्द एव न उत्थापयिष्यति ।]

Ganadāsa. Please to hear me, queen. This is how people will think. So now,

if you will not permit me, although I am willing to show my skill in teaching in this contest,
I would understand that you have deserted me. (19)

(*Rises from his seat.*)

Queen. (*To herself*) What help ! (*Aloud*) The teacher has every authority over his pupil.

Gaṇadāsa. I was filled with vain apprehensions so long. (*Looking at the king*) So the queen consents. Let the king give orders : in what particular piece of acting should I show my skill ?

King. As the revered lady commands.

Parivrājikā. There is something on the queen's mind. So I am a bit doubtful.

Queen. You may speak without fear. I shall certainly have power over my servants.

King. Say also over mine too.

Queen. Revered lady, speak then.

Parivrājikā. The chalita which depends upon four verse-quadrants is accounted to be difficult to act. Let us, therefore, witness the performance of both, by one and the same piece of acting. That will show clearly the difference in the teaching of both the gentlemen.

Both. As the revered lady commands.

Vidūsaka. Well then, let both the parties arrange all the accessories of music in the theatre and send a messenger to his highness. Or rather the sound of the drum will be a signal for us to rise.

२१ **हरदत्तः**—तथा । (इत्युत्तिष्ठति ।) (गणदासो देवीं विलोकयति ।)

देवी—ण खु विअअपच्चत्थिणी अहं अज्जस्स । विअई होहि ।

[न खलु विजयप्रत्यर्थिन्यहमार्यस्य । विजयी भव ।]

(उभौ प्रस्थितौ ।)

२५ **परिव्राजिका**—इतस्तावदाचार्यौ ।

उभौ—(परिवृत्य) इमौ स्वः ।

२७ **परिव्राजिका**—निर्णयाधिकारे ब्रवीमि । सर्वाङ्गसौष्ठवाभिव्यक्तये विरलनेपथ्ययोः पात्रयोः प्रवेशोऽस्तु ।

आचार्यौ—नेदमावयोरुपदेश्यम् । (इति निष्क्रान्तौ ।)

३० **देवी** (राजानवमलोक्य ।)—जइ राअकज्जेसु वि ईरिसी उवाअणिउणदा अज्जउत्तस्स तदा सोहणं हवे ।

[यदि राजकार्येष्वपीदृश्युपायनिपुणतार्यपुत्रस्य तदा शोभनं भवेत् ।]

३३ **राजा**—देवि

अलमन्यथा गृहीत्वा
न खलु मनस्विनि मया प्रयुक्तमिदम् ।
प्रायः समानविद्याः
परस्परयशःपुरोभागाः ॥ २० ॥

(नेपथ्ये मृदङ्गशब्दः । सर्वे कर्णं ददति ।)

परिव्राजिका—हन्त प्रवृत्तं सङ्गीतकम् । तथा ह्येषा

जीमूतस्तनितविशङ्किभिर्मयूरै-
रुद्ग्रीवैरनुरसितस्य पुष्करस्य ।
निर्ह्रादिन्युपहितमध्यमस्वरोत्था
मायूरी मदयति मार्जना मनांसि ॥ २१ ॥

राजा—देवि सामाजिका भवामः

Haradatta. Let it be. (*Rises. Gaṇadāsa looks at the queen.*)

Queen. I am indeed not against your gaining victory. May you be victorious.

(*Both start to leave.*)

Parivrājikā. Here, please, professors.

Both. (*turning round*) Here we are.

Parivrājikā. I speak in the capacity of a judge. Let the actors enter in thin stage-costumes in order to exhibit the graces of all their limbs.

Teachers. That need not be told us. (*Exeunt both.*)

Queen.— (*Looking to the king*) If my noble lord shows the same command of means in political affairs, it would be to much advantage.

King. Do not misjudge me; this is not my doing, proud lady. Generally persons of equal learning are envious of one another's fame (20).

(*The sound of drum is heard from behind the scenes ; all listen.*)

Parivrājikā. Why, they have already started music! For this

sound of the drum, dear to the peacocks and answered by them with upstretched neck as they suspect it to be the rumble of clouds, deeply resonating, and set to the middle note, delights the mind (21).

King. My queen, let us join the audience.

देवी (स्वगतम्)—अहो अविणयो अज्जउत्तस्स ।

३ [अहो अविनय आर्यपुत्रस्य ।] (सर्वे उत्तिष्ठन्ति)

विदूषकः(अपवार्य ।)—भो वयस्स धीरं गच्छ । मा तत्तहोदी धारिणी विसंवादइस्सदि ।

६ [भो वयस्य धीरं गच्छ । मा तत्रभवती धारिणी विसंवादयिष्यति ।]

राजा—

धैर्यावलम्बिनमपि
त्वरयति मां मुरजवाद्यरागोऽयम् ।
अवतरतः सिद्धिपथं
शब्दः स्वमनोरथस्येव ॥ २२ ॥

[इति निष्क्रान्ताः सर्वे ।]

इति प्रथमोऽङ्कः ।

Queen. (*To herself*) O this indecorum of my lord!

(*All rise.*)

Vidūṣaka. (*Aside*) Keep calm, my friend, lest the queen Dhāriṇī should countermand (the whole proceeding).

King.

The sound of the drum makes me impatient in spite of my efforts to keep calm, as though it is the voice of my own desire that is treading down the path of fulfilment. (22)

Exeunt Omnes.

End of Act One.

द्वितीयोऽङ्कः ।

(ततः प्रविशति सङ्गीतरचनायां कृतायामासनस्थः सवयस्यो राजा धारिणी परिव्राजिका विभवतश्च परिवारः ।)

राजा—भगवति अत्रभवतोराचार्ययोः कतरस्य प्रथममुपदेशं द्रक्ष्यामः ।

परिव्राजिका—ननु समानेऽपि ज्ञानवृद्धभावे वयोवृद्धत्वाद्गणदासः पुरस्कारमर्हति ।

राजा—तेन हि मौद्गल्य एवमत्रभवतोरावेद्य स्वनियोगमशून्यं कुरु ।

कञ्चुकी—यदाज्ञापयति देवः । (इति निष्क्रान्तः)

(प्रविश्य) **गणदासः**—देव शर्मिष्ठायाः कृतिर्लयमध्या चतुष्पदा । तस्याश्चतुर्थवस्तुकं प्रयोगमेकमनाः श्रोतुमर्हति देवः ।

राजा—आचार्य बहुमानादवहितोऽस्मि । (निष्क्रान्तो गणदासः ।)

राजा—(जनान्तिकम्) वयस्य

नेपथ्यगृहगतायाश्चक्षुर्दर्शनसमुत्सुकं तस्याः ।
संहर्तुमधीरतया व्यवसितमिव मे तिरस्करणीम् ॥१॥

विदूषकः—(अपवार्य ।) भो उवट्ठिदं णअणमहु । सण्णिहिदमक्खिअं अ । ता अप्पमत्तो दाणिं पेक्खदु भवं ।

[भो उपस्थितं नयनमधु । सन्निहितमक्षिकं च । तदप्रमत्त इदानीं प्रेक्षतां भवान् ।]

(ततः प्रविशत्याचार्यप्रत्यवेक्ष्यमाणाङ्गसौष्ठवा मालविका)

विदूषकः (जनान्तिकम) पेक्खदु भवं । ण खु से पडिच्छन्दादो परिहीअदि महुरदा । [प्रेक्षतां भवान् । न खल्वस्याः प्रतिच्छन्दात् परिहीयते मधुरता ।]

ACT II.

(Then, after orchestral arrangements are got ready, enter seated the king with his friend, Dhāriṇī, Parivrājikā, and the attendants according to their rank.)

King. Revered Madam, of which of the two venerable teachers shall we first witness (the skill in) teaching?

Parivrājikā. Although they are equally old in learning, yet Gaṇadāsa deserves precedence on account of his being the elder.

King. Well then, Maudgalya, do communicate this to the gentlemen and then go about your business.

Chamberlain. As the king commands. (*Exit.*)

(*Entering*)

Gaṇadāsa. King, there is Śarmisṭhā's composition of four parts and sung in medium time; it behoves the king to listen to the performance of one-fourth of it very attentively.

King. Well, professor, I am respectfully attentive.

(*Exit Gaṇadāsa.*)

King. (*Aside*) friend,

mine eyes, eager to behold her who is now in
the tiring-room, are as it were proceeding to
remove the curtain owing to their impatience. (1)

Vidūsaka. (*Aside*) Friend, the honey of your eyes is come, but the wasp is close by; so be vigilant and watch.

(Enter Mālavikā with the teacher contemplating the grace of her limbs).

Vidūsaka. Behold, Sir. I am sure her charms do not fall short of the picture.

९ राजा (जनान्तिकम्) —वयस्य

चित्रगतायामस्यां कान्तिविसंवादशङ्कि मे हृदयम् ।
सम्प्रति शिथिलसमाधिं मन्ये येनेयमालिखिता ॥ २ ॥

गणदासः—वत्से मुक्तसाध्वसा सत्त्वस्था भव ।

राजा (आत्मगतम्) — अहो सर्वस्थानानवद्यता रूपस्य ।

दीर्घाक्षं शरदिन्दुकान्ति वदनं बाहू नतावंसयोः
सङ्क्षिप्तं निबिडोन्नतस्तनमुरः पार्श्वे प्रमृष्टे इव ।
मध्यः पाणिमितो नितम्बि जघनं पादावरालाङ्गुली
छन्दो नर्तयितुर्यथैव मनसि श्लिष्टं तथास्याः वपुः ॥३॥

मालविका—(उपवहनं कृत्वा चतुष्पदं वस्तु गायति)

दुल्लहो पिओ तस्सिं भव हिअअ णिरासं
अम्हो अपङ्गओ मे पप्फुरइ किं वि वामओ ।
एसो सो चिरदिट्ठो कहं उवणइदव्वो
णाह मं पराहीणं तुइ गणअ सतिण्हं ॥ ४ ॥

(इति यथारसमभिनयति ।)

[दुर्लभः प्रियस्तस्मिन् भव हृदय निराशम्
३ अहो अपाङ्गको मे प्रस्फुरति किमपि वामकः ।
एष स चिरदृष्टः कथमुपनेतव्यो
नाथ मां पराधीनां त्वयि गणय सतृष्णाम् ॥]

६ विदूषकः (जनान्तिकम्)—भो वयस्स चउप्पदवत्थुअ दुवारीकदुअ तुइ उवक्खित्तो विअ अप्पा तत्तहोदीए । [भो वयस्य, चतुष्पदवस्तुकं द्वारीकृत्य त्वय्युपक्षिप्त इवात्मा तत्रभवत्या ।]

King. *(Aside)* Friend,

when I beheld her picture, I thought she would belie the loveliness of it ; but now I think that the painter who limned her likeness had not secured full concentration. (2).

Gaṇadāsa. Child, give up fear and be composed.

King. *(To himself)* How flawless in every part is her form !

Her long eyes ; her face lovely like the moon of autumn ; the arms sloping at the shoulders ; her compact bosom with the plump and swelling breasts ; her sides as if polished ; her waist measurable by the palm of the hand ; her hips expansive ; her feet with their curved toes ; her whole body thus seems framed to suit the fancy of her teacher of dancing. (3).

Mālavikā. (*After a preliminary trying of the notes she sings the musical piece of four lines.*)

The dear one is far above thee ; my heart, despair. Ah, how the corner of my left eye throbs somewhat ! How should he, seen after a long time, be approached ? My lord, helpless that I am, know me to be filled with passion for you. (4)

(She expresses the emotion through acting.)

Vidūṣaka. (*Aside*) Ah, my friend, taking occasion of this musical piece of four parts, she seems to have given herself over to you.

राजा (जनान्तिकम्)—सखे एवमात्रयोर्हृदयम् । अनया खलु

जनमिममनुरक्तं विद्धि नाथेति गेये
वचनमभिनयन्त्या स्वाङ्गनिर्देशपूर्वम् ।
प्रणयगतिमदृष्ट्वा धारिणीसन्निकर्षा-
दहमिव सुकुमारप्रार्थनाव्याजमुक्तः ॥ ५ ॥

(मालविका गीतान्ते निष्क्रमितुमिच्छति ।)

विदूषकः—भोदि चिट्ठ । किं वि वो विसुमरिदो कमभेदो । तं
३ दाव पुच्छिस्सम् । [भवति तिष्ठ । किमपि वो विस्मृतः क्रमभेदः ।
तं तावत्प्रक्ष्यामि ।]

गणदासः—वत्से स्थीयताम् । उपदेशविशुद्धा यास्यसि ।

(मालविका निवृत्य स्थिता ।)

७ **राजा** (आत्मगतम्)—अहो सर्वास्ववस्थासु चारुता शोभां
पुष्यति । तथा हि ।

वामं सन्धिस्तिमितवलयं न्यस्य हस्तं नितम्बे
कृत्वा श्यामाविटपसदृशं स्रस्तमुक्तं द्वितीयम् ।
पादाङ्गुष्ठालुलितकुसुमे कुट्टिमे पातिताक्षं
नृत्तादस्याः स्थितमतितरां कान्तमृज्वायतार्धम् ॥६॥

देवी—णं गोदमवअणं वि अज्जो हिअए करेदि । [ननु गौतम-
वचनमप्यार्यो हृदये करोति]

३ **गणदासः**—देवि मा मैवम् । देवप्रत्ययात्सम्भाव्यते सूक्ष्मदर्शिता
गौतमस्य । पश्य ।

King. *(Aside)* friend, such the state of our hearts. For

" Know me to be devoted to you, my lord ": as she accompanied these words of the song with gestures in which she pointed to the different parts of her body, she seemed to address me under cover of the graceful plaint, as she could see no other way of showing her love for me owing to Dhāriṇī's presence. (5)

(Mālavikā makes as if she would leave at the end of the song.)

Vidūṣaka. Wait, lady. You seem to have forgotten somewhat the proper sequence. I will, therefore, ask about it.

Gaṇadāsa. Stay, child. You will leave, when your performance will have been declared to be flawless.

(Mālavikā turns round and stays.)

King. *(To himself)* How loveliness gains fresh charms under all conditions! For

the left hand with its bracelet resting on the wrist, placed upon her hip, and the right hand hanging loosely down like a branch of the Śyāmā creeper; the eyes cast on the pavement where the flowers are pressed by the toes of her feet—this her posture, with the upper part of the body stretched upright, is far more attractive than her dancing (posture). (6)

Queen. Now, sir, would you mind the words even of Gautama?

Gaṇadāsa. Not so, queen. Owing to the confidence which the king reposes in him, it is possible to expect acute perception in him. See

मन्दोऽप्यमन्दतामेति संसर्गेण विपश्चितः ।
पङ्कच्छिदः फलस्येव निकषेणाविलं पयः ॥ ७ ॥

(विदूषकं विलोक्य।) शृणुमो विवक्षितमार्यस्य ।

विदूषकः (गणदासं विलोक्य ।)—सक्खिणिं दाव पुच्छ । पच्छा
३ जो मए कमभेदो लक्खिदो तं भणिस्सं । [साक्षिणीं तावत्पृच्छ । पश्चाद्यो मया क्रमभेदो लक्षितः तं भणिष्यामि ।]

गणदासः—भगवति, यथादृष्टमभिधीयतां गुणो वा दोषो वा ।

६ **परिव्राजिका**—यथादर्शनं सर्वमनवद्यम् । कुतः ।

अङ्गैरन्तर्निहितवचनैः सूचितः सम्यगर्थः
पादन्यासो लयमनुगतस्तन्मयत्वं रसेषु ।
शाखायोनिर्मृदुरभिनयस्तद्विकल्पानुवृत्तौ
भावो भावं नुदति विषयाद्रागबन्धः स एव ॥ ८ ॥

गणदासः— देवः कथं मन्यते ।

राजा—गणदास, स्वपक्षे शिथिलाभिमाना वयं संवृत्ताः ।

३ **गणदासः**—अद्य नर्तयितास्मि ।

उपदेशं विदुः शुद्धं सन्तस्तमुपदेशिनः ।
श्यामायते न युष्मासु यः काञ्चनमिवाग्निषु ॥ ९ ॥

देवी—दिट्ठिआ परिक्खआराहणेण अहिअं वड्ढइ अज्जो ।
[दिष्ट्या परीक्षकाराधनेनाधिकं वर्धत आर्यः ।]

even a dull person becomes sharp of intelligence by association with the wise, as turbid water attains transparency by contact with the mud-removing fruit. (7)

(*Looking at the Vidūṣaka*) We should like to heaı what the gentleman wants to say.

Vidūṣaka. (*Looking at Gaṇadāsa*) Ask the judge in the first place. Afterwards will I speak of the violation of sequence which I have observed.

Gaṇadāsa. Revered lady, speak out whatever you observed, whether merits or defects.

Parivrājikā. Everything was blameless and in accordance with the rules of the art.

The meaning was well suggested by her limbs that were eloquently expressive; the movement of the feet was in perfect time, and she was perfectly absorbed in the (various) sentiments; the acting was delicate—of which the instrument of expression was the branch-like hand; and while in the successive exhibition of its various shades one fleeting emotion seemed to drive away another from the field, yet the main sentiment (of love) remained the same throughout. (8)

Gaṇadāsa. What does his majesty think?

King. I no longer hold the same high regard for my protege.

Gaṇadāsa. Now (I feel) I am in truth a professor of dancing.

Wise men consider that the instruction given by a teacher is pure when the same is found to be without any fault by such as you, as they consider gold to be pure when it does not get blackened in fire. (9)

Queen. I congratulate you, sır, on being so fortunate as to satisfy your judges.

गणदासः—देवीपरिग्रहश्च मे वृद्धिहेतुः । (विदूषकं विलोक्य।) गौतम, वदेदानीं यत्ते मनसि वर्तते ।

विदूषकः—पुढमोवदेसदंसणे पुढमं बम्हणस्स पूआ कादव्वा । सा णं वो विसुमरिदा । [प्रथमोपदेशदर्शने प्रथमं ब्राह्मणस्य पूजा कर्तव्या । सा ननु वो विस्मृता ।]

परिव्राजिका—अहो प्रयोगाभ्यन्तरः प्रश्नः ।

विदूषकः—अइ पण्डितंमण्णे किं अण्णं । मोदअखण्डणे वि असमत्था तुमं किं जाणासि । पसण्णचन्दपादसरिसेहिं केसपासेहिं एदाणं भीसिअसि । [अयि पण्डितंमन्ये, किमन्यत् । मोदकखण्डनेऽप्यसमर्था त्वं किं जानासि । प्रसन्नचन्द्रपादसदृशैः केशपाशैरेतान् भीषयसे ।]

(सर्वे प्रहसिताः । मालविका च मन्दस्मितं करोति ।)

राजा (आत्मगतम्)—उपात्तसारश्चक्षुषा मे स्वविषयः । यदनेन

> **स्मयमानमायताक्ष्याः**
> **किंचिदभिव्यक्तदशनशोभि मुखम् ।**
> **असमग्रलक्ष्यकेसर-**
> **मुच्छ्वसदिव पङ्कजं दृष्टम् ॥ १० ॥**

गणदासः—महाब्राह्मण, न खलु नेपथ्यसङ्गीतकमिदम् । अन्यथा कथं त्वामर्चनीयं नार्चयिष्यामः ।

विदूषकः—मए णाम मुद्धचादएण विअ सुक्खघणगज्जिदे अन्दरिक्खे जलपाणं इच्छिदं । [मया नाम मुग्धचातकेनेव शुष्कघनगर्जितेऽन्तरिक्षे जलपानमिष्टम् ।]

परिव्राजिका—एवमेव ।

Gaṇadāsa. The queen's favour, too, is responsible for my good fortune. *(Looking at the Vidūṣaka)* Now, Gautama, say what you have in your mind.

Vidūṣaka. The first time that skill is exhibited a Brāhmaṇa must be honoured ; and that you have forgotten to do.

Parivrājikā. Ha ! Ha ! What a vital point in acting!

Vidūṣaka. What else, you conceited woman! What, indeed, do you know, when you are not able to break even balls of sweets ? You merely frighten these people here by your abundant hair that are white like the clear rays of the moon.

(They all laugh; Mālavikā too gently smiles.)

King. *(To himself)* my eye has perceived the most beautiful of the objects of sight. For

> it has beheld the smiling face of the long-eyed one, lovely with the teeth but half visible, like an opening lotus with its filaments partially seen. (10)

Gaṇadāsa. Great Brāhamaṇa, this is not a musical piece in regular stage-costume. How, otherwise, could we have failed to do you honour who deserve to be honoured ?

Vidūṣaka. I, indeed, like the simple Cātaka had asked for a drink of water when the sky was filled with the rumble of a rainless cloud.

Parivrājikā. Yes, even so.

विदूषकः—भअवदि, पण्डिदपरिदोसप्पच्चआ णं मूढा जादी । जइ भअवदीए सोहणं भाणिदं तदो इमं से पारितोसिअं पयच्छम्मि।

९ (इति राज्ञो हस्तात्कटकमाकर्षति ।) [भगवति, पण्डितपरितोषप्रत्यया ननु मूढा जातिः । यदि भगवत्या शोभनं भणितं तत इदमस्यै पारितोषिकं प्रयच्छामि ।]

१२**देवी**—चिट्ठ चिट्ठ । गुणन्तरं अआणन्तो किंति तुमं आहरणं देसि । [तिष्ठ तिष्ठ । गुणान्तरमजानन्किमिति त्वमाभरणं ददासि ।]

विदूषकः—परकेरअं ति कदुअ । [परकीयमिति कृत्वा ।]

१५**देवी** (आचार्यं विलोक्य)—अज्ज गणदास, णं दंसिदोवदेसा वो सिस्सा । [आर्य गणदास, ननु दर्शितोपदेशा वः शिष्या ।]

गणदासः—वत्से प्रतिष्ठस्वेदानीम् । (मालविका सहाचार्येण निष्क्रान्ता।)

१८**विदूषकः** (राजानं विलोक्य । जनान्तिकम् ।)—एत्तिओ मे मदिविहवो भवन्तं सेविदुम् । [एतावान्मे मतिविभवो भवन्तं सेवितुम्।]

राजा (जनान्तिकम् ।)—अलमलं परिच्छेदेन । अद्य हि

भाग्यास्तमयमिवाक्ष्णोर्हृदयस्य महोत्सवावसानमिव ।
द्वारपिधानमिव धृतेर्मन्ये तस्यास्तिरस्करणम् ॥११॥

विदूषकः—साहु तुमं दरिद्दो आदुरो विअ वेज्जेण उवणिज्जमाणं ओसहं इच्छसि । [साधु त्वं दरिद्र आतुर इव वैद्येनोपनीयमान-
३मौषधमिच्छसि ।]

(प्रविश्य ।) **हरदत्तः**—देव मदीयमिदानीमुपदेशमवलोकयितुं क्रियतां प्रसादः ।

६**राजा** (आत्मगतम् ।)—अवसितो मे दर्शनार्थः । (दाक्षिण्यमवलम्ब्य । प्रकाशम् ।) हरदत्त, ननु पर्युत्सुका एव वयम् ।

Vidūṣaka. Revered lady, those who are ignorant have to depend upon the satisfaction of the learned. If you commend her, here would I give her a present. (*So saying, he draws off a bracelet from the king's hand.*)

Queen. Hold, hold. How could you bestow the ornament before you have known a different kind of merit ?

Vidūṣaka. Because it belongs to another.

Queen. *(Looking at the professor)* Noble Gaṇadāsa, your pupil has indeed exhibited her proficiency.

Gaṇadāsa. Child, you may leave now. (*Mālavikā departs with her teacher.)*

Vidūṣaka. (*Looking at the king, aside*) Thus far only can my ingenuity help you.

King. Have done with setting a limit to your power. For now

I regard her disappearance to be like the
obscuration of the prosperity of mine eyes, or
like the end of the great festivity of my heart,
or like the closing of the portals of my joy. (11)

Vidūṣaka. Ah, well ! Like a poor patient you desire the physician to procure you medicine.

(*Entering*)

Haradatta. King please now favour me by witnessing the exhibition of my skill in teaching.

King. (*To himself*) The object of my vision has vanished ; *(Courteously, aloud)* friend Haradatta, indeed, we are so eager !

हरदत्तः—अनुगृहीतोऽस्मि ।

वैतालिकः–(नेपथ्ये) विजयतां देवः । उपारूढो मध्याह्नः । तथाहि ।

पत्रच्छायासु हंसा मुकुलितनयना दीर्घिकापद्मिनीनां
सौधान्यत्यर्थतापाद्वलभिपरिचयद्वेषिपारावतानि ।
बिन्दूत्क्षेपान्पिपासुः परिपतति शिखी भ्रान्तिमद्वारियन्त्रं
सर्वैरुस्रैः समग्रस्त्वमिव नृपगुणैर्दीप्यते सप्तसप्तिः ॥ १२ ॥

विदूषकः—अविहा अविहा । बम्हणस्स भोअणवेला संवुत्ता । अत्तहोदो वि । उइदवेलादिक्कमे चिकिस्सआ दोसं उदाहरन्ति । हरदत्त किं दाणिं भणसि । [अविहा अविहा । ब्राह्मणस्य भोजनवेला संवृत्ता । अत्रभवतोऽपि । उचितवेलातिक्रमे चिकित्सका दोषमुदाहरन्ति । हरदत्त, किमिदानीं भणसि ।]

हरदत्तः—नास्ति मे वचनस्यान्यस्यावकाशोऽत्र ।

राजा (हरदत्तमवलोक्य ।)—तेन हि त्वदीयमुपदेशं श्वो वयं द्रक्ष्यामः । विश्राम्यतु भवान् ।

हरदत्तः—यदाज्ञापयति देवः । (इति निष्क्रान्तः ।)

देवी—णिव्वत्तेदु अज्जउत्तो मज्जणविहिं । [निर्वर्तयत्वार्यपुत्रो मज्जनविधिम् ।]

विदूषकः—होदि, विसेसेण भोअणं तुवरावेदु । [भवति, विशेषेण भोजनं त्वरयतु ।]

परिव्राजिका (उत्थाय ।)—स्वस्ति भवते ।

(इति सपरिजनया देव्या सह निष्क्रान्ता)

विदूषकः—भो ण केवलं रूवे सिप्पे वि अद्दुदीया मालविआ । [भोः न केवलं रूपे शिल्पेऽप्यद्वितीया मालविका ।]

Haradatta. I feel favoured.

(*Behind the scenes*)

A bard.

Victory to our king! It is mid-day. Thus
the swans with closed eyes nestle under the
shadows of the leaves of the lotus-plants in the
ponds; while the pigeons hate to be on the
terrace-tops on account of the blazing heat; the
peacock dashes to the revolving water-wheel
desiring to lick up the splashing drops; and the
sun too, endowed with all his rays, as you with
kingly virtues, is shining brilliantly. (12)

Vidūṣaka. O confound it! It is time for this Brāhmaṇa to feed himself, so likewise for your majesty; and the physicians warn us that it is a grave mistake to transgress the proper time. How do you think, Haradatta?

Haradatta. There is no occasion for words other than these from me.

King. (*Looking at Haradatta*) Well, then, we shall witness your instruction to-morrow. Rest you.

Haradatta. As the king commands. (*Exit*)

Queen. Let my noble Lord finish his bath.

Vidūṣaka. You will be particularly quick in getting the meal ready.

Parivrājikā. (*Rising*) Blessings on you.

(*Leaves along with the queen and attendants.*)

Vidūṣaka. Sir, not in loveliness alone, but also in the art is she peerless.

राजा—वयस्य

अव्याजसुन्दरीं तां विज्ञानेन ललितेन योजयता ।
परिकल्पितो विधात्रा बाणः कामस्य विषदिग्धः॥ १३॥

किं बहुना, चिन्तयितव्योऽस्मि ते ।

विदूषकः—भवदा वि अहं । दिढं खु विवणिकन्दू विअ उअरब्भन्दरं डज्झइ । [भवताप्यहम् । दृढं खलु विपणिकन्दुरिवोदराभ्यन्तरं दह्यते ।]

राजा—एवमेव भवान् सुहृदर्थे त्वरताम् ।

विदूषकः—गहिदक्खणोम्हि । किं दु मेहावलीरुद्धजोह्ना विअ पराहीणदंसणा तत्तहोदी मालविआ । भवं वि सूणोवरिअरो गिद्धो विअ आमिसलोलुओ भीरुओ अ । ता अणादुरो भविअ कज्जसिद्धिं पत्थयन्तो मे रुच्चइ । [गृहीतक्षणोऽस्मि । किं तु मेघावलीरुद्धज्योत्स्नेव पराधीनदर्शना तत्रभवती मालविका । भवानपि सूनोपरिचरो गृध्र इव आमिषलोलुपो भीरुकश्च । तस्मादनातुरो भूत्वा कार्यसिद्धिं प्रार्थयमानो मे रोचसे ।]

राजा—सखे कथमनातुरो भविष्यामि । यदा

सर्वान्तःपुरवनिताव्यापारं प्रति निवृत्तहृदयस्य ।
सा वामलोचना मे स्नेहस्यैकायनीभूता ॥ १४ ॥

(इति निष्क्रान्ताः सर्वे ।)

इति द्वितीयोऽङ्कः ।

King. Friend,

the creator now by uniting this knowledge of the fine arts to her artless charms has surely devised a shaft of love smeared with poison. (13)

What more! You have ever to be solicitous about me.

Vidūṣaka. You too about me. For the inside of me is grilling like the frying pan in the market-place.

King. Even so, do you be quick to accomplish your friend's desire.

Vidūṣaka. I undertake the venture. But like moonlight veiled by clouds the sight of the lady Mālavikā is dependent upon another ; while you, like the vulture wheeling over the slaughter-house, desire the flesh yet fear to venture. I shall, therefore, much appreciate your exercising patience while you seek success in this venture.

King. Friend, how can I curb my impatience when

that sweet-eyed beauty has become the one centre of the affection of my heart which has withdrawn its interest from all the ladies of my harem ? (14).

(Exeunt Omnes.)

Here ends the Second Act.

तृतीयोऽङ्कः ।

(ततः प्रविशति परिव्राजिकायाः परिचारिका ।)

परिचारिका—आणत्तम्हि भअवदीए । उवाअणत्थं बीजपूरअं गेण्हिअ आअच्छत्ति । ता जाव पमदवणपालिअं महुअरिअं अण्णेसामि । (परिक्रम्य अवलोक्य च ।) एसा तवणीआसोअं ओलोअन्ती चिट्ठइ । जाव णं उवसप्पे । [आज्ञतास्मि भगवत्या । 'उपायनार्थं बीजपूरकं गृहीत्वागच्छ' इति । तद्यावत् प्रमदवनपालिकां मधुकारिकामान्विष्यामि । एषा तपनीयाशोकमवलोकयन्ती तिष्ठति । यावदेनामुपसर्पामि ।]

(ततः प्रविशत्युद्यानपालिका ।)

परभृतिका (उपसृत्य ।)—महुअरिए अवि सुहो दे उज्जाणव्वावारो । [मधुकरिके, अपि सुखस्त उद्यानव्यापारः ।]

मधुकरिका—अम्मो परहुदिआ । सहि साअदं दे । [अम्मो परभृतिका । सखि स्वागतं ते ।]

परभृतिका—हला भअवदी आणवेदि अरित्तपाणिणा अम्हारिसजणेण तत्तहोदी देवी देक्खिदव्वा । ता बीजपूरएण सुस्सूसिदुं इच्छम्मित्ति । [हला, भगवत्याज्ञापयति 'अरिक्तपाणिनास्मादृशजनेन तत्रभवती देवी द्रष्टव्या । तद्बीजपूरकेण शुश्रूषितुमिच्छामि' इति ।]

मधुकरिका—णं सण्णिहिदं एव्व बीजपूरअं । कहेहि दाव अण्णोण्णसङ्घरिसिदाणं णट्टाअरिआणं उवदेसं देक्खिअ कदरो भअवदीए पसंसिदो । [ननु सन्निहितमेव बीजपूरकम् । कथय तावदन्योन्यसङ्घर्षितयोर्नाट्याचार्ययोरुपदेशं दृष्ट्वा कतरो भगवत्या प्रशंसितः ।]

परभृतिका—दुवे वि किल आअमिणो पओअणिउणा अ । किंदु सिस्सागुणविसेसेण उण्णमिदो गणदासो । [द्वावपि किलागमिनौ प्रयोगनिपुणौ च । किं तु शिष्यागुणविशेषेण उन्नमितो गणदासः ।]

ACT III.

(Enter the maid-servant of the Parivrājikā).

Maid-servant. I have been ordered by the reverend lady to fetch for her a fruit of the citron for offering as a present. I will, therefore, find out Madhukarikā, the keeper of the Pramadavana garden. *(Moving about and looking).* Here she is, looking at the gold Aśoka tree; so I will go to her.

(Enter the keeper of the Garden.)

Parabhṛtikā. *(Approaching)* Madhukarikā, I hope you find your work in the garden quite pleasant.

Madhukarikā. Ah ! Friend Parabhṛtikā, you are welcome.

Parabhṛtikā. Friend, the reverend lady says :— people like us ought not to approach the queen with empty hands. I, therefore, desire to make her the gift of a citron and wait upon her.

Madhukarikā. Oh, here is a citron quite at hand. But tell me which of the two professors of dancing that had quarrelled was praised by the reverend lady after she had witnessed their skill in teaching ?

Parabhṛtikā. Both are, indeed, known to be very learned and skilful teachers. But Ganadāsa was adjudged the superior of the two, owing to the excellent merits of his pupil.

मधुकरिका——अह मालविआगदं कोलीणं कहं सुणीअदि। [अथ मालविकागतं कौलीनं कथं श्रूयते ।]

परभृतिका——बलिअं खु साहिलासो भट्टा तस्सिं । केवलं देवीए धारिणीए चित्तं रक्खन्तो अत्तणो पहुत्तणं ण दंसेदि । मालविआ वि इमेसु दिअहेसु अणुहूदमुत्ता विअ मालदीमाला मिलायमाणा लक्खिअदि । अदो वरं ण आणे । विसज्जेहि मं । [बलवत् खलु साभिलाषो भर्ता तस्याम् । केवलं देव्या धारिण्याश्चित्तं रक्षन्नात्मनः प्रभुत्वं न दर्शयति । मालविकाप्येषु दिवसेष्वनुभूतमुक्तेव मालतीमाला म्लायमाना लक्ष्यते । अतः परं न जाने । विसर्जय माम् ।]

मधुकरिका——एदं साहावलम्बि बीजपूरअं गेह्ण । [एतच्छाखावलम्बि बीजपूरकं गृहाण ।]

परभृतिका (नाट्येन गृहीत्वा)—हला तुमं वि इदो वरं पेसलअरं साहुअणसुस्सूसाए फलं पाविदा होहि । [हला त्वमपि इतः परं पेशलतरं साधुजनशुश्रूषायाः फलं प्राप्ता भव ।]

(इति प्रस्थिता ।)

मधुकरिका——सहि समं एव्व गच्छम्ह । अहं वि इमस्स चिराअमाणकुसुमुग्गमस्स तवणीआसोअस्स दोहदणिमित्तं देवीए विण्णवेमि । [सखि सममेव गच्छावः । अहमप्यस्य चिरायमाणकुसुमोद्गमस्य तपनीयाशोकस्य दोहदनिमित्तं देव्यै विज्ञापयामि ।]

परभृतिका—जुज्जइ । अहिआरो खु तुह । [युज्यते ! अधिकारः खलु तव ।] (इति निष्क्रान्ते ।)

प्रवेशकः ।

(ततः प्रविशति कामयमानावस्थो राजा विदूषकश्च ।)

राजा (आत्मानं विलोक्य)—

शरीरं क्षामं स्यादसति दयितालिङ्गनसुखे
भवेत्सास्रं चक्षुः क्षणमपि न सा दृश्यत इति ।

Madhukarikā. Well, but what is this scandal about Mālavikā ?

Parabhṛtikā. The king has conceived a strong passion for her. Only out of regard for the feelings of queen Dhāriṇī, he does not exercise his power. Mālavikā, too, during all these days has grown pale like a jasmine garland worn and cast away. Beyond this I know nothing. Well, allow me to go.

Madhukarikā. Take the citron that hangs on yonder bough.

Parabhṛtikā. *(Acting as if she picks up the citron)* Ah, may you get a far more glorious fruit than this for your readiness to serve the saintly lady.

(Starts to go.)

Madhukarikā. Friend, we will go together. For I want to request the queen regarding the longing of this gold Aśoka tree which is delaying to burst into blossom.

Parabhrtikā. Quite right. Indeed, it is your duty.

(Exeunt both.)

Here ends the introductory scene.

(Enter the king in a love-lorn state, and the Vidūṣaka.)

King. *(Looking at himself)*

The body may get emaciate in the absence of the pleasure of the beloved's embrace, and the eyes tearful, as they do not get even a moment's

तया सारङ्गाक्ष्या त्वमसि न कदाचिद्विरहितं
प्रसक्ते निर्वाणे हृदय परितापं वहसि किम् ॥ १ ॥

विदूषकः—अलं भवदो धीरदं उज्झिअ परिदेविदेण। दिट्ठा मए तत्तहोदीए मालविआए पिअसही बउलावलिआ। सुणाविदा अ मए जं भवदा सन्दिट्ठं। [अलं भवतो धीरतामुज्झित्वा परिदेवितेन। दृष्टा मया तत्रभवत्या मालविकायाः प्रियसखी बकुलावलिका। श्राविता च मया यद्भवता सन्दिष्टम्।]

राजा—ततः किमुक्तवती।

विदूषकः—विण्णवेहि भट्टारं। अणुगहीदम्हि इमिणा णिओएण। किं दु सा तवस्सिणी देवीए अहिअदरं रक्खिअमाणा णाअरक्खिदो विअ णिही ण सुहं समासादइदव्वा भविस्सदि। तह वि घडइस्सं ति। [विज्ञापय भर्तारम्। 'अनुगृहीतास्मि अनेन नियोगेन। किं तु सा तपस्विनी देव्या अधिकतरं रक्ष्यमाणा नागरक्षित इव निधिर्न सुखं समासादयितव्या भविष्यति। तथापि घटयिष्यामि' इति।]

राजा—भगवन् सङ्कल्पयोने, प्रतिबन्धवत्स्वपि विषयेष्वभिनिवेश्य तथा प्रहरसि यथा जनोऽयं कालान्तरक्षमो न भवति। (सविस्मयं)

क्व रुजा हृदयप्रमाथिनी क्व च ते विश्वसनीयमायुधम्।
मृदु तीक्ष्णतरं यदुच्यते तदिदं मन्मथ दृश्यते त्वयि॥२॥

विदूषकः—णं भणामि तस्सिं साहणिज्जे कज्जे किदो मए उवाओवक्खेवो। ता पज्जवत्थावेदु भवं अत्ताणं। [ननु भणामि तस्मिन् साधनीये कार्ये कृतो मयोपायोपक्षेपः। तत्पर्यवस्थापयतु भवानात्मानम्।]

राजा—अथेमं दिवसशेषमुचितव्यापारविमुखेन चेतसा क्व न खलु यापयामि।

विदूषकः—णं भवं अज्ज पुढमं वसन्दावदारसूअआइं रत्तासोअकोरआइं उवाअणं पेसिअ णववसन्दूसवावदेसेण इरावदीए

glimpse of her; but, my heart, never art thou severed from that fawn-eyed one: how then dost thou suffer agony even when thou gettest the highest bliss? (1)

Vidūṣaka. Do not give up fortitude and lament. I have seen Bakulāvalikā, the dear friend of the lady Mālavikā. I have also conveyed to her your message.

King. What was her reply to that?

Vidūṣaka. 'Request the king: I feel favoured by this command. But the poor girl is being more carefully guarded by the queen like a treasure by a cobra, and, therefore, will not be obtained with ease. Still I will do my best.'

King. Oh revered God of love, although you impel me to long for an inaccessible object, yet you smite me so sorely that I am not able to brook any delay. (*Wonderingly*)

What great disparity is there between this heart-wrenching ache, and your weapon seemingly so harmless! What is described as both soft and piercing hard—that indeed is seen in you, O love. (2)

Vidūṣaka. Well, I say, I have devised means for the (attainment) of the object desired. Do you, therefore, compose yourself.

King. Where shall I pass the rest of the day when my mind feels such aversion for my proper duties?

Vidūṣaka. Well, you have already heard through Nipuṇikā the request of Irāvatī, who taking occasion

णिउणिआमुहेण पत्थिदो । इच्छामि अज्जउत्तेण सह डोलाहिरोहणं अणुहोदुं ति । भवदा वि से पडिण्णादं । ता पमदवणं एव्व गच्छम्ह । [ननु भवानद्य प्रथमं वसन्तावतारसूचकानि रक्ताशोककोरकाण्युपायनं प्रेष्य नववसन्तोत्सवापदेशेन इरावत्या निपुणिकामुखेन प्रार्थितः ‘इच्छाम्यार्यपुत्रेण सह दोलाधिरोहणमनुभवितुम्’ इति । भवताप्यस्यै प्रतिज्ञातम् । तत्प्रमदवनमेव गच्छावः ।]

राजा—न क्षममिदम् ।

विदूषकः—कहं विअ । [कथमिव ।]

राजा—वयस्य निसर्गनिपुणाः स्त्रियः । कथं मामन्यसङ्क्रान्तहृदयमुपलालयन्तमपि ते सखी न लक्षयिष्यति । अतः पश्यामि ।

उचितः प्रणयो वरं विहन्तुं
बहवः खण्डनहेतवो हि दृष्टाः ।
उपचारविधिर्मनस्विनीनां
न तु पूर्वाभ्यधिकोऽपि भावशून्यः ॥ ३ ॥

विदूषकः—णारुहदि भवं सव्वं अन्देउरपडिट्ठिदं दक्खिण्णं एक्कपदे पिट्ठदो कादुं । [नार्हति भवान् सर्वमन्तःपुरप्रतिष्ठितं दाक्षिण्यमेकपदे पृष्ठतः कर्तुम् ।]

राजा (विचिन्त्य)—तेन हि प्रमदवनमार्गमादेशय ।

विदूषकः—इदो इदो भवं । [इत इतो भवान् ।]

(उभौ परिक्रामतः ।)

विदूषकः—णं एदं पमदवणं पवणचलिदाहिं पल्लवंगुलीहिं तुअरावेदि विअ भवन्दं । ता पविसदु भवं । [नन्वेतत्प्रमदवनं पवनचलिताभिः पल्लवाङ्गुलीभिस्त्वरयतीव भवन्तम् । तत्प्रविशतु भवान् ।]

of spring's advent has first sent you as present the buds of the red Aśoka tree indicative of the arrival of that season : " I long to enjoy sitting on the swing together with my lord." You too have promised her. So we shall proceed to the Pramadavana garden.

King. That is impossible.

Vidūṣka. How do you mean ?

King. Friend, women are naturally so cunning. Do you think she will not notice—spite of all my love-caressings—that my heart is devoted to another ? Therefore, I see clearly

> that it is better to decline this request, although it is a proper one to make at this season, for I know many excuses for declining it than to go through the form of showing regard to these proud women, may be, with greater fervour than before, when one feels not even a shred of affection for them. (3)

Vidūṣaka. You ought not all of a sudden to throw aside your unfailing courtesy to the ladies of your harem.

King. (*Reflecting*) well, then, lead the way to the Pramadavana.

Vidūṣaka. This way, this way, my friend. (*Both move about.*)

Vidūṣaka. Here we come to the Pramadavana which seems to beckon you to hurry up with its fingers of leaves waving in the wind ; so please to enter.

राजा—(स्पर्शसुखं रूपयित्वा ।)—अभिजातः खलु वसन्तः। सखे
१२ पश्य

> **आमत्तानां श्रवणसुभगैः कूजितैः कोकिलानां**
> **सानुक्रोशं मनसिजरुजः सह्यतां पृच्छतेव ।**
> **अङ्गे चूतप्रसवसुरभिर्दक्षिणो मारुतो मे**
> **सान्द्रस्पर्शः करतल इव व्यापृतो माधवेन ॥ ४ ॥**

विदूषकः—एहि । पविस णिव्वुदिलाहाअ । [एहि । प्रविश निर्वृतिलाभाय ।] (उभौ प्रविशतः ।)

३ **विदूषकः**—भो वअस्स अवहाणेण दिट्ठिं देहि । एदं खु भवन्दं विलोहइदुकामाए पमदवणलच्छीए जुवइवेसलज्जत्तअं वसंदकुसुमणेवत्थं गहिदं । [भो वयस्य अवधानेन दृष्टिं देहि । एतत्खलु भवन्तं विलोभयितुकामया प्रमदवनलक्ष्म्या युवतिवेषलज्जयितृकं वसन्तकुसुमनेपथ्यं गृहीतम् ।]

राजा—ननु विस्मयादवलोकयामि ।

> **रक्ताशोकरुचा विशेषितगुणो बिम्बाधरालक्तकः**
> **प्रत्याख्यातविशेषकं कुरबकं श्यामावदातारुणम् ।**
> **आक्रान्ता तिलकक्रियापि तिलकैर्लग्नद्विरेफाञ्जनैः**
> **सावज्ञेव मुखप्रसाधनविधौ श्रीर्माधवी योषिताम् ॥५॥**

(उभौ उद्यानशोभां निरूपयतः ।)

(ततः प्रविशति पर्युत्सुका मालविका ।)

३ **मालविका**—अविण्णादहिअअं भट्टारं अहिलसन्ती अत्तणो वि दाव लज्जेमि । कुदो विहवो सिणिद्धसहिअणस्स इमं वुत्तन्तं आअक्खिदुं । ण आणे अप्पडीआरगरुअं वेअणं केत्तिअं कालं
६ मअणो मं णइस्सदि । (कतिचित्पदानि गत्वा ।) कहिं णु खु पत्थिदम्हि । (विचिन्त्य) आं सन्दिट्ठम्हि देवीए जह 'मालविए गोदमचावलादो डोलापरिब्भट्ठाए सरुजा मह चलणा । तुमं दाव

King. (*Gesticulating that he feels the pleasure of touch*) How noble is spring : see friend,

by the sweet notes of the slightly intoxicated koil, he seems to be compassionately inquiring whether I can bear the torture of love; while the south breeze with its soft touch and its incense of mango-blossoms is like the palm of spring's hand stroking my limbs. (4)

Vidūṣaka. : Come, enter and repose yourself. (*Both enter.*)

Vidūṣaka. Look attentively, my friend. Surely the presiding goddess of the Pramadavana desiring to allure you has put on the garment of spring-flowers that puts to shame the dress of a young lady.

King. Indeed, I behold it and am filled with wonderment.

The gleaming red of the Aśoka excels the paint that is applied to the bimba-like lip ; the Kurabaka with its (variety of colours) dark, and bright, and red, surpasses the paintings on the forehead ; the Tilaka blossoms with the bees clinging to them like collyrium, have thoroughly grasped the art of adorning the forehead with the tilaka mark ; thus vernal beauty seems to hold up to ridicule the art of adorning the face as practised by women. (5)

(*Both of them observe the beauty of the garden. Enter Mālavikā in a state of longing.*)

Mālavikā. How I feel ashamed of myself for being in love with the king, whose heart is unknown to me

तवणीआसोअस्स दोहलं णिव्वट्टेहि। जइ सो पञ्चरत्तब्भन्दरे कुसुमं दंसेदि तदो अहं तुह (अन्तरा निश्वस्य) अहिलासपूरइत्तअं पसादं दाइस्सं ' ति । ता जाव णिओअभूमिं पुढमं गदा होमि । जाव अणुपदं मह चलणालङ्कारहत्थाए बउलावलिआए आअन्तव्वं। परिदेविस्सं दाव विस्सद्धं मुहुत्तअं। (इति परिक्रामति) [अविज्ञात-हृदयं भर्तारमभिलषन्त्यात्मनोऽपि तावल्लज्जे। कुतो विभवः स्निग्धसखी-जनस्येमं वृत्तान्तमाख्यातुम् । न जाने अप्रतीकारगुरुकां वेदनां कियन्तं कालं मदनो मां नेष्यति। कुत्र नु खलु प्रस्थितास्मि। आम् सन्दिष्टास्मि देव्या यथा ' मालविके गौतमचापलाद् दोला-परिभ्रष्टायाः सरुजौ मम चरणौ । त्वं तावत्तपनीयाशोकस्य दोहदं निर्वर्तय । यदि स पञ्चरात्राभ्यन्तरे कुसुमं दर्शयति ततोऽहं तव (अन्तरा निःश्वस्य) अभिलाषपूरयितृकं प्रसादं दास्यामि ' इति । तद्यावन्नियोगभूमिं प्रथमं गता भवामि। यावदनुपदं मम चरणा-लङ्कारहस्तया बकुलावलिकया आगन्तव्यम् । परिदेविष्ये तावद् विस्रब्धं मुहूर्तकम् ।]

विदूषकः (दृष्ट्वा)--ही ही इअं खु सीहुपाणुव्वेजिदस्स मच्छण्डिआ उवणदा । [ही ही इयं खलु शीधुपानोद्वेजितस्य मत्स्यण्डिका उपनता ।]

राजा—अये किमेतत् ।

विदूषकः—एसा खु णादिपज्जत्तवेसा पज्जूसुआ विअ एआइणी मालविआ अदूरे वट्टइ । [एषा खलु नातिपर्याप्तवेषा पर्युत्सुकेव एकाकिनी मालविका अदूरे वर्तते ।]

राजा (सहर्षम्)—कथं मालविका ।

विदूषकः—अह इं । [अथ किम्]

राजा—शक्यमिदानीमात्मानमवलम्बितुम् ।

त्वदुपलभ्य समीपगतां प्रियां
हृदयमुच्छ्वसितं मम विक्लवम् ।

Where have I the courage to speak of the circumstance to my dear friend? I do not know how long will love submit me to this irremediably severe agony. (*Moving a few steps*) Where, indeed, am I going? (*Reflecting*) Ah, the queen has ordered me: 'Mālavikā, having had a fall from the swing owing to the heedlessness of Gautama, I am still suffering pain in my feet. Do you, therefore, perform the ceremony of fulfilling the longing of the golden Aśoka. If within five nights from this time it shows flowers, then will I (*Heaves a sigh in the middle of her speech*) bestow on you a favour which will gratify your desire.' I will, therefore, first proceed to the place where I am to perform this duty. For immediately after me will Bakulāvalikā come with the ornaments to adorn my feet. Let me then for a while freely bewail my state. (*Moves about.*)

Vidūṣaka. (*Observing*) Here is treacle offered to you who have been troubled with drinking wine.

King. Ah, what is this?

Vidūṣaka. Here is Mālavikā, not far (from us) but scantily dressed, who looks like one afflicted, and all alone.

King. (*With joy*) How? Mālavikā?

Vidūṣaka. Certainly.

King. Now it is possible to support my life.

When I learnt from you that my beloved
was quite close (to us) my distracted heart (at
once) revived like that of a thirsty traveller,

तरुवृतं पथिकस्य पिपासतः
सलिलमारासितादिव सारसात् ॥ ६ ॥

अथ क तत्रभवती ।

विदूषकः—एषा णं तरुराइमज्झादो णिक्कन्ता इदो एव्व
३ परिवट्टन्ती दीसइ । [एषा ननु तरुराजिमध्यान्निष्क्रान्ता इत एव परिवर्तमाना दृश्यते ।]

राजा—वयस्य पश्याम्येनाम्

विपुलं नितम्बबिम्बे मध्ये क्षामं समुन्नतं कुचयोः ।
अत्यायतं नयनयोर्मम जीवितमेतदायाति ॥ ७ ॥

सखे पूर्वस्मादवस्थान्तरमुपारूढा तत्रभवती । तथा हि ।

शरकाण्डपाण्डुगण्डस्थलेयमाभाति परिमिताभरणा ।
माधवपरिणतपत्रा कतिपयकुसुमेव कुन्दलता ॥८॥

विदूषकः—एसा वि भवं विअ मअणव्वाहिणा परामिट्ठा भविस्सदि । [एषापि भवानिव मदनव्याधिना परामृष्टा भविष्यति ।]

३**राजा**—सौहार्दमेवं पश्यति ।

मालविका—अअं सो सुउमारदोहलावेक्खी अगहिदकुसुमणे-
वत्थो उक्कण्ठिदं मं अणुकरेदि असोओ । जाव से पच्छाअ-
६सीदले सिलापट्टए णिसण्णा अत्ताणं विणोदेमि । [अयं स सुकुमार-
दोहदापेक्षी अगृहीतकुसुमनेपथ्य उत्कण्ठितां मामनुकरोत्यशोकः । याव-
९दस्य प्रच्छायशीतले शिलापट्टके निषण्णात्मानं विनोदयामि ।]

विदूषकः—सुदं भवदा उक्कण्ठिदम्हित्ति तत्तहोदीए मन्तिदं । [श्रुतं भवता उत्कण्ठितास्मीति तत्रभवत्या मन्त्रितम् ।]

१२**राजा** —नैतावता भवन्तं प्रसन्नतर्कं मन्ये । कुतः ।

वोढा कुरबकरजसां किसलयपुटभेदशीकरानुगतः ।
अनिमित्तामुत्कण्ठामपि जनयति मलयवातोऽयम् ॥९॥

when from the cry of the Sārasa he gathers that some river surrounded by trees is near. (6)

Well, where is she?

Vidūsaka. Here she emerges from the rows of trees and seems to be turning in this very direction.

King. Well, friend, I see her.

Ample in the hips and thin in the waist, uplifted in the bosom and very broad in the eyes she, my very life, is coming. (7)

Friend, how she seems to have changed from the former state! For

scantily decked, her broad cheeks pale like the stalk of a reed, she resembles a Kunda creeper having its leaves ripened by spring and with only a few flowers. (8)

Vidūsaka. It is likely that she too like yourself is affected with love-sickness.

King. It is only friendship that sees thus.

Mālavikā. This Aśoka awaiting the fulfilment of its delicate longing, and not assuming its robe of flowers, seems to imitate me in my love-sick condition. So I will sit on the cool slab under its shade and divert myself.

Vidūsaka. Did you hear? She said she was in a love-sick state.

King. That is not enough to assure me of the correctness of your inference.

This Malaya breeze laden with the pollen of the Kurabaka flowers, and charged with the drops of water issuing from the opening folds of the tender sprouts, produces longing in the heart without any definite cause. (9)

5

(मालविका उपविष्टा ।)

राजा—वयस्य इतस्तावदावां लतान्तरितौ भवाव: ।

विदूषकः—इरावदिं विअ अदूरे समत्थेमि । [इरावतीमिवादूरे समर्थये ।]

राजा—न हि कमलिनीं दृष्ट्वा ग्राहमवेक्षते मतङ्गजः ।

(इति विलोकयन्स्थितः ।)

मालविका—हिअअ णिरवलम्बादो मणोरहादो विरम । किं मं आआसेसि । [हृदय निरवलम्बान्मनोरथाद्विरम । किं मामायासयसि ।]

(विदूषकः राजानमवेक्षते ।)

राजा (आत्मगतम्)—प्रिये पश्य वामतां स्नेहस्य ।

औत्सुक्यहेतुं विवृणोषि न त्वं
तत्त्वावबोधैकरसो न तर्कः ।
तथापि रम्भोरु करोमि लक्ष्य-
मात्मानमेषां परिदेवितानाम् ॥ १० ॥

विदूषकः—सम्पदं भवदो णिस्संसअं भविस्सदि । एसा अप्पिदमअणसन्देसा विवित्ते णं बउलावलिआ उवट्ठिदा । [सांप्रतं भवतो निःसंशयं भविष्यति । एषार्पितमदनसन्देशा विविक्ते ननु बकुलावलिकोपस्थिता ।]

राजा—अपि स्मरेदस्मदभ्यर्थनाम् ।

विदूषकः—किं दाणिं एसा दासीए सुदा तुह गरुअं सन्देसं विसुमरिस्सदि । अहं वि दाव दाणिं एदं ण विसुमरेमि । [किमिदानीमेषा दास्याः सुता तव गुरुकं सन्देशं विस्मरिष्यति । अहमपि तावदिदानीमेतं न विस्मरामि ।]

(प्रविश्य चरणालङ्कारहस्ता बकुलावलिका ।)

बकुलावलिका—अवि सुहं सहीए । [अपि सुखं सख्याः ।]

(*Mālavikā sits down.*)

King. Friend, come here, let us hide behind the creepers.

Vidūṣaka. I think Irāvatī, too, is not far from here.

King. But the elephant recks not of the alligator, when he sees a lotus-plant.

(*Stands gazing.*)

Mālavikā. My heart, cease from cherishing this fruitless longing. Why should you torture me ?

(*The Vidūṣaka looks at the king.*)

King. (*To himself*) Beloved, look, how perverse is love.

> You do not reveal the cause of your longing
> nor does conjecture invariably give the truth ;
> nevertheless, fair one, I regard myself as the
> theme of these lamentations. (10)

Vidūṣaka. Now will be dispelled all your doubts. For is not that Bakulāvalikā to whom I gave your message of love arriving in this solitary place ?

King. I wonder if she remembers my request.

Vidūṣaka. How would that daughter of a female slave forget your weighty message now ? Why, even I remember it perfectly well at this moment.

(*Enter Bakulāvalikā with ornaments for the feet in her hand.*)

Bakulāvalikā. Is my friend happy ?

मालविका—अम्मो बउलावलिआ। सहि साअदं दे। उवविस। [अम्मो बकुलावलिका। सखि स्वागतं ते। उपविश।]

बकुलावलिका(उपविश्य)–हला तुमं दाव दाणिं देवीए जोग्गदाए णिउत्ता। ता एक्कं दे चलणं उवणेहि। जाव सालत्तअं सणेउरं करेमि। [हला त्वं तावदिदानीं देव्या योग्यतया नियुक्ता। तदेकं ते चरणमुपनय। यावत्सालक्तकं सनूपुरं करोमि।]

मालविका (स्वगतम्)—हिअअ अलं सुहिददाए अअं विहवो उवट्ठिदोत्ति। कहं दाणिं अत्ताणं मोचएअं। अहवा एदं एव्व मह मिच्चुमण्डणं भविस्सदि। [हृदय अलं सुखिततया अयं विभव उपस्थित इति। कथमिदानीमात्मानं मोचयेयम्। अथवा एतदेव मे मृत्युमण्डनं भविष्यति।]

बकुलावलिका—किं विआरेसि। उस्सुआ खु एदस्स तवणीआसोअस्स कुसुमुग्गमे देवी। [किं विचारयसि। उत्सुका खल्वेतस्य तपनीयाशोकस्य कुसुमोद्गमे देवी।]

राजा—कथमशोकदोहदनिमित्तोऽयमारम्भः।

विदूषकः—किं णु खु ण आणासि अकालणादो देवी इमं अन्देउरणेवत्थेण ण संजोअइस्सदित्ति। [किं नु खलु न जानासि अकारणाद्देवी इमां अन्तःपुरनेपथ्येन न संयोजयिष्यतीति।]

मालविका (पादमुपहरन्ती)—हला मरिसेहि दाणिं। [हला मर्षयेदानीम्।]

बकुलावलिका—अइ सरीरं सि मे। (नाट्येन चरणालङ्कारमारभते।) [अयि शरीरमसि मे।]

राजा— **चरणान्तनिवेशितां प्रियायाः**
सरसां पश्य वयस्य रागरेखाम्।
प्रथमामिव पल्लवप्रसूतिं
हरदग्धस्य मनोभवद्रुमस्य॥ ११॥

Mālavikā. Ah! Bakulāvalikā is come! Friend you are welcome. Sit down.

Bakulāvalikā. (*Sitting down*) Friend, you have indeed been appointed by the queen, owing to your fitness. So give me one of your feet; so that I might lay on it the Alaktaka die and put the anklet on it.

Mālavikā. (*To herself*) My heart, do not be happy that greatness comes to you. How can I secure my freedom? Or rather this will serve as the ornament to adorn me at death.

Bakulāvalikā. Why are you hesitating? The queen indeed, is anxious that the golden Aśoka should burst into flowers.

King. So all this preparation is due to the longing of the Aśoka!

Vidūṣaka. Why! Don't you know that the queen will not without reason make her put on the attire of the harem?

Mālavikā. (*Bringing close her foot*) Friend, please to pardon me.

Bakulāvalikā. You are indeed as dear to me as my very body. (*She gesticulates adorning her foot.*)

King. Friend, look at this streak of wet paint laid upon her foot, which is like the first burgeoning of leaves on the tree of love consumed by Hara. (11)

विदूषकः—चलणाणुरूवो खु तत्तहोदीए अहिआरो उवक्खित्तो। [चरणानुरूपः खलु तत्रभवत्या अधिकार उपक्षिप्तः ।]

राजा—सम्यगभिहितं भवता।

> नवकिसलयरागेणाग्रपादेन बाला
> स्फुरितनखरुचा द्वौ हन्तुमर्हत्यनेन।
> अकुसुमितमशोकं दोहदापेक्षया वा
> प्रणिहितशिरसं वा कान्तमार्द्रापराधम् ॥१२॥

विदूषकः—पारइस्ससि तत्तहोदीए अवरध्दुं। [पारयिष्यसि तत्रभवत्या अपराद्धुम् ।]

राजा—प्रतिगृहीतं वचः सिद्धिदर्शिनो ब्राह्मणस्य।

(ततः प्रविशति युक्तमदा इरावती चेटी च ।)

इरावती—हञ्जे णिउणिए सुणामि बहुसो मदो किल इत्थिआजणस्स विसेसमण्डणं ति। अवि सच्चो अअं लोअवादो। [हञ्जे निपुणिके श्रृणोमि बहुशो मदः किल स्त्रीजनस्य विशेषमण्डनमिति। अपि सत्योऽयं लोकवादः।]

निपुणिका—पुढमं लोअवादो एव्व। अज्ज उण सच्चो संवुत्तो। [प्रथमं लोकवाद एव। अद्य पुनः सत्यः संवृत्तः।]

इरावती—अल मइ सिणेहेण। कुदो दाणिं अवगदं डोलाघरं पुढमं गदो भट्टात्ति। [अलं मयि स्नेहेन। कुत इदानीमवगतं दोलागृहं प्रथमं गतो भर्तेति।]

निपुणिका—भट्टिणीए अखण्डिदादो पणआदो। [भट्टिन्या अखण्डितात्प्रणयात्।]

इरावती—अलं सेवाए। मज्झत्थदं गेण्हिअ भणाहि। [अलं सेवया। मध्यस्थतां गृहीत्वा भण।]

निपुणिका—वसन्दोवाअणलोलुवेण अज्जगोदमेण कहिदं। तुवरदु भट्टिणी। [वसन्तोपायनलोलुपेनार्यगौतमेन कथितम्। त्वरतां भट्टिनी।]

Vidūsaka. The queen indeed has laid upon her foot a duty of which it is worthy.

King. You speak well.

With the toes of her foot red-hued like young foliage; and flashing with the lustre of the nails this girl deserves to smite two objects—the Aśoka awaiting the fulfilment of its longing before it would blossom, and the lover who, having only recently given offence, stands with bowed head. (12)

Vidūsaka. You will soon be able to give some offence.

King. I accept these words of a Brahmin who prophesies success.

(*Enter Irāvatī in a state of intoxication and an attendant.*)

Irāvatī. Girl Nipunikā, I heard it often said that intoxication is a special ornament to women. Is there any truth in this popular saying ?

Nipunikā. First it was a popular saying merely-but now it has become true.

Irāvatī. Have done with this affection towards me. How did you know that my lord went first to the house in which the swing is ?

Nipunikā. From my unfailing affection for my mistress.

Irāvatī. Give up this servile attitude—speak like one independent.

Nipuṇikā. It was the noble Vasantaka, greedy to receive presents offered in the month of spring, who told me so.

इरावती—(अवस्थासदृशं परिक्रम्य ।) हञ्जे मएण मिलाअमाणं मं अज्जउत्तदंसणे हिअअं तुवरावेदि । चलणा उण मग्गे ण प्पसरन्ति। [हञ्जे मदेन म्लायमानां मामार्यपुत्रदर्शने हृदयं त्वरयति । चरणौ पुनर्मार्गे न प्रसरतः ।]

निपुणिका—णं सम्पत्तम्ह डोलाघरअं । [ननु संप्राप्ते स्वो दोलागृहम ।]

इरावती—णिउणिए ण एत्थ अज्जउत्तो दीसइ । [निपुणिके नात्रार्यपुत्रो दृश्यते ।]

निपुणिका—ओलोएदु भट्टिणी । परिहासणिमित्तं कहिं वि गूढेण भट्टिणा होदव्वं । अम्हे वि इमं पिअङ्गुलदापरिक्खित्तं असोअसिलापट्टअं पविसम्ह । [अवलोकयतु भट्टिनी । परिहासनिमित्तं कुत्रापि गूढेन भर्त्रा भवितव्यम् । आवामपीमं प्रियङ्गुलतापरिक्षिप्तमशोकशिलापट्टकं प्रविशावः ।]

(इरावती तथा करोति ।)

निपुणिका (परिक्रम्य विलोक्य ।)—ओलोएदु भट्टिणी । चूदङ्कुरं विइण्णन्तीणं अम्हाणं पिपीलिआहिं दट्ठं । [अवलोकयतु भट्टिनी । चूताङ्कुरं विचिन्वत्योरावयोः पिपीलिकाभिर्दष्टम् ।]

इरावती—किं विअ एदं । [किमिवैतत् ।]

निपुणिका—एसा बउलावलिआ असोअपाअवच्छाआए मालविआए चलणालङ्कारं णिव्वट्टेदि । [एषा बकुलावलिका अशोकवृक्षच्छायायां मालविकायाश्चरणालङ्कारं निर्वर्तयति ।]

इरावती (शङ्कां रूपयित्वा ।)—अभूमी इअं मालविआए । किं तक्केसि । (अभूमिरियं मालविकायाः । किं तर्कयसि ।)

निपुणिका—तक्केमि डोलापरिब्भट्टाए सलुजचलणाए असोअदोहलाहिआरे णिउत्ता मालविअत्ति । अण्णहा कहं देवी सअं

Irāvatī. (*Moving in a manner befitting her condition*) Girl, my heart hastens me that have grown languid through intoxication, to see my lord ; but my feet do not move on the way.

Nipunikā. Well, we have come to the house where the swing is.

Irāvatī. Nipuṇikā, my lord is not to be seen here.

Nipuṇikā. Look about you, my mistress ; for the king, simply to make fun, may have lain hidden. We too shall sit down on this slab of stone under the Asoka tree which is twined round with the Priyangu creeper.

(*Irāvatī does as described.*)

Nipunikā. (*Moving about and observing* Look, mistress. While searching for mango-sprouts we have been bitten by ants.

Irāvatī. What is it ?

Nipunikā. Here is Bakulāvalikā adorning Mālavikā's foot in the shade of the Aśoka tree.

Irāvatī. (*Expressing doubt*) This is not a place where Mālavikā can have access. What do you think, then ?

Nipunikā. I think that the queen, having had a fall from the swing and got pain in her feet, has appointed Mālavikā to perform the ceremony of fulfilling the long-

धारिदं णेउरजुअलं परिअणस्स अणुजाणिस्सदि। [तर्कयामि दोलापरिभ्रष्टया-सरुजचरणया देव्या अशोकदोहदाधिकारे नियुक्ता मालविकेति । अन्यथा कथं देवी स्वयं धारितं नूपुरयुगलं परिजनस्यानुज्ञास्यति]

इरावती—महदी खु से सम्भावणा । [महती खल्वस्याः सम्भावना ।]

निपुणिका—किं उण ण अण्णेसीअदि भट्टा । [किंपुनर्नान्विष्यते भर्ता ।]

इरावती—हंजे मे चलणा अण्णदो ण प्पवट्टन्ति । मणो वि किं वि विआरेदि । आसङ्किदस्स दाव अन्तं गमिस्सं । (मालविकां निर्वर्ण्य आत्मगतम् ।) ठाणे खु कादरं मे हिअअं । [हञ्जे मे चरणावन्यतो न प्रवर्तेते । मनोऽपि किमपि विचारयति । आशङ्कितस्य तावदन्तं गमिष्यामि । स्थाने खलु कातरं मे हृदयम् ।]

बकुलावलिका (चरणं दर्शयन्ती ।)—हला मालविए अवि रोअदि दे अअं चलणराअरेहाविण्णासो । [हला मालविके अपि रोचते तेऽयं चरणरागरेखाविन्यासः ।]

मालविका—अत्तणो चलणगदोत्ति लज्जेमि णं पसंसिदुं। कहेहि केण पसाहणकलाए अहिविणीदासि । [आत्मनश्चरणगत इति लज्जे एनं प्रशंसितुम् । कथय केन प्रसाधनकलायामभिविनीतासि ।]

बकुलावलिका—एत्थ खु भट्टिणो सिस्सम्हि । [अत्र खलु भर्तुः शिष्यास्मि ।]

विदूषकः—तुवरेहि दाणिं गुरुदक्खिणाए । [त्वरस्वेदानीं गुरुदक्षिणायै ।]

मालविका—दिट्ठिआ ण गव्विदासि । [दिष्टया न गर्वितासि ।]

बकुलावलिका—उवदेसाणुरूवे चलणे लम्भिअ दाणिं गव्विदा भविस्सं । (स्वगतम् ।) हन्त सिद्धं मे दोच्चं । (रागं विलोक्य प्रकाशम् ।) सहि एक्कस्स दे चलणस्स अवसिदो राअणिक्खेवो ।

ing of the Aśoka tree; how, otherwise, could the queen allow a mere servant to wear the anklets worn by herself?

Irāvatī. She has, indeed, been highly honoured.

Nipunikā. But why should we not seek the king?

Irāvatī. Well, girl, my feet do not move from this place, and my mind too is filled with some suspicions; I shall first get to the end of them. (*Looking at Mālavikā, to herself*) It is but proper that my heart is filled with fear.

Bakulāvalikā. (*Pointing to the foot*) friend Mālavikā. how do you like these lines of paint on your foot?

Mālavikā. I am ashamed of praising it, as it is on my own foot. Tell me who taught you this art of decoration.

Bakulāvalikā. I am the pupil of the king in this (art).

Vidūsakā. Be quick now to receive the present due to a teacher.

Mālavikā. Happily you are free from conceit.

Bakulāvalikā. Surely I shall be full of conceit, now that I can exhibit my skill on worthy feet. (*To herself*) O joy, my mission is done. (*Looking at the paint, aloud*)

केवलं मुहमारुदो लम्भइदव्वो । अहवा पवादो एव्व अअं पदेसो । [उपदेशानुरूपे चरणे लब्ध्वा इदानीं गर्विता भविष्यामि । हन्त, सिद्धं मे दौत्यम् । सखि एकस्य ते चरणस्यावसितो रागनिक्षेपः । केवलं मुखमारुतो लम्भयितव्यः । अथवा प्रवात एवायं प्रदेशः ।]

राजा—सखे पश्य पश्य ।

आर्द्रालक्तकमस्याश्चरणं मुखमारुतेन वीजयितुम् ।
प्रतिपन्नः प्रथमतरः सम्प्रति सेवावकाशो मे ॥ १३ ॥

विदूषकः—कुदो दे अणुसओ । चिरं भवदा एदं कमेण अणुहोदव्वं । [कुतस्तेऽनुशयः । चिरं भवतैतत्क्रमेणानुभवितव्यम् ।]

बकुलावलिका—सहि अरुणसदपत्तं विअ सोहदि दे चलणं । सव्वहा भट्टिणो अङ्कपरिवट्टिणी होहि । [सखि अरुणशतपत्रमिव शोभते ते चरणम् । सर्वथा भर्तुरङ्कपरिवर्तिनी भव ।]

(इरावती निपुणिकामुखमवेक्षते ।)

राजा—ममेयमाशीः ।

मालविका—हला अवअणीअं मन्तेसि । [हला अवचनीयं मन्त्रयसे ।]

बकुलावलिका—मन्तिदव्वं एव्व मए मन्तिदं । [मन्त्रयितव्यमेव मया मन्त्रितम् ।]

मालविका—पिआ खु अहं तुह । [प्रिया खल्वहं तव ।]

बकुलावलिका—ण केवलं मह । [न केवलं मम]

मालविका—कस्स वा अण्णस्स । [कस्य वान्यस्य ।]

बकुलावलिका—गुणेसु अहिणिवेसिणो भट्टिणो वि । [गुणेष्वभिनिवेशिनो भर्तुरपि ।]

मालविका— अलिअं मन्तासि । एदं एव्व मइ णत्थि । [अलीकं मन्त्रयसे । एतदेव मयि नास्ति ।]

बकुलावलिका—सच्चं तुइ णत्थि । भट्टिणो किसेसु सुन्दरपण्डुरेसु

Friend, I have finished laying the paint on one of your feet. Only it requires to be blown upon by the mouth; or rather there is a good breeze here.

King. Mark, my friend, mark.

Here is an admirable opportunity for me to wait upon her by blowing upon her foot with the breath of my mouth—her foot which has the paint still wet upon it. (13)

Vidūṣaka. Where is the occasion for regret? Soon you will be enjoying (this privilege) for a long time.

Bakulāvalikā. My friend, your foot looks as lovely as a red lotus. May you, by all means, sit in the king's lap.

(Irāvatī looks at Nipuṇikā's face.)

King. To me it is a blessing.

Mālavikā. Well you are chattering absurdly.

Bakulāvalikā. I have said what I ought to say.

Mālavikā. Surely you love me.

Bakulāvalikā. Not only I but—

Mālavikā. Who else?

Bakulāvalikā. The king also who is attracted by good qualities.

Mālavikā. You don't speak the truth; for I haven't secured the king's love.

Bakulāvalikā. You haven't indeed! Only it is to

अङ्गेसु दीसइ । [सत्यं त्वयि नास्ति । भर्तुः कृशेषु सुन्दरपाण्डुरेष्वङ्गेषु दृश्यते ।]

निपुणिका—पुढमगणिदं विअ हदासाए उत्तरं । [प्रथमगणितमिव हताशाया उत्तरम् ।]

बकुलावलिका—अणुराओ अणुराएण परिक्खिदव्वोत्ति सुअणवअणं पमाणीकरेहि । [अनुरागोऽनुरागेण परीक्षितव्य इति सुजनवचनं प्रमाणीकुरु ।)

मालविका—किं अत्तणो छन्देण मन्तेसि । [किमात्मनश्छन्देन मन्त्रयसे ।]

बकुलावलिका—णहि णहि । भट्टिणो खु एदाइं पणअमउआइं बिम्बन्तरिदाइं अक्खराइं । [नहि नहि । भर्तुः खल्वेतानि प्रणयमृदुकानि बिम्बान्तरितान्यक्षराणि ।]

मालविका—हला देविं चिन्तिअ ण मे हिअअं विस्ससदि । [हला देवीं चिन्तयित्वा न मे हृदयं विश्वसिति !]

बकुलावलिका—मुद्धे भमरसम्बाधोत्ति वसन्तावदारसव्वस्सभूदो किं ण चूदपसवो ओदंसणिज्जो । [मुग्धे भ्रमरसम्बाध इति वसन्तावतारसर्वस्वभूतः किं न चूतप्रसवोऽवतंसनीयः ।]

मालविका—तुमं दाव दुज्जादे मह अच्चन्तसहाइणी होहि । [त्वं तावद् दुर्जाते ममात्यन्तसहायिनी भव ।]

बकुलावलिका—विमद्दसुरही बउलावलिआ खु अहं । [विमर्दसुरभिर्बकुलावलिका खल्वहम् ।]

राजा—साधु बकुलावलिके साधु ।

भावज्ञानानन्तरं प्रस्तुतेन
प्रत्याख्याने दत्तयुक्तोत्तरेण ।
वाक्येनेयं स्थापिता स्वे निदेशे
स्थाने प्राणाः कामिनां दूत्यधीनाः ॥ १४ ॥

be seen in the beautifully pale and thin limbs of the king.

Nipuṇikā. How the accursed wench gives her answers as if she had got them all up beforehand.

Bakulāvalikā. You must accept the words of the good people as authoritative : love is tested by love.

Mālavikā. How do you talk as suits your fancy ?

Bakulāvalikā. No, no ; these are but the words of the king echoed by me which are so sweet through love.

Mālavikā. Friend, my heart grows diffident as I think of the queen.

Bakulāvalikā. You simple girl, is the mango-shoot-spring's all in all not to be used as an ear-ornament because bees are clinging to it ?

Mālavikā. But, surely, you will help me greatly in my distress.

Bakulāvalikā. Well, am I not a Bakula garland which gives out fragrance when crushed ?

King. Good, Bakulāvalikā, good.

Surely she has held her to her purpose by her words which were spoken after ascertaining her feelings, and which effectively answered all her objections ; it is quite proper that the life of a lover is dependent on a love-messenger. (14)

इरावती—हञ्जे पेक्ख पेक्ख। कारिदा एव्व एदस्सिं बउलावलिआए पदं मालविआ। [हञ्जे पश्य पश्य। कारितैवैतस्मिन् बकुलावलिकया पदं मालविका।]

निपुणिका—भट्टिणि णिव्विआरस्स वि ऊसुअदाजणओ उवदेसो। [भट्टिनि निर्विकारस्याप्युत्सुकताजनक उपदेशः।]

इरावती—ठाणे सङ्किदं मे हिअअं। गहिदत्था अणन्तरं चिन्तइस्सं। [स्थाने शङ्कितं मे हृदयम्। गृहीतार्थानन्तरं चिन्तयिष्यामि।]

बकुलावलिका—एसो दुदीओ वि समत्तपडिकम्मो दे चलणो। जाव दुवे वि सणेउरे करेमि। (नाट्येन नूपुरयुगलमामुच्य।) हला उट्ठेहि अणुचिट्ठ देवीए असोअविआसइत्तअं णिओअं। (उभे उत्तिष्ठतः।) [एष द्वितीयोऽपि समाप्तपरिकर्मा ते चरणः। यावद् द्वावपि सनूपुरौ करोमि। हला उत्तिष्ठ। अनुतिष्ठ देव्या अशोकविकासयितृकं नियोगम्।]

इरावती—सुदं देवीए णिओओत्ति दाणिं। [श्रुतं देव्या नियोग इतीदानीम।]

बकुलावलिका—एसो उवारूढराओ उवभोअक्खमो पुरदो दे दीसइ। [एष उपारूढराग उपभोगक्षमः पुरतस्ते दृश्यते।]

मालविका (सहर्षम्)—किं भट्टा। [किं भर्ता।]

बकुलावलिका (सस्मितम्)—ण दाव भट्टा। एसो असोअसाहावलम्बी पल्लवगुच्छो। ओदंसेहि दाव णं। [न तावद्भर्ता। एषोऽशोकशाखावलम्बी पल्लवगुच्छः। अवतंसय तावदेनम।]

विदूषकः—अवि सुदं भवदा। [अपि श्रुतं भवता।]

राजा—सखे पर्याप्तमेतावता कामिनाम्।

अनातुरोत्कण्ठितयोः प्रसिध्यता
समागमेनापि रतिर्न मां प्रति।
परस्परप्राप्तिनिराशयोर्वरं
शरीरनाशोऽपि समानुरागयोः॥ १५॥

Irāvatī. Mark, girl, mark. Already has she made Mālavikā aspire after him.

Nipuṇikā. Mistress, even a person free from passion would become restless by such teaching.

Irāvatī. I was rightly apprenhensive. After getting at the facts, I will think (what to do).

Bakulāvalikā. I have finished painting this your other foot also. So now I will put anklets on them. *(Acting loosening the pair of anklets)* Friend, rise, do the queen's bidding of causing the Aśoka to blossom. (*Both rise.*)

Irāvatī. So now we learn that it is the queen's bidding.

Bakulāvalikā. Here before you stands one flushed (of increased redness, passion) and fit to enjoy.

Mālavikā. (*With joy)* What ? The king ?

Bakulāvalikā. *(Smiling)* Not the king, but a spray of leaves on a bough of the Aśoka. Make an ear-ornament of it.

Vidūṣaka. Did your highness hear ?

King. Friend, this much is enough for lovers.

For to me there is no pleasure in the union of lovers one of whom is ardent and the other indifferent, although it may be successfully accomplished ; better it is that those whose love is equal pine away through despair of securing their union. (15)

6

(मालविका रचितपल्लवावतंसा सलीलमशोकाय पादं प्रहिणोति ।)

राजा—वयस्य पश्य ।

आदाय कर्णकिसलयमस्मादियमत्र चरणमर्पयति ।
उभयोः सदृशविनिमयादात्मानं वञ्चितं मन्ये ॥१६॥

मालविका—अवि णाम अम्हाणं संभावणा सफला हवे । [अपि नाम आवयोः सम्भावना सफला भवेत् ।]

बकुलावलिका—हला णत्थि दे दोसो णिग्गुणो अअं असोओ जइ कुसुमुब्भेदमन्थरो भवे जो ईरिसं चरणसक्कारं लहेइ । [हला नास्ति ते दोषः निर्गुणोऽयमशोकः यदि कुसुमोद्भेदमन्थरो भवेद्य ईदृशं चरणसत्कारं लभते ।]

राजा—

अनेन तनुमध्यया मुखरनूपुराराविणा
नवाम्बुरुहकोमलेन चरणेन सम्भावितः ।
अशोक यदि सद्य एव कुसुमैर्न सम्पत्स्यसे
वृथा वहसि दोहदं ललितकामिसाधारणम् ॥ १७ ॥

सखे वचनावसरपूर्वं प्रवेष्टुमिच्छामि ।

विदूषकः—एहि णं परिहासइस्सं । [एह्येनां परिहासयिष्यामि ।]

(उभौ प्रवेशं कुरुतः ।)

निपुणिका—भट्टिणि भट्टा एत्थ एव्व पविसदि । [भट्टिनि भर्ता अत्रैव प्रविशति ।]

इरावती—इदं मह पुढमं चिन्तिदं हिअएण । [इदं मम प्रथमं चिन्तितं हृदयेन ।]

विदूषकः (उपसृत्य)—होदि जुत्तं णाम अत्तहोदो पिअवअस्सो असोओ अअं वामपादेण ताडिदुं । [भवति युक्तं नामात्रभवतः प्रियवयस्योऽशोकोऽयं वामपादेन ताडयितुम् ।]

उभे (ससम्भ्रमम्)—अम्मो भट्टा । [अम्मो भर्ता ।]

(Mālavikā after arranging the tender leaves into an ear-ornament gracefully raises her foot towards the Aśoka.)

King. Friend, see.

Having taken a sprig for the ear of this (Aśoka) she is presenting to it her foot. By this mutual exchange of similar gifts I feel that I have been deluded. (16)

Mālavikā. Will this honour rendered by us to the Aśoka bear fruit ?

Bakulāvalikā. Friend, it won't be your fault; for if after receiving this honour from your foot, the Aśoka is tardy in blossoming out, it would be devoid of any good qualities.

King. Honoured with her foot delicate as a fresh lotus and loud-tinkling with the jingling anklets by this slender-waisted one, O Aśoka, if you are not immediately covered with blossoms, then in vain do you cherish the delicate longing which is also cherished by sportive lovers. (17)

Friend, I desire to show myself when an opportunity for interposing a remark presents itself.

Vidūṣaka. Come I will make fun of her. (*Both enter.*)

Nipuṇikā. Mistress, here comes the king on the scene.

Irāvatī. This was what my heart had already anticipated.

Vidūṣaka. (*Approaching*) Lady, is it proper to strike with the foot this Aśoka, the dear friend of the king ?

Both. (*confusedly*) O, the king !

विदूषकः—बउलावलिए तुए गहिदत्थाए ईरिसं अविणअं करेन्ती किं सही ण णिवारिदा । [बकुलावलिके त्वया गृहीतार्थया ईदृशमविनयं कुर्वती किं सखी न निवारिता ।]

(मालविका भयं रूपयति ।)

निपुणिका—भट्टिणि पेक्ख किं पवुत्तं अज्जगोदमेण । [भट्टिनि पश्य किं प्रवृत्तमार्यगौतमेन ।]

इरावती—कहं बम्हबन्धू अण्णहा जिविस्सदि । [कथं ब्रह्मबन्धुरन्यथा जीविष्यति ।]

बकुलावलिका—अज्ज एसा देवीए णिओअं अणुचिट्ठदि । एदस्सिं अदिक्कमे परवदी इअं । पसीददु भट्टा । [आर्य एषा देव्या नियोगमनुतिष्ठति । एतस्मिन्नतिक्रमे परवतीयम् । प्रसीदतु भर्ता ।] (आत्मना सममेनां प्रणिपातयति ।)

राजा—यद्येवमनपराद्धासि । उत्तिष्ठ भद्रे । (हस्तेन गृहीत्वोत्थापयति ।)

विदूषकः—जुज्जइ । देवी एत्थ माणइदव्वा । [युज्यते । देव्यत्र मानायितव्या ।]

राजा (विहस्य)—

किसलयमृदोर्विलासिनि कठिने निहितस्य पादपस्कन्धे ।
चरणस्य न ते बाधा सम्प्रति वामस्य वामोरु ॥ १८ ॥

(मालविका लज्जां नाटयति ।)

इरावती (सासूयम्)—अहो अविणीदहिअओ खु अज्जउत्तो । [अहो अविनीतहृदयः खल्वार्यपुत्रः ।]

मालविका—बउलावलिए एहि । अणुट्ठिदं अत्तणो णिओअं देवीए णिवेदेम्ह । [बकुलावलिके एहि । अनुष्ठितमात्मनो नियोगं देव्यै निवेदयावः ।]

बकुलावलिका—तेण हि विण्णवेहि भट्टारं विसज्जेहि त्ति । [तेन हि विज्ञापय भर्तारं विसर्जयेति ।]

Vidūsaka. Bakulāvalikā, why did not you, who knew it, prevent this your friend from doing the immodest deed?

(Mālavikā gesticulates fear.)

Nipuṇikā. Mistress, see what the noble Gautama is about.

Irāvatī. How else could that accursed Brahmin find a living?

Bakulāvalikā. Sir, she is doing the queen's bidding; she cannot help this transgression. Let the king be compassionate. (*She makes Mālavikā bow along with herself.*)

King. If it is thus, you are innocent. Rise, good girl.

(*Takes her by the hand and raises her.*)

Vidūṣaka. That is proper; for the queen must be respected.

King. (*Smiling*)

Fair one, full of graces, I hope you have not
hurt your foot soft as a young shoot by placing
it on the hard stem of the tree, now. (18)

(*Mālavikā gesticulates bashfulness.*)

Irāvatī. (*Angrily*) How wanton in thought is my lord.

Mālavikā. Bakulāvalikā, come, let us go and report to the queen that we have done her bidding.

Bakulāvalikā. Well, then request the king to give you leave to depart.

राजा—भद्रे यास्यसि । मम तावदुपपन्नावसरमर्थित्वं श्रूयताम् ।

बकुलावलिका—अवहिदा सुणाहि । आणवेदु भट्टा । [अवहिता शृणु । आज्ञापयतु भर्ता ।]

राजा—

धृतिपुष्पमयमपि जनो बध्नाति न तादृशं चिरात्प्रभृति ।
स्पर्शामृतेन पूरय दोहदमस्याप्यनन्यरुचेः ॥ १९ ॥

इरावती (सहसोपसृत्य)—पूरेहि पूरेहि । असोओ कुसुमं दंसेदि ण वा । अअं उण पुप्फइ फलइ अ । [पूरय पूरय । अशोकः कुसुमं दर्शयति न वा । अयं पुनः पुष्प्यति फलति च ।]

(सर्वे इरावतीं दृष्ट्वा सम्भ्रान्ताः ।)

राजा (अपवार्य)—वयस्य का प्रतिपत्तिरत्र ।

विदूषकः—किं अण्णं । जङ्घाबलं एव्व । [किमन्यत् । जङ्घाबलमेव ।]

इरावती—बउलावलिए साहु तुए उवक्कन्तं । मालविए तुमं दाव करेहि सफलपत्थणं अज्जउत्तं । [बकुलावलिके साधु त्वयोपक्रान्तम् । मालविके त्वं तावत् कुरु सफलप्रार्थनमार्यपुत्रम् ।]

उभौ—पसीददु भट्टिणी । का अम्हे भट्टिणो पणअपरिग्गहस्स । [प्रसीदतु भट्टिनी । के आवां भर्तुः प्रणयपरिग्रहस्य ।]

(इति निष्क्रान्ते ।)

इरावती—अहो अविस्ससणीआ पुरिसा । मए क्खु अत्तणो वञ्चणा वाहजणगीदिरत्ताए हरिणीए विअ असङ्किदाए ण विण्णादा । [अहो अविश्वसनीयाः पुरुषाः । मया खल्वात्मनो वञ्चना व्याधजनगीतिरक्तया हरिण्येवाशङ्कितया न विज्ञाता ।]

विदूषकः (जनान्तिकम्)—पडिओजेहि किं वि दाणिं । किं अण्णं कम्मगहिदेण कुम्भीलएण सन्धिच्छेअणं सिक्खिदोम्हित्ति वत्तव्वं होइ । [प्रतियोजय किमपीदानीम् । किमन्यत् कर्मगृहीतेन कुम्भीलकेन सन्धिच्छेदनं शिक्षितोऽस्मीति वक्तव्यं भवति ।]

King. Fair one, you will go (presently). But listen to this request which is proper to the occasion.

Bakulāvalikā. Listen attentively. Let the king command.

King.

I too have not for a long time borne the
flower of happiness ; with the nectar of touch
do you satisfy the longing of one who has relish
left for nothing else now. (19).

Irāvatī. (*Suddenly presenting herself*) Satisfy, satisfy ; the Aśoka may or may not bear blossoms ; but this on the other hand not only flowers but also bears fruit.

(*All are confused at the sight of Irāvatī.*)

King. (*Aside*) Friend, what is the recourse now ?

Vidūsaka. What save taking to our heels ?

Irāvatī. Bakulāvalikā, you have begun well! Mālavikā, do you fulfil my lord's longing.

Both. Be pleased, mistress. Who are we to receive such favours from the king ? (*Exeunt*)

Irāvatī. What traitors men are ! But, guileless like a deer attracted by the hunter's sŏng, I did not realise my deception.

Vidūsaka. (*Aside*) Invent something now. What else : a burglar caught red-handed should say that he was but learning house-breaking.

राजा—सुन्दरि, न मे मालविकायां कश्चिदर्थः । मया त्वं चिरायसीति यथाकथंचिदात्मा विनोदितः ।

इरावती—विस्ससणीओ सि । मए ण विण्णादं ईरिसं विणोदवत्थुअं अज्जउत्तेण उवलद्धंति । अण्णहा मन्दभाइणीए एव्वं ण किज्जइ । [विश्वसनीयोऽसि। मया न विज्ञातमीदृशं विनोदवस्तुकमार्यपुत्रेणोपलब्धमिति । अन्यथा मन्दभागिन्या एवं न क्रियते ।]

विदूषकः—मा दाव अत्तहोदी अत्तहोदो दक्खिण्णस्स उवरोहं भणादु । समावत्तिदिट्ठेण देवीए परिअणेण संकहा वि जइ अवराहो ठाविअदि एत्थ तुमं एव्व पमाणं । [मा तावदत्रभवती अत्रभवतो दाक्षिण्यस्योपरोधं भणतु । समापत्तिदृष्टेन देव्याः परिजनेन सङ्कथापि यद्यपराधः स्थाप्यते अत्र त्वमेव प्रमाणम् ।]

इरावती—णं संकहा णाम होदु। किंति अत्ताणं आआसइस्सं। [ननु संकथा नाम भवतु । किमित्यात्मानमायासयिष्ये ।]

[रुष्टा प्रस्थिता।]

राजा (अनुसरन्)—प्रसीदतु भवती ।

[इरावती रशनासन्दितचरणा व्रजत्येव ।]

राजा—सुन्दरि न शोभते प्रणयिजने निरपेक्षता ।

इरावती—सढ, अविस्ससणीअहिअओ सि । [शठ, अविश्वसनीयहृदयोऽसि ।]

राजा—

> **शठ इति मयि तावदस्तु ते**
> **परिचयवत्यवधीरणा प्रिये ।**
> **चरणपतितया न चण्डि तां**
> **विसृजसि मेखलयापि याचिता ॥ २० ॥**

इरावती—इअं वि हदासा तुमं एव्व अणुसरदि । [इयमपि हताशा त्वामेवानुसरति ।]

King. Darling, I care not for Mālavikā. I was just amusing myself as you were late.

Irāvatī. You are to be relied upon. I did not know that my lord had secured such a means of amusement; otherwise luckless that I am, I would not have acted thus.

Vidūsaka. Let not my lady by her words repel his civilities. For if mere conversation with the queen's attendant met by chance is put down as an offence, then you should direct (what is proper and improper.)

Irāvatī. Be it mere conversation! Why should I worry myself? *(Starts to go in anger.)*

King. *(following)* Be pleased my lady—

(Irāvatī moves, although her feet are entangled by the girdle.)

King. Fair one, it is not good to be indifferent to a lover.

Irāvatī. Traitor, you are wholly unreliable.

King.

> With the word, traitor, you may show your
> usual scorn of me; but why not give it up, Oh
> angry one, although besought by your girdle
> that has fallen at your feet? (20)

Irāvatī. How this accursed one also sides with you?

(इति रशनामादाय राजानं ताडयितुमिच्छति ।)

राजा--वयस्य एषा हि

बाष्पासारा हेमकाञ्चीगुणेन
श्रोणीबिम्बादव्यपेक्षाच्युतेन ।
चण्डी चण्डं हन्तुमभ्युद्यता मां
विद्युद्दाम्ना मेघराजीव विन्ध्यम् ॥ २१ ॥

इरावती--किं मां भूओ वि अवरद्धं करेसि । [किं मां भूयोऽप्यपराद्धां करोषि ।] (इति रशनां हस्तेनावलम्बते ।)

राजा--

अपराधिनि मयि दण्डं संहरसि किमुद्यतं कुटिलकेशि ।
वर्धयसि विलसितं त्वं दासजनायात्र कुप्यसि च ॥ २२ ॥

(आत्मगतम्) नूनमिदानीमनुज्ञातम् । (इति पादयोः पतति ।)

इरावती--ण क्खु इमे मालविआए चलणा जे दे फरिसदोहलं
३ पूरइस्संति । [न खल्विमौ मालविकायाश्चरणौ यौ ते स्पर्शदोहदं पूरयिष्यतः ।] (इति सचेटी निष्क्रान्ता ।)

विदूषकः--उट्ठेहि । किदप्पसादो सि । [उत्तिष्ठ । कृतप्रसा-
६ दोऽसि ।]

राजा (उत्थाय इरावतीमपश्यन् ।)--कथं गतैव प्रिया ।

विदूषकः--वयस्स देवेहिं इमस्स अविणअस्स अपसारिदा णिअंतणा ।
९ दाव सिग्घदरं अवक्कमाम जाव अङ्गारओ रासिं विअ सा अणुवक्कं
ण करेइ । [वयस्य देवैरस्याविनयस्यापसारिता नियन्त्रणा । ताव-
१२ च्छीघ्रतरमपक्रमावः यावदङ्गारको राशिमिव सा अनुवक्रं न करोति ।]

राजा--अहो मनसिजवैषम्यम् ।

मन्ये प्रियाहृतमनास्तस्याः प्रणिपातलङ्घनं सेवाम् ।
एवं प्रणयवती सा मयि शक्यमुपेक्षितुं कुपिता ॥ २३ ॥

(इति परिक्रम्य निष्क्रान्ताः सर्वे)

इति तृतीयोऽङ्कः ॥

(*Takes the girdle and desires to strike the king.*)

King. Friend,

This angry lady, shedding streams of tears, is ready to strike me cruelly, with the cord of her golden girdle slipped accidently from her ample hips, as the row of clouds, full of showers of water, strikes the Vindhya mountain with the streak of lightning. (21)

Irāvatī. Why drive me to offend you a second time? (*Catches hold of the girdle.*)

King. Why withdraw the scourge uplifted against my guilty self, O curly-haired one? While (thus) you add to your charms, you are still angry with your slave here. (22)

(*To himself*) Surely I shall find favour now. (*Falls prostrate at her feet.*)

Irāvatī. Surely these are not Mālavikā's feet to fulfil your longing to be touched by them !

(*Withdraws along with her maid.*)

Vidūsaka. Rise, you have found favour.

King. (*Rising and not seeing Irāvatī*) How, my darling is really gone ?

Vidūsaka. The gods have, indeed, removed the constraint in these your improper relations with Mālavikā. Let us speedily depart before she comes back again, like (angry) Mars retrogressing to his mansion in the Zodiac.

King. How perverse is love !

With the mind attracted by the loved one, I consider it a favour that she has slighted my prostration. Yet I should not neglect her, although she is so very angry with me, as she is so much attached to me. (23)

(*All walk about and exeunt.*)

Here ends the third Act.

चतुर्थोऽङ्कः ।

(ततः प्रविशति पर्युत्सुको राजा प्रतीहारी च ।)

राजा (आत्मगतम् ।)—

तामाश्रित्य श्रुतिपथगतामास्थया लब्धमूलः
सम्प्राप्तायां नयनविषयं रूढरागप्रवालः ।
हस्तस्पर्शैर्मुकुलित इव व्यक्तरोमोद्गमत्वात्
कुर्यात्क्लान्तं मनसिजतरुर्मां रसज्ञं फलस्य ॥ १ ॥

(प्रकाशम्) सखे गौतम ।

प्रतीहारी — जेदु भट्टा । असण्णिहिदो गोदमो । [जयतु भर्ता । असन्निहितो गौतमः ।]

राजा (आत्मगतम्)—आः, मालविकावृत्तान्तज्ञानाय प्रेषितः ।

विदूषकः—(प्रविश्य) जेदु भवं । [जयतु भवान् ।]

राजा—जयसेने जानीहि तावत् क्व देवी धारिणी कथं वा सरुजचरणत्वाद्विनोद्यत इति ।

प्रतीहारी—जं देवो आणवेदि । [यद्देव आज्ञापयति ।] (इति निष्क्रान्ता ।)

राजा—गौतम को वृत्तान्तस्तत्रभवत्यास्ते सख्याः ।

विदूषकः—जो बिडालगहिदाए परहुदिआए । [यो बिडालगृहीतायाः परभृतिकायाः ।]

राजा (सविषादम्)—कथमिव ।

विदूषकः—सा खु तवस्सिणी ताए पिङ्गलच्छीए सारभण्डभूमिगेहे मिच्चुमुहे विअ णिक्खित्ता । [सा खलु तपस्विनी तया पिङ्गलाक्ष्या सारभाण्डभूमिगृहे मृत्युमुख इव निक्षिप्ता ।]

राजा—ननु मत्सम्पर्कमुपलभ्य ।

ACT IV.

(Enter king in a love-sick state and a door-keeper.)

King. (*To himself*)

The tree of love which had for its object the lady about whom I had heard, struck its root when I felt interested in her ; and when I saw her it put forth the shoot of passion ; when I touched her hands it blossomed as my hair stood visibly erect through delight ; may that same tree of love make me, weary that I am, taste the flavour of its fruit. (1).

(*Aloud*) Friend Gautama !

The door-keeper. Victory to the king ! Gautama is not here.

King. (*To himself*) Ha ! He has been sent to get news about Mālavikā.

(*Entering*)

Vidūsaka. Victory to your honour !

King. Jayasenā, go and just ascertain where queen Dhāriṇī is, and how does she beguile herself, now that she has pain in her feet.

Door-keeper. As the king commands. (*Exit*).

King. Gautama, how is the lady—your friend ?

Vidūṣaka. Very much like a cuckoo seized by a cat.

King. *(despondently)* How is that ?

Vidūṣaka. The poor lady has been flung into the cellar where all precious things are stored up, as if into the jaws of death by that fiery-eyed one.

King. Was it because of her meeting me ?

विदूषकः—अह इं। [अथ किम्।]

राजा—गौतम क एवं विमुखोऽस्माकं येन चण्डीकृता देवी।

विदूषकः—सुणादु भवं। परिव्वाजिआ मे कहेदि। हिओ किल तत्तहोदी इरावदी रुजाविहत्थचलणं देविं सुहपुच्छिआ आअदा। [शृणोतु भवान्। परिव्राजिका मे कथयति। ह्यः किल तत्रभवती इरावती रुजाविहस्तचरणां देवीं सुखपृच्छिका आगता।]

राजा—ततस्ततः।

विदूषकः—तदो देवीए सा पुच्छिदा किं उण लक्खिदो वल्लहजणोत्ति। तदो ताए उत्तं कुदो वा दे उवआरो। जं दे परिअणस्स वल्लहत्तणं जाणन्ती वि पुच्छसित्ति। [ततो देव्या सा पृष्टा किं पुनर्लक्षितो वल्लभजन इति। ततस्तयोक्तं कुतो वा ते उपचारः। यत्तव परिजनस्य वल्लभत्वं जानत्यपि पृच्छसीति।]

राजा—निर्भेदादृतेऽपि मालविकायामयमुपन्यासः शङ्कयति। ततस्ततः।

विदूषकः—तदो ताए अणुबन्धिज्जमाणाए भवदो अविणअं अन्तरेण परिग्गहिदत्था किदा देवी। [ततस्तयानुबध्यमानया भवतोऽविनयमन्तरेण परिगृहीतार्था कृता देवी।]

राजा—अहो दीर्घरोषता तत्रभवत्याः। अतः परं कथय।

विदूषकः—किं अदो वरं। मालविआ बउलावलिआ अ णिअलवदीओ अदिट्ठसुज्जपादं पादालवासं णाअकण्णआ विअ अणुहोन्ति। [किमतःपरम्। मालविका बकुलावलिका च निगलवत्यावदृष्टसूर्यपादं पातालवासं नागकन्यके इवानुभवतः।]

राजा—कष्टं कष्टम्।

मधुररवा परभृतिका भ्रमरी च विबुद्धचूतसङ्गिन्यौ।
कोटरमकालवृष्ट्या प्रबलपुरोवातया गमिते॥ २॥

वयस्य, अप्यत्र कस्यचिदुपक्रमस्य गतिः स्यात्।

Vidūsaka. Exactly.

King. Gautama, who indeed hates me so that he makes the queen angry with me?

Vidūsaka. Listen, sir! The Parivrājikā tells me as a fact that yesterday the lady Irāvatī came to inquire after the health of the queen, whose feet are disabled with pain.

King. What then?

Vidūsaka. Then the queen asked her "Have you seen the loved person lately?", whereupon she replied; "why this formality when knowing as you do the way he loves (me) your servant, you ask such a question?"

King. This mode of speech must have made the queen suspect Mālavikā even when it is so vague.

Vidūsaka. And when the queen importuned her, she informed the queen of your misdemeanour.

King. How unforgiving is that Lady! Tell me what happened next?

Vidūṣaka. What happened next! Mālavikā and Bakulāvalikā are now in fetters, and are now enjoying residence in the underworld where not a ray of the sun penetrates, like two snake-maidens.

King. Alas! alas!

The sweet-voiced cuckoo and the bee clinging
to the opened mango-blossom have been driven
to seek a hollow by an unseasonable shower
preceded by a strong gale (2).

My friend, can there be an opening here for any stratagem?

विदूषकः—कहं भविस्सदि । जं सारभण्डे वावुदा माहविआ देवीए सन्दिट्ठा । मह अङ्गुलीअअमुद्दं अदेक्खिअ ण मोत्तव्वा तुए इअं हदासा मालविआ बउलावलिआ अ त्ति । [कथं भविष्यति । यत्सारभाण्डे व्यापृता माधविका देव्या सन्दिष्टा । ममाङ्गुलीयकमुद्रामदृष्ट्वा न मोक्तव्या त्वयेयं हताशा मालविका बकुलावलिका चेति ।]

राजा (निश्वस्य सपरामर्शम् ।)—सखे किमत्र कर्तव्यम् ।

विदूषकः (विचिन्त्य)—अत्थि एत्थ उवाओ। [अस्त्यत्रोपायः ।]

राजा—क इव ।

विदूषकः (सदृष्टिक्षेपम्)—को वि अदिट्ठो सुणादि । कण्णे दे कहेमि । (उपश्लिष्य कर्णे ।) एव्वं विअ । [कोऽप्यदृष्टः शृणोति । कर्णे ते कथयामि । एवमिव ।]

राजा—साधु प्रयुज्यतां सिद्धये ।

प्रतीहारी—(प्रविश्य) देव पवादसअणे देवी णिसण्णा रत्तचन्दणधारिणा परिअणहत्थगदेण चलणेण भअवदीए कहाहिं विणोदीअमणा चिट्ठदि । [देव प्रवातशयने देवी निषण्णा रक्तचन्दनधारिणा परिजनहस्तगतेन चरणेन भगवत्या कथाभिर्विनोद्यमाना तिष्ठति ।]

राजा —अस्मत्प्रवेशयोग्योऽयमवसरः ।

विदूषकः—ता गच्छदु भवं । अहं वि देविं पेक्खिदुं अरित्तपाणी भविस्सं। [तस्मात् गच्छतु भवान् । अहमपि देवीं द्रष्टुमरिक्तपाणिर्भविष्यामि ।]

राजा—जयसेनायास्तावत्संवेद्य गच्छ ।

विदूषकः—तह। (कर्णे) भोदि एव्वं विअ । (इति निष्क्रान्तः।) [तथा । भवति एवमिव ।]

राजा—जयसेने तेन हि प्रवातशयनमार्गमादेशय ।

प्रतीहारी—इदो इदो देवो । [इत इतो देवः ।]

(ततः प्रविशति शयनस्था देवी परिव्राजिका विभवतश्च परिवारः ।)

Vidūṣaka. How can there be? For the queen has commanded Mādhavikā in charge of the treasure-house: you will not set free Mālavikā and Bakulāvalikā unless you see the seal of my ring.

King. *(Sighing and musing.)* Friend, what shall we do in the matter?

Vidūṣaka. *(Reflecting.)* Yes, there is a remedy for this.

King. What is it?

Vidūṣaka. *(Glancing around.)* Somebody might overhear; so I will whisper it in your ear. ***(Draws near and whispers in his ear.)*** It is thus.

King. Excellent! Put it in execution and may it succeed.

(Entering)

A door-keeper. King, the queen is reclining on a couch in a breezy place, her foot smeared with the red sandal resting in the hand of her attendant; and she is being regaled with stories by the reverend lady.

King. This is a proper occasion for me to enter.

Vidūṣaka. Well, then, you go. I too will provide myself with some present and see the queen.

King. Speak to Jayasenā and then go.

Vidūṣaka. All right. ***(Whispers in her ear.)*** Lady, it is thus.

(Exit)

King. Jayasenā, lead the way to where the queen reclines on a couch in the open air.

Door-keeper. This way, this way, king.

(Then enter the queen reclining on a bed, the Parivrājikā and the attendants at a respectful distance.)

7

देवी—भअवदि अदिरमणीअं कहावत्थु । तदो तदो । [भगवति अतिरमणीयं कथावस्तु । ततस्ततः ।]

परिव्राजिका (सदृष्टिक्षेपम्)—अतः परं पुनः कथयिष्यामि । तत्रभवानीश्वरः सम्प्राप्तः ।

देवी—अम्मो भट्टा । (अभ्युत्थातुमिच्छति ।) [अम्मो भर्ता ।]

राजा—अलमलमुपचारयन्त्रणया ।

अनुचितनूपुरविरहं नार्हसि तपनीयपीठिकालम्बम् ।
चरणं रुजापरीतं कलभाषिणि मां च पीडयितुम् ॥ ३ ॥

देवी—जेदु अज्जउत्तो । [जयत्वार्यपुत्रः ।]

परिव्राजिका—विजयतां देवः ।

राजा (परिव्राजिकां प्रणम्योपविश्य ।) देवि अपि सह्या ते वेदना ।

देवी—अत्थि मे विसेसो । [अस्ति मे विशेषः ।]

(ततः प्रविशति यज्ञोपवीतबद्धाङ्गुष्ठः सम्भ्रान्तो विदूषकः ।)

विदूषकः—परित्ताअदु परित्ताअदु । सप्पेण मिच्चुणा दट्ठोम्हि । [परित्रायतां परित्रायताम् । सर्पेण मृत्युना दष्टोऽस्मि ।]

(सर्वे विषण्णाः ।)

राजा—कष्टं कष्टम् । क भवान् परिभ्रान्तः ।

विदूषकः—देविं पेक्खिस्सं ति आआरपुप्फग्गहणकालणादो पमदवणं गदोम्हि । [देवीं द्रक्षामीत्याचारपुष्पग्रहणकारणात्प्रमदवनं गतोऽस्मि ।]

देवी—हद्धि हद्धि । णं अहं एव्व बम्हणस्स जीविअसंसअणिमित्तं जादा । [हा धिक् हा धिक् । नन्वहमेव ब्राह्मणस्य जीवितसंशयनिमित्तं जाता ।]

विदूषकः—तहिं असोअत्थवअस्स कालणादो पसारिदे मे हत्थे कोडरणिग्गदेण सप्परूवेण कालेण दट्ठोम्हि । णं एदाइं दुवे दन्तपदाइं । [तत्राशोकस्तबककारणात्प्रसारिते मे हस्ते कोटर-

Queen. Revered lady, the plot of the story is so interesting. What next ?

Parivrājikā. (*Looking about her*) I shall tell you further on some other occasion. Here comes the king.

Queen. Ah ! my lord ! (*Desires to rise.*)

King. Do not worry yourself with the distressing formality.

> Sweet-voiced one, it is not proper to trouble
> your aching foot, unused to the severance from
> anklets, and resting on the golden foot-stool,
> and cause me much pain. (3)

Queen. Victory to my noble lord !

Parivrājikā. Victory attend the king !

King. (*Bowing to the Parivrājikā and taking his seat*) My queen, I hope you find the pain bearable ?

Queen. I feel better now.

(*Then Enter Vidūṣaka in a hurry, his thumb tied up by the sacred thread.*)

Vidūṣaka. Help, help ! I am bitten by death in the form of a serpent.

(*All are distressed .*)

King. Alas ! alas ! where were you wandering ?

Vidūṣaka. As I wanted to see the queen, I went to the Pramadavana garden to collect flowers for the customary offering.

Queen. O fie ! fie ! That I should have been the cause of putting his life in danger !

Vidūśaka. As I stretched forth my hand to get at the cluster of Aśoka flowers, I was bitten by death in

निर्गतेन सर्परूपिणा कालेन दष्टोऽस्मि । नन्वेते द्वे दन्तपदे ।] (इति दर्शयति ।)

परिव्राजिका—तेन हि दंशच्छेदः पूर्वकर्मेति श्रूयते । स तावदस्य क्रियताम् ।

छेदो दंशस्य दाहो वा क्षतेर्वा रक्तमोक्षणम् ।
एतानि दष्टमात्राणामायुषः प्रतिपत्तयः ॥ ४ ॥

राजा—सम्प्रति विषवैद्यानां कर्म । जयसेने क्षिप्रमाहूयतां ध्रुवसिद्धिः ।

प्रतीहारी—जं देवो आणवेदि । [यद्देव आज्ञापयति ।] (इति निष्क्रान्ता ।)

विदूषकः—अहो पावेण मिच्चुणा गहीदोम्हि । [अहो पापेन मृत्युना गृहीतोऽस्मि ।]

राजा—मा कातरो भूः । अविषोऽपि कदाचिद्दंशो भवेत् ।

विदूषकः—कहं ण भाइस्सं । सिमसिमाअन्ति मे अङ्गाइं । [कथं न भेष्यामि । सिमसिमायन्ति मे अङ्गानि ।] (इति विषवेगं रूपयति ।)

देवी—ही ही असुहं दंसिदं विआरेण । हला अवलम्बह णं । [ही ही अशुभं दर्शितं विकारेण । हला अवलम्बध्वमेनम् ।]

(परिजनः ससम्भ्रममवलम्बते ।)

विदूषकः (राजानमवलोक्य ।) —भो भवदो बालवअस्सोम्हि । ता अविआरेण वुड्ढाए मे जणणीए जोअक्खेमं वहेहि । [भो भवतो बालवयस्योऽस्मि । तदविचारेण वृद्धाया मे जनन्या योगक्षेमं वह ।]

राजा—मा भैषीः । अचिरात्त्वां विषवैद्यश्चिकित्सते । स्थिरो भव ।

जयसेना—(प्रविश्य) देव धुवसिद्धी विण्णवेदि । इह एव्व आणीअदु गोदमोत्ति । [देव ध्रुवसिद्धिर्विज्ञापयति । इहैवानीयतां गौतम इति ।]

the form of a serpent issuing out of its hollow—why, here are the two marks of its fangs. (*Shows them.*)

Parivrājikā. Then, indeed. they say that the first thing to be done, is the excision of the bitten part. Let that be done to him.

> Excision of the bitten part, or the burning of it, or letting off blood from the wound, these are the remedies to save the lives of persons just when they are bitten. (4)

King. Now it is the work of a doctor who specialises in the treatment of poison. Jayasenā, quickly fetch Dhruvasiddhi.

Door-keeper. As my lord commands. (*Exit*)

Vidūsaka. Ah ! How accursed death has seized me !

King. Don't lose heart. May be, the bite is without poison.

Vidūsaka. How can I help being afraid ? How all my limbs are tingling with pain ! (*Gesticulates the working of poison.*)

Queen. Alas ! alas ! the bite shows itself to be fatal. Help him, ho !

(*The attendants hurriedly support him.*)

Vidūsaka. (*Looking at the king*) I have been your friend since childhood. You will therefore have no hesitation in looking after the welfare of my old mother.

King. Do not be afraid. The poison-doctor will speedily cure you. Be composed.

(*Entering*)

Jayasenā. Your majesty, Dhruvasiddhi requests that Gautama should be removed to his place.

राजा—तेन हि वर्षवरपरिगृहीतमेनं तत्रभवतः सकाशं प्रापय ।

जयसेना—तह । [तथा ।]

विदूषकः (देवीं विलोक्य)—भोदि जीवेअं वा ण वा । जं मए अत्तभवन्तं सेवन्तेण दे अवरद्धं तं मरिसेहि । [भवति जीवेयं वा न वा । यन्मया अत्रभवन्तं सेवमानेन तेऽपराद्धं तन्मर्षय ।]

देवी—दीहाऊ होहि । [दीर्घायुर्भव ।]

(निष्क्रान्तो विदूषकः प्रतीहारी च ।)

राजा—प्रकृतिभीरुस्तपस्वी । ध्रुवसिद्धेरपि यथार्थनाम्नः सिद्धिं मन्ये ।

जयसेना—(प्रविश्य) जेदु भट्टा । धुवसिद्धी त्रिण्णवेदि । उअकुम्भविहाणे सप्पमुद्दिअं किं वि कप्पइदव्वं । ता अण्णेसीअदु त्ति । [जयतु भर्ता । ध्रुवसिद्धिर्विज्ञापयति । उदकुम्भविधाने सर्पमुद्रितं किमपि कल्पयितव्यम् । तदन्विष्यतामिति ।]

देवी—इदं सप्पमुद्दिअं अंगुलीअअं । पच्छा मह एव्व हत्थे देहि णं । [इदं सर्पमुद्रितमङ्गुलीयकम् । पश्चान्ममैव हस्ते देह्येतत् ।]

(इति प्रयच्छति । जयसेना नाट्येन गृह्णाति ।)

राजा—जयसेने कर्मसिद्धावाशु प्रतिपत्तिमानय ।

जयसेना—जं देवो आणवेदि । [यद्देव आज्ञापयति ।] (इति निष्क्रान्ता ।)

परिव्राजिका—देव यथा मे हृदयमाचष्टे तथा निर्विषो गौतमः ।

राजा—भूयादेवम् ।

जयसेना—(प्रविश्य) देव णिउत्तविसवेओ अज्जगोदमो मुहुत्तेण पइदित्थो संवुत्तो । [देव निवृत्तविषवेग आर्यगौतमो मुहूर्तेन प्रकृतिस्थः संवृत्तः ।]

देवी—दिट्ठिआ वअणीआदो मुत्तम्हि । [दिष्टया वचनीयान्मुक्तास्मि ।]

King. Well, then, take him into his presence borne by the eunuchs of the harem.

Jayasenā. As your majesty orders.

Vidūsaka. (*Looking at the queen*) Queen, I may or may not live ; I beg (therefore) to be forgiven whatever offence I may have given you while serving the king.

Queen. May you live on to a good old age.

(*Exeunt Vidūṣaka and door-keeper.*)

King. The poor fellow is nervous by nature. I hope Dhruvasiddhi-rightly named the infallible one-will succeed.

(*Entering*)

Jayasenā. Victory to the king ! Dhruvasiddhi requests that something bearing a serpent-seal should be found out for putting on the water-pitcher. Do, therefore, make a search.

Queen. Here is a ring with a serpent-seal. Later on give it back to me only. (*Offers it, Jayasenā makes as if she takes it.*)

King. Jayasenā, quickly bring word that success has been attained.

Jayasenā. As the king commands. (*Exit*)

Parivrājikā. King, as my heart tells me, Gautama is cured of poison.

King. I hope so.

(*Entering*) Jayasenā—My lord, cured of the effect of poison, the noble Gautama after a while became quite his usual self.

Queen. Happily I am free from blame.

जयसेना—एसो उण अमच्चो वाहदओ विण्णवेदि । राअकज्जं बहु मन्तिदव्वं । ता दंसणेण अणुग्गहं इच्छामित्ति । [एष पुनरमात्यो वाहतको विज्ञापयति । राजकार्यं बहु मन्त्रयितव्यम् । तद्दर्शनेनानुग्रहमिच्छामीति ।]

देवी—गच्छदु अज्जउत्तो कज्जसिद्धीए । [गच्छत्वार्यपुत्रः कार्यसिद्धये ।]

राजा (उत्थाय)—देवि आतपाक्रान्तोऽयमुद्देशः । शीतक्रिया चास्य प्रशस्ता । तदन्यत्र नीयतां शयनीयम् ।

देवी—बालिआ अज्जउत्तवअणं अणुचिट्ठइ । [बालिकाः आर्यपुत्रवचनमनुतिष्ठत ।]

परिजनः—तह । [तथा]

(इति निष्क्रान्ता देवी परिव्राजिका परिजनश्च ।)

राजा—जयसेने गूढपथेन मां प्रमदवनं प्रापय ।

जयसेना—इदो इदो देवो । [इत इतो देवः ।]

राजा (परिक्रम्य)—जयसेने ननु समाप्तकृत्यो गौतमः ।

जयसेना—अह इं । [अथ किम् ।]

राजा—

इष्टाधिगमनिमित्तं प्रयोगमेकान्तसाधुमपि मत्वा ।
सन्दिग्धमेव सिद्धौ कातरमाशङ्कते चेतः ॥ ५ ॥

विदूषकः—(प्रविश्य) जेदु भवं । सिद्धाइं मे सव्वमङ्गलकम्माइं । [जयतु भवान् । सिद्धानि मे सर्वमङ्गलकर्माणि ।]

राजा—जयसेने त्वमपि नियोगमशून्यं कुरु ।

जयसेना—जं देवो आणवेदि । [यद्देव आज्ञापयति]

(इति निष्क्रान्ता ।)

राजा—वयस्य क्षुद्रा माधविका । न खलु किंचिद्विचारितमनया ।

Jayasenā. The minister Vāhataka now requests : I have to discuss a good many affairs of the state, and so I seek to be favoured with an audience.

Queen. May my lord leave and attain success in his undertakings.

King. *(Rising)* My queen, this place is exposed to the sun, while this requires a cooling remedy; so let the bed be removed to a different place.

Queen. Girls, carry out the command of my lord.

Servants. As you bid.

(Exeunt queen, Parivrājikā and retinue.)

King. Jayasenā, take me to the Pramadavana by the secret way.

Jayasena. This way, this way, king.

King. (*moving about*) Jayasenā I hope Gautama has finished his work.

Jayasenā. Just so.

King. Although I think the devise to be decisively the best for the accomplishment of my purpose, yet my timid heart feels dubious about its attainment. (5)

(Entering)

Vidūsaka. Victory to your highness. Success attends all our auspicious undertakings.

King. Jayasenā, you too attend to your duty.

Jayasenā. As the king commands.

(Exit).

King. Friend, Mādhavikā is such a dullard ; did not she hesitate a bit ?

विदूषकः—देवीए अंगुलीअअमुद्दिअं पेक्खिअ कहं विआरेदि। [देव्या अङ्गुलीयकमुद्रिकां दृष्ट्वा कथं विचारयति।]

राजा—न खलु मुद्रामधिकृत्य ब्रवीमि। तयोर्बद्धयोः किंनिमित्तोऽयं मोक्षः। किं वा देव्या परिजनमतिक्रम्य भवान्सन्दिष्टः। इत्येवमनया प्रष्टव्यम्।

विदूषकः—णं पुच्छिदोम्हि। पच्चुप्पण्णबुद्धिणा मए कहिदम्। [ननु पृष्टोऽस्मि। प्रत्युत्पन्नबुद्धिना मया कथितम्।]

राजा—कथ्यताम्।

विदूषकः—भणिदं मए। देव्वचिन्तएहिं विण्णाविदो राआ। सोवसग्गं वो णक्खत्तं। सव्वबन्धमोक्खो करीअदु त्ति। [भणितं मया। दैवचिन्तकैर्विज्ञापितो राजा। सोपसर्गं वो नक्षत्रम्। सर्वबन्धमोक्षः क्रियतामिति।]

राजा (सहर्षम्)—ततस्ततः।

विदूषकः—तं सुणिअ देवीए इरावदीए चित्तं रक्खन्तीए राआ किल मोएदि त्ति तुमं एव्व णं मोएहि त्ति अहं सन्दिट्ठोम्हि त्ति। तदो जुज्जइ त्ति ताए सम्पादिदो अत्थो। [तच्छ्रुत्वा देव्या इरावत्याश्चित्तं रक्षन्त्या राजा किल मोचयतीति त्वमेवैनां मोचयेत्यहं सन्दिष्टोऽस्मि इति। ततो युज्यत इति तया सम्पादितोऽर्थः।]

राजा (विदूषकं परिष्वज्य)—सखे प्रियोऽहं तव।

> **न हि बुद्धिगुणेनैव सुहृदामर्थदर्शनम्।**
> **कार्यसिद्धिपथः सूक्ष्मः स्नेहेनाप्युपलभ्यते॥ ६॥**

विदूषकः—तुवरदु भवं। समुद्दघरए पिअसहीसहिअं मालविअं ठाविअ भवन्तं पच्चुग्गदोम्हि। [त्वरतां भवान्। समुद्रगृहके प्रियसखीसहितां मालविकां स्थापयित्वा भवन्तं प्रत्युद्गतोऽस्मि।]

राजा—अहमेनां सम्भावयामि। गच्छाग्रतः।

Vidūsaka. How could she hesitate at sight of the Queen's ring ?

King. I do not talk of the ring. But she should certainly have asked as to why these prisoners were to be liberated; and why to the exclusion of all her attendants, the queen commissioned you to bring the message.

Vidūsaka. Indeed, she asked me; and I immediately with a ready wit told her.

King. Tell me.

Vidūsaka. I said—the astrologers told the king that the constellation presiding over the king's fortunes was possessed of a malignant influence. Therefore let all prisoners be set free.

King. What then ?

Vidūsaka. On hearing that, the queen with a view to spare the feelings of Irāvatī ordered me to release them and give out that the king wanted them set at liberty; she granted my request, saying that it was quite all right.

King. (*Embracing the Vidūṣaka*) Friend, you, indeed, love me.

> For not only by force of intellect does one see how to promote a friend's interest; love too points out the narrow path to success in one's undertaking. (6)

Vidūsaka. Let your highness make haste. I have put Mālavikā and her dear friend in the Ocean-pavilion and have come to meet you.

King. Well, I will honour her. Do you go ahead.

विदूषकः—एदु भवं। (परिक्रम्य) एदं समुद्दघरअं। [एतु भवान्। इदं समुद्रगृहम्।]

राजा (साशङ्कम्) —वयस्य एषा कुसुमापचयव्यग्रहस्ता सख्यास्ते इरावत्याः परिचारिका चन्द्रिका समागच्छति। इतस्तावदावां भित्ति-निगूढौ भवावः।

विदूषकः—अहो कुम्भीलएहिं कामुएहिं अ पलिहलणिज्जा खु चन्दिआ। [अहो कुम्भीलकैः कामुकैश्च परिहरणीया चन्द्रिका।]

(उभौ यथोक्तं कुरुतः।)

राजा—गौतम कथं नु ते सखी मां प्रतिपालयति। एह्येनां गवाक्ष-माश्रित्यावलोकयावः।

विदूषकः—तह। तथा। (इति विलोकयन्तौ स्थितौ।)

(ततः प्रविशति मालविका बकुलावलिका च।)

बकुलावलिका—हला पणम भट्टारं। [हला प्रणम भर्तारम्।]

राजा—मन्ये प्रतिकृतिं मे दर्शयतीति।

मालविका (सहर्षम्) णमो दे (द्वारमवलोक्य सविषादम्) कहिं भट्टा। हला विप्पलम्भेसि मं। [नमस्ते। कुत्र भर्ता। हला। विप्रलम्भयसि माम्।]

राजा—सखे हर्षविषादाभ्यामत्रभवत्याः प्रीतोऽस्मि।

सूर्योदये भवति या सूर्यास्तमये च पुण्डरीकस्य।
वदनेन सुवदनायास्ते समवस्थे क्षणादूढे॥ ७॥

बकुलावलिका—णं एसो चित्तगदो भट्टा। [नन्वेष चित्रगतो भर्ता।]

उभे (प्रणिपत्य) जेदु भट्टा। [जयतु भर्ता।]

मालविका—हला तदा अहं सम्मुहट्ठिदा भट्टिणो रूवस्स तह ण वितिण्हम्हि जह अज्ज मए विभाविदो चित्तगदो भट्टा। [हला

Vidūṣaka. Come, your highness. (*moving about*) Here is the Ocean-pavilion.

King. (*Apprehensively*) Friend, here comes Candrikā, the maid of your friend Irāvatī, her hands engaged in gathering flowers. Let us, therefore, hide ourselves behind this wall here.

Vidūṣaka. Ah, thieves and lovers have to avoid the moon-light.

(*Both do what was said.*)

King. Gautama how must your friend be awaiting me ? Come, let us watch her from the window.

Vidūṣaka. Well.

(*They stand looking in.*)

(*Enter Mālavikā and Bakulāvalikā.*)

Bakulāvalikā. Come, friend, salute the king.

King. I think she is showing her my likeness.

Mālavikā. *(With joy)* I salute you. *(Looking at the door, with disappointment)* Where is the king ? Friend, you deceive me.

King. Friend I feel delighted at the lady's joy and disappointment both.

For in a moment the face of the lovely faced one has assumed the two appearances of the lotus—that which it wears at sun-rise and that other which it wears at sunset. (7)

Bakulāvalikā. Well, I say, here is the king in the picture.

Both *(Saluting)* Victory to the king !

Mālavikā. Friend, at that time when I stood face to face with the king, I was not so well satisfied with

तदाहं सम्मुखस्थिता भर्तू रूपस्य तथा न वितृष्णास्मि यथाद्य मया विभाविताश्चित्रगतो भर्ता ।]

विदूषकः—सुदं भवदा । अत्तहोदीए जह दिट्ठो चित्ते ण तह दिट्ठो भवं ति मंतिदं । मुहा दाणिं मञ्जूसा विअ रअणभण्डं जोव्वणगव्वं वहेसि । [श्रुतं भवता । अत्रभवत्या यथा दृष्टश्चित्रे न तथा दृष्टो भवानिति मन्त्रितम् । मुधेदानीं मञ्जूषेव रत्नभाण्डं यौवनगर्वं वहसि ।]

राजा—सखे कुतूहलवानपि निसर्गशालीनः स्त्रीजनः । पश्य—

> **कात्स्न्येंन निर्वर्णयितुं च रूप-**
> **मिच्छन्ति तत्पूर्वसमागतानाम् ।**
> **न च प्रियेष्वायतलोचनानां**
> **समग्रपातीनि विलोचनानि ॥ ८ ॥**

मालविका—हला का एसा ईसिपरिवत्तिदवअणा भट्टिणा सिणिद्धाए दिट्ठीए णिज्झाईअदि । [हला कैषा ईषत्परिवर्तितवदना भर्त्रा स्निग्धया दृष्ट्या निध्यायते ।]

बकुलावलिका—णं इअं भट्टिणो पासगदा इरावदी । [नन्वियं भर्तुः पार्श्वगतेरावती ।]

मालविका—हला भट्टा अदक्खिणो विअ पडिभादि । जो सव्वं देवीजणं उज्झिअ एक्काए मुहे बद्धलक्खो । [हला भर्ता अदक्षिण इव प्रतिभाति । यः सर्वं देवीजनमुज्झित्वा एकस्या मुखे बद्धलक्ष्यः ।]

बकुलावलिका (आत्मगतम्)—चित्तगदं भट्टारं परमत्थं गेह्णिअ असूअदि इअं । होदु कीलिस्सं दाव एदाए । (प्रकाशम्) हला भट्टिणो वल्लहा एसा । [चित्रगतं भर्तारं परमार्थं गृहीत्वाऽसूयतीयम् । भवतु क्रीडिष्यामि तावदेतया । हला भर्तुर्वल्लभैषा ।]

मालविका—तदो किं दाणिं अत्ताणं आआसेमि । [ततः किमिदानींमात्मानमायासयामि ।] (इति सासूयं परावर्तते ।)

his beauty as at the present moment with looking at him in the picture.

Vidūṣaka. Has your honour heard ? The lady says you did not look as you do here in the picture. Vainly do you bear the pride of youth as a casket a store of gems.

King. Friend, women, though filled with curiosity, are yet by nature so bashful. Observe,

> they do desire to study completely the features of those whom they meet for the first time and yet the long-eyed ones will not allow their eyes to fall full upon the beloved persons. (8)

Mālavikā. Friend, who is this with her slightly averted face whom the king is regarding with an affectionate gaze ?

Bakulāvalikā. Surely this is Irāvatī at his side.

Mālavikā. Friend, the king seems to me to be somewhat rude, that he should neglect all his queens and fix his glance on her face alone.

Bakulāvalikā. (To *herself)* She takes the king's picture for the king himself and exhibits jealousy towards it. Well, then, let me chaff her a bit. (*Aloud*) friend, she is beloved of the king.

Mālavikā. If that be so, why should I trouble myself in vain? (*Turns away pettishly*).

१५ **राजा**—पश्य सख्या मुखम् ।

भ्रूभङ्गभिन्नतिलकं स्फुरिताधरोष्ठं
सासूयमाननमितः परिवर्तयन्त्या ।
कान्तापराधकुपितेष्वनया विनेतुः
सन्दर्शितेव ललिताभिनयस्य शिक्षा ॥९॥

विदूषकः—अणुणअसज्जो दाणिं होहि । [अनुनयसज्ज इदानीं भव ।]

३ **मालविका**—अज्जगोदमो वि एत्थ एव्व सेवदि णं । [आर्यगौतमोऽप्यत्रैव सेवत एनम् ।] (पुनः स्थानान्तराभिमुखी भवितुमिच्छति)

बकुलावलिका—(मालविकां रुध्वा)–ण खु कुविदा दाणिं तुमं । [न खलु कुपितेदानीं त्वम् ।]

मालविका—जइ मं चिरं कुविदं मण्णासि एसो पच्चाणीअदि कोवो । [यदि मा चिरं कुपितां मन्यसे एष प्रत्यानीयते कोपः ।]

९. **राजा** (उपसृत्य)—

कुप्यसि कुवलयनयने चित्रार्पितचेष्टया किमेवमयि ।
ननु तव साक्षादयमहनन्यसाधारणो दासः ॥ १० ॥

बकुलावलिका—जेदु भट्टा । [जयतु भर्ता ।]

मालविका (आत्मगतम्) **कहं चित्तगदो भट्टा मए असूइदो ।** [कथं चित्रगतो भर्ता मयासूयितः ।] (सव्रीडवदना अञ्जलिं करोति । राजा मदनकातर्यं रूपयति ।)

विदूषकः—किं भवं उदासीणो विअ । [किं भवानुदासीन इव ।]

६ **राजा**—अविश्वसनीयत्वात्सख्यास्ते ।

विदूषकः—मा दाव । अत्तहोदी तुह अविस्ससणीआ । [मा तावत् । अत्रभवती तवाविश्वसनीया ।]

King. Observe the face of your friend.

As in anger she turned her face away from the (picture) so that the tilaka mark on the forehead was blurred, by the knitting of the brows, and the lower lip was made to quiver, she seemed to exhibit the graceful expression taught her by her teacher as being appropriate in the fits of anger caused by the faults of a lover. (9)

Vidūsaka. Prepare yourself now to propitiate her.

Mālavikā. And the noble Gautama too is waiting upon her in this place. (*She again desires to turn away in another direction.*)

Bakulāvalikā. (*Preventing Mālavikā*) Surely you are not angry now.

Mālavikā. If you desire me to be angry for long, here I recall my anger.

King. (*Advancing*)

Oh Lotus-eyed one, why should you be angry thus at an action represented in the picture? Do I not here stand in my own person, a slave devoted to you alone? (10)

Bakulāvalikā. Victory to the king!

Mālavikā. (*To herself*) What? Did I get angry with the king in the picture?

(*With an apologetic expression, she folds her hands together.*)

(*The king acts as if he is distracted with love.*)

Vidūsaka. Why do you appear to be so apathetic?

King. Because your friend is so unreliable.

Vidūsaka. How! Do you distrust the lady?

१ **राजा**—श्रूयताम् ।

पथि नयनयोः स्थित्वा स्वप्ने तिरोभवति क्षणात्
सरति सहसा बाह्वोर्मध्यं गताप्यबला सती ।
मनसिजरुजा क्लिष्टस्यैवं समागममायया
कथमिव सखे विश्रब्धं स्यादिमां प्रति मे मनः ॥११॥

बकुलावलिका—सहि बहुसो किल तुए विप्पलद्धो भट्टा । ता दाव अत्ता विस्ससणिज्जो करीअदु । [सखि बहुशः किल त्वया
२ विप्रलब्धो भर्ता । तत्तावदात्मा विश्वसनीयः क्रियताम्]

मालविका—सहि मम उण मन्दभाइणीए सिविणअसमाअमो वि भट्टिणो दुल्लहो आसि । [सखि मम पुनर्मन्दभागिन्याः स्वप्नसमा-
६ गमोऽपि भर्तुर्दुर्लभ आसीत् ।]

बकुलावलिका—भट्टा देउ से उत्तरं । [भर्ता ददात्वस्या उत्तरम् ।]

९**राजा**—

उत्तरेण किमात्मैव पञ्चबाणाग्निसाक्षिकम् ।
तव सख्यै मया दत्तो न सेव्यः सेविता रहः ॥ १२ ॥

बकुलावलिका—अणुगहिदम्हि । [अनुगृहीतास्मि ।]

विदूषकः (परिक्रम्य ससम्भ्रमम् ।)—बउलावलिए एसो बालासो-
३अरुक्खस्स पल्लवाइं हरिणो लङ्घिदुं आअच्छदि । एहि णिवारेम णं । [बकुलावलिके एष बालाशोकवृक्षस्य पल्लवानि हरिणो लङ्घितुमागच्छति । एहि निवारयाव एनम् ।]

६**बकुलावलिका**—तह । [तथा ।] (इति प्रस्थिता ।)

राजा—एवमस्मद्रक्षणे वयस्येनावहितेन भवितव्यम् ।

विदूषकः—एदं वि गोदमो णं सन्दिस्सीअदि । [एतदपि गौतमो
९ ननु सन्दिश्यते ।]

King. Listen: your friend appears before me in a dream, and yet in a moment she vanishes from my sight; and though clasped between my arms, she suddenly slips away from them, (frail) woman though she be, how can my mind repose any trust in her while I am afflicted by the anguish of love caused by a delusive union? (II)

Bakulāvalikā. Friend, often has the king been deceived; so now prove yourself to be a person worthy of trust.

Mālavikā. But, my friend, unluckly that I am, I find union with the king even in a dream so hard to obtain.

Bakulāvalikā. King, please now to give her answer.

King.

What is the use of making any answer? For in the very presence of the fire of love have I given myself over to your friend. I am not her master, but her servant in secret. (12)

Bakulāvalikā. I am beholden to you for this answer.

Vidūṣaka. (*Walking round*) Bakulāvalikā, here is a deer, cropping the shoots of the young Aśoka tree; let us drive it off.

Bakulāvalikā. Very well. (*Starts off.*)

King. Friend, even thus must you be on the look-out at this moment when we deserve to be guarded.

Vidūṣaka. Does Gautama require to be instructed thus?

बकुलावलिका—अज्ज गोदमो अहं अप्पआसे चिट्ठामि । तुमं दुवाररक्खओ होहि । [आर्य गौतम अहमप्रकाशे तिष्ठामि । त्वं द्वाररक्षको भव ।]

विदूषकः—जुज्जइ । [युज्यते ।] (निष्क्रान्ता बकुलावलिका ।)

विदूषकः (परिक्रम्यावलोक्य च ।)—इदं दाव फलिहत्थलं । आसीणो होमि । (तथा कृत्वा ।) अहो सुहप्फरिसदा सिलाविसेसस्स । [इदं तावत्स्फाटिकस्थलम् । आसीनो भवामि । अहो सुखस्पर्शता शिलाविशेषस्य ।] (निद्रायते)

(मालविका ससाध्वसा तिष्ठति ।)

राजा--

विसृज सुन्दरि सङ्गमसाध्वसं
तव चिरात्प्रभृति प्रणयोन्मुखे ।
परिगृहाण गते सहकारतां
त्वमतिमुक्तलताचरितं मयि ॥ १३ ॥

मालविका--देवीए भएण अत्तणो वि पिअं कादु ण पारेमि । [देव्या भयेनात्मनोऽपि प्रियं कर्तुं न पारयामि ।]

राजा--अयि न भेतव्यं न भेतव्यम् ।

मालविका—जो ण भाएदि सो मए भट्टिणीदंसणे दिट्ठसमवत्थो भट्टा णं । [यो न बिभेति स मया भट्टिनीदर्शने दृष्टसमवस्थो भर्ता ननु ।]

राजा—

दाक्षिण्यं नाम बिम्बोष्ठि बैम्बिकानां कुलव्रतम् ।
तन्मे दीर्घाक्षि ये प्राणास्ते त्वदाशानिबन्धनाः॥१४॥

तदयमनुगृह्यतां चिरानुरक्तो जनः । (इति संश्लेषमभिनयति । मालविका नाट्येन परिहरति ।)

Bakulāvalikā. *(Walking about)* Noble Gautama, I shall remain hidden from sight, and you will guard the entrance.

Vidūṣaka. That is quite proper. *(Exit Bakulāvalikā.)*

Vidūṣaka. In the meanwhile I shall lean against this crystal column. *(Doing as he says.)* How pleasant the feel of this delicious stone! *(Falls asleep.)*

(Mālavikā is overcome with fear.)

King. Give up, Oh sweet one, this fear of union, and now that I, who have for long been devoted to you, have become like the Mango-tree, do you assume the part of the Atimukta creeper towards me. (13)

Mālavikā. For fear of the queen, I cannot do what even my heart approves.

King. Well, you need have no fear.

Mālavikā. I have witnessed the courage of the king, who is now so fearless, in the presence of the queen.

King. Politeness indeed, Oh Bimba-lipped one, is the family tradition of the descendants of Bimbaka; nevertheless what life I possess depends entirely on the hope of thy favour. (14)

So favour me who am for long enamoured of thee. *(Goes close to her ; Mālavikā averts him.)*

राजा (आत्मगतम्)—रमणीयः खलु नवाङ्गनानां मदनविषयावतारः । एषा हि ।

हस्तं कम्पवती रुणद्धि रशनाव्यापारलोलाङ्गुलिं
हस्तौ स्वौ नयति स्तनावरणतामालिङ्ग्यमाना बलात् ।
पातुं पक्ष्मलचक्षुरुन्नमयतः साचीकरोत्याननं
व्याजेनाप्यभिलाषपूरणसुखं निर्वर्तयत्येव मे ॥ १५ ॥

(ततः प्रविशति इरावती निपुणिका च ।)

इरावती—हञ्जे निउणिए सच्चं तुए संदिट्ठं चन्दिआए समुद्दघरआलिन्दए अज्जगोदमो एआई दिट्ठोत्ति । [हञ्जे निपुणिके सत्यं त्वया सन्दिष्टं चान्द्रिकया समुद्रगृहालिन्दे आर्यगौतम एकाकी दृष्ट इति ।]

निपुणिका—अण्णहा कहं भट्टिणीए विण्णएमि । [अन्यथा कथं भट्टिन्यै विज्ञापयामि ।]

इरावती—तेण हि तहिं एव्व गच्छम्ह । संसआदो मुत्तं भट्टिणो पिअवअस्सं पेक्खिदुं अ । [तेन हि तत्रैव गच्छावः । संशयान्मुक्तं भर्तुः प्रियवयस्यं प्रेक्षितुं च ।]

निपुणिका—सविसेसं विअ भट्टिणीए वअणं । [सविशेषमिव भट्टिन्या वचनम् ।]

इरावती—आम् । चित्तगदं भट्टारं पसादेदुं । [आम् । चित्रगतं भर्तारं प्रसादयितुम् ।]

निपुणिका—अह दाणिं भट्टा एव्व किं ण पच्चणुणीअदि । [अथेदानीं भर्तैव किं न प्रत्यनुनीयते ।]

इरावती—मुद्धे जारिसो चित्तगदो भट्टा ण तारिसो एव्व । अण्णसङ्कन्ताहिअओ अज्जउत्तो । केवलं उवआरादिक्कमं पमज्जिदुं अम्हाणं अअं आरम्भो । [मुग्धे यादृशश्चित्रगतो भर्ता न तादृश एव । अन्यसङ्क्रान्तहृदय आर्यपुत्रः । केवलमुपचारातिक्रमं प्रमार्ष्टुमस्माकमयमारम्भः ।]

King. (*To himself*) How sweet the stepping of young women into the province of love ; for

she moves about her hand, and stops my
Trembling, she stops my hand with its fingers moving about the girdle, she côvers her breasts with her hands as perforce I embrace her; she turns aside her face with its eyes possessed of long eyelashes, as I try to raise it that I may sip it: thus does she grant me the happiness of enjoying the fulfilment of my desire even under a pretext. (15)

(*Then enter Irāvatī and Nipuṇikā.*)

Irāvatī. Nipuṇikā, my girl, did Candrikā really tell you that she saw the noble Gautama alone on the terrace of the ocean-pavilion ?

Nipuṇikā. How otherwise should I have ventured to tell your highness so ?

Irāvatī. Let us then proceed there that we might inquire after the health of the dear friend of my husband rescued from imminent peril—

Nipuṇikā. Your highness seems to have something further to say.

Irāvatī. And also to beg of my husband in the picture to forgive me.

Nipuṇikā. But how even now you don't endeavour to gain him over ?

Irāvtī. Silly girl, my husband is no longer what he appears to be in the picture. He has transferred the devotion of his heart to another woman. My present purpose is therefore to atone for my transgression of the proper decorum.

निपुणिका—इदो इदो भट्टिणी। [इत इतो भट्टिनी।]

(उभे परिक्रामतः।)

चेटी (प्रविश्य)—जेदु भट्टिणी। देवी भणादि। ण मे एसो मच्छरस्स कालो। केवलं तुह खु बहुमाणं वड्ढेदुं वअस्सिआए सह णिअलबन्धणे किदा मालविआ। जइ अणुमण्णेसि अज्जउत्तं वि तुह किदे विण्णविस्सं। जं तुह इच्छिदं तं भणाहित्ति। [जयतु भट्टिनी। देवी भणति—न मे एष मत्सरस्य कालः। केवलं तव खलु बहुमानं वर्धयितुं वयस्यया सह निगलबन्धने कृता मालविका। यद्यनुमन्यसे आर्यपुत्रमपि तव कृते विज्ञापयिष्यामि। यत्तवेष्टं तद्भण इति।]

इरावती—णाअरिए, विण्णवेहि देविं। का वअं भट्टिणिं णिओएदुं। परिअणणिग्गहेण मइ दंसिदो सिणेहो। कस्स वा अण्णस्स पसादेण अअं जणो वड्ढदित्ति। [नागरिके, विज्ञापय देवीम्। का वयं भट्टिनीं नियोजयितुम्। परिजननिग्रहेण मयि दर्शितः स्नेहः। कस्य वान्यस्य प्रसादेनायं जनो वर्धत इति।]

चेटी—तह। [तथा।] (इति निष्क्रान्ता।)

निपुणिका (परिक्रम्यावलोक्य च।)—भट्टिणी एसो दुवारुच्छङ्गे समुद्दघरस्स विवणिगदो विअ वुसहो अज्जगोदमो आसीणो एव्व णिद्दाअदि। [भट्टिनी एष द्वारोत्सङ्गे समुद्रगृहस्य विपणिगत इव वृषभ आर्यगौतम आसीन एव निद्रायते।]

इरावती—अच्चाहिदं। ण क्खु सावसेसविसविआरो भवे। [अत्याहितम्। न खलु सावशेषविषविकारो भवेत्।]

निपुणिका—पसण्णमुहो दीसइ। अवि अ धुवसिद्धिणा चिइच्छिदो। ता से असङ्कणिज्जं पावं। [प्रसन्नमुखो दृश्यते। अपि च ध्रुवसिद्धिना चिकित्सितः। तदस्य अशङ्कनीयं पापम्।]

Nipuṇikā. This way, your highness, this way.

(Both walk round.)

(Entering)

A female servant. Victory to your highness! The queen says " My time of showing jealousy is past and therefore only with a view to increase the great respect (in which you are held) that I put in fetters Mālavikā and her friend; if you give me leave, I will request my husband on your behalf Let me therefore know your wish. "

Irāvatī. Nāgarikā, tell the queen: who am I that I should commission the queen to do my bidding? She has shown great favour to me by punishing her servants; indeed what other person has shown me such favours?

Servant. I will do so. *(Exit)*

Nipuṇikā. *(Walking round and looking)* Your highness, here is the noble Gautama sleeping even in a sitting posture on the threshold of the ocean-pavilion like an ox in the market-place.

Irāvatī. What a pity! Surely it cannot be that the effects of the poison still remain.

Nipuṇikā. The expression of his face is serene. Besides Dhruvasiddhi has ministered to him. Therefore we need not be afraid that his life is in peril.

विदूषकः (उत्स्वप्नायते ।)—होदि मालविए । [भवति मालविके ।]

निपुणिका—सुदं भट्टिणीए । कस्स वि एसो अत्तणीणो हदासो किदवो । सव्वकालं इदो एव्व सोत्थिवाअणमोदएहिं कुक्खिं पूरिअ सम्पदं मालविअं उस्सिविणावेदि । [श्रुतं भट्टिन्या । कस्याप्येष आत्मनीनो हताशः कितवः । सर्वकालमित एव स्वस्तिवाचनमोदकैः कुक्षिं पूरयित्वा साम्प्रतं मालविकां उत्स्वप्नायते ।]

विदूषकः—इरावदिं अदिक्कामन्ती होहि । [इरावतीमतिक्रामन्ती भव ।]

निपुणिका—सुदं एदं अच्चाहिदं । भुअङ्गभीरुअं बम्हबन्धुं इमिणा भुअङ्गकुडिलेण दण्डकट्ठेण थम्भन्तरिदा भविअ भीसअम्हि । [श्रुतमेतदत्याहितम् । भुजङ्गभीरुकं ब्रह्मबन्धुमनेन भुजङ्गकुटिलेन दण्डकाष्ठेन स्तम्भान्तारिता भूत्वा भीषयिष्ये ।]

इरावती—एसो अरुहदि किदवो सप्पदंसस्स । [एषोऽर्हति कितवः सर्पदंशस्य ।]

(निपुणिका विदूषकस्योपरि दण्डकाष्ठं पातयति ।)

विदूषकः— (सहसा प्रतिबुध्य ।) अविहा अविहा । भो दव्वीअरो मे उवरि पडिदो । [अविहा अविहा । भो दर्वीकरो मे उपरि पतितः ।]

राजा (सहसोपसृत्य ।)—सखे न भेतव्यं न भेव्यतम् ।

मालविका—(अनुसृत्य) भट्टा मा दाव सहसा णिक्कम । सप्पोत्ति भणादि । [भर्तः मा तावत्सहसा निष्काम । सर्प इति भणति ।]

इरावती—हद्धि हद्धि भट्टा इदो एव्व धावइ । [हा धिक् हा धिक् भर्ता इत एव धावति ।]

विदूषकः (सप्रहासम्) —कहं दण्डकट्ठं एदं । अहं उण जाणे जं मए केदईकण्टएहिं दंसं करिअ सप्पस्स विअ दंसो किदो तं फलिदंति।

Vidūsaka. (*Talks in his sleep*) Lady Mālavikā—

Nipuṇikā. Did your highness hear ? What sire begot this accursed rogue I wander ! This accursed wretch, constantly filling his belly with complimentary sweetmeats given here, is now talking in his sleep about Mālavikā !

Vidūṣaka. May you supplant Irāvatī.

Nipuṇikā. Heard this piece of ill luck ? I will hide behind the pillar and with this stick of mine, which is crooked like a snake, frighten this vile Brahmin who is afraid of serpents.

Irāvatī. Surely the traitor deserves some misfortune.

(*Nipuṇikā hurls her stick at the body of the Vidūṣaka.*)

Vidūṣaka. *(Suddenly waking up)* Woe is me! Friend, a serpent has fallen upon me.

King. *(Rushing out immediately)* Do not be afraid, my friend, do not be afraid.

Mālavikā. *(following)* Husband, do not rush out all of a sudden ; he says there is a snake there.

Irāvatī. Alas ! alas ! my lord is running in this very direction.

Vidūsaka. *(Laughing aloud)* How now ? This is a mere stick. But I think this is the just reward for the blame I had the presumption to cast upon a imitating its bite with Ketakī thorns.

७२ [कथं दण्डकाष्ठमेतत् । अहं पुनर्जाने यन्मया केतकीकण्टकाभ्यां दंशं
कृत्वा सर्पस्येव दंशः कृतः तत्फलितमिति ।]

(ततः प्रविशति पटाक्षेपेण बकुलावलिका ।)

७८ **बकुलावलिका**—मा दाव भट्टा पविसदु । इह कुडिलगई सप्पो
विअ दीसइ। [मा तावत् भर्ता प्रविशतु । इह कुटिलगतिः सर्प
इव दृश्यते ।]

८१ **इरावती** (राजानं सहसोपसृत्य)—अवि णिव्विग्घमणोरहो दिवा-
सङ्केदो मिहुणस्स । [अपि निर्विघ्नमनोरथो दिवासङ्केतो मिथुनस्य ।]
(सर्वे इरावतीं दृष्ट्वा सम्भ्रान्ताः ।)

८४ **राजा**—प्रिये अपूर्वोऽयमुपचारः ।

इरावती—बउलावलिए दिट्ठिआ दोच्चहिआरविसआ संपुण्णा दे
पडिण्णा । [बकुलावलिके दिष्ट्या दूत्यधिकारविषया सम्पूर्णा ते प्रतिज्ञा ।]

८७ **बकुलावलिका**—पसीददु भट्टिणी । किं णु खु दद्दुरा वाहरन्तित्ति
देवो पुढविं विसुमरेदि । किं मए किदंति देवो पुच्छिदव्वो [प्रसी-
दतु भट्टिनी । किं नु खलु दर्दुरा व्याहरन्तीति देवः पृथिवीं विस्मरति ।
९० किं मया कृतमिति देवः प्रष्टव्यः ।]

विदूषकः—मा दाव । होदीए दंसणमेत्तेणं अत्तभवं पणिवादलङ्घणं
विसुमरिदो । होदी उण अज्ज वि पसादं ण गेह्णादि । [मा तावत् ।
९३ भवत्या दर्शनमात्रेणात्रभवान् प्रणिपातलङ्घनं विस्मृतः । भवती पुनः
अद्यापि प्रसादं न गृह्णाति ।]

इरावती—कुविदा वि दाणिं किं करिस्सं । [कुपितापीदानीं किं
९६ करिष्यामि ।]

राजा—अस्थाने कोप इत्येतदनुपपन्नं त्वयि । तथा हि—

कदा मुखं वरतनु कारणादृते
तवागतं क्षणमपि कोपपात्रताम् ।

(Then enter Bākulavalikā with a hurried toss of the curtain.)

Bakulāvalikā. Do not enter, Oh king; for it seems it is a serpent going in a zigzag course.

Irāvatī. *(concealing herself behind the pillar and advancing towards the king)* Did the couple find their mid-day meeting yield them the desire of their heart without any obstruction ?

(All are confused at sight of Irāvatī.)

King. Darling, this is indeed a novel form of greeting.

Irāvatī. Bakulāvalikā, I congratulate you upon your making good the promise of acting as a go-between.

Bakulāvalikā. Let your highness have compassion on me; for does Indra cease to shower rain on the divine earth because the frogs croak ? You may ask the king as to what I have done.

Vidūṣaka. Please, don't go on in this way. For merely on beholding you his honour forgot your repudiation of his humble prostration ; but you would not be friendly with him even now.

Irāvatī. What can I do now even though I am angry ?

King. It is not proper for you to be angry without cause. For

fair one, when did your face exhibit anger without cause ? Would the night have the orb

अपर्वणि ग्रहकलुषेन्दुमण्डला
विभावरी कथय कथं भविष्यति ॥ १६ ॥

इरावती—अट्ठाणे त्ति सुट्ठु वाहरिदं अज्जउत्तेण । अण्णसङ्कन्तेसु अम्हाणं भाअहेएसु जइ उण कुप्पेअं अहं हस्सा हविस्सम् । [अस्थान इति सुष्ठु व्याहृतमार्यपुत्रेण । अन्यसङ्क्रान्तेष्वस्माकं भागधेयेषु यदि पुनः कुप्येयम् ततोऽहं हास्या भवेयम्]

राजा—त्वमन्यथा कल्पयसि । अहं पुनः सत्यमेवात्र कोपस्थानं न पश्यामि । कुतः

नार्हति कृतापराधोऽप्युत्सवदिवसेषु परिजनो दण्डम् ।
इति मोचिते मयैते प्रणिपतितुं मामुपगते च ॥ १७ ॥

इरावती—णिउणिए गच्छ देविं विण्णवेहि । दिट्ठं देवीए पक्खवाइत्तणं अज्ज त्ति । [निपुणिके गच्छ देवीं विज्ञापय । दृष्टं देव्याः पक्षपातित्वमद्येति ।]

निपुणिका—तह । [तथा ।] (इति निष्क्रान्ता ।)

विदूषकः (आत्मगतम्)—अहो अणत्थो संवुत्तो । बन्धणब्भट्ठो घरकवोदआ बिडालिआलोए पडिदो । [अहो अनर्थः संवृत्तः । बन्धनभ्रष्टो गृहकपोतको बिडालिकालोके पतितः ।]

निपुणिका—(प्रविश्य) भट्टिणि जदिच्छादिट्ठाए माधविआए आचक्खिदं । एवं खु एदं णिव्वुत्तं । (इति कर्णे कथयति ।) [भट्टिनि यदृच्छादृष्टया माधविकयाख्यातम्—एवं खल्वेतन्निर्वृत्तमिति ।]

इरावती (आत्मगतम्)—उववण्णं सव्वं । बम्हबन्धुणा उब्भिण्णो दुप्पओओ । (विदूषकं विलोक्य प्रकाशम् ।) इअं इमस्स कामतन्तसइवस्स णीदी । [उपपन्नं सर्वम् । ब्रह्मबन्धुनोद्भिन्नो दुष्प्रयोगः । इयमस्य कामतन्त्रसचिवस्य नीतिः ।]

विदूषकः—होदि जइ णीदीए एक्कं वि अक्खरं पढेअं तदो णं

of the moon obscured by Rāhu except on the full-moon day ? (16)

Irāvatī. 'Not proper'—that is a proper expression used by my husband. For now that my good fortune has passed on to another, I should only be making myself ridiculous if I were to get angry again.

King. You take it differently ; but I, on my part, really do not see any cause for anger.

For it was in obedience to the precept
that on festive days attendants ought not to
be punished even when they have committed
an offence, that I let them free and now they
come to pay me their respects. (17).

Irāvatī. Nipuṇikā, go and inform the queen that I have to-day witnessed her partiality.

Nipuṇikā. Very well. (*Exit.*)

Vidūṣaka. (*To himself*) Alas ! a calamity has befallen : the house-pigeon has escaped from confinement (only) to come within sight of the cat.

(*Entering*)

Nipuṇikā. (*Aside*) Queen, Mādhavikā whom I happened to meet informed me that it happened thus.

(*Whispers in her ear.*)

Irāvatī. (*To herself*) I have it now. Surely this must be an intrigue of that scoundrelly Brahmin's planning. (*Looking at the Vidūṣaka.*) This is the policy of this minister versed in the treatises on love.

गाअत्तिं वि विसुमरेअं। [भवति यदि नीत्यां एकमप्यक्षरं पठेयं ततो ननु गायत्रीमपि विस्मरेयम् ।]

राजा (स्वगतम्)—कथं नु खलु सङ्कटादस्मादात्मानं मोचयिष्यामि ।

(प्रविश्य) **जयसेना** (सावेगम्)–देव कुमारी वसुलच्छी कन्दुअं अणुधावन्ती पिङ्गलवाणरेण बलिअं उत्तासिदा अङ्कणिसण्णा देवीए पवादकिसलअं विअ वेवमाणा दाणिं वि पकिदिं ण पडिवज्जइ। [देव कुमारी वसुलक्ष्मीः कन्दुकमनुधावन्ती पिङ्गलवानरेण बलवदुत्त्रासिताङ्कनिषण्णा देव्याः प्रवातकिसलयमिव वेपमाना इदानीमपि प्रकृतिं न प्रतिपद्यते ।]

राजा—कष्टम् कष्टम् । कातरो बालभावः ।

इरावती (सावेगम्)—तुवरदु तुवरदु अज्जउत्तो णं समासासइदुं। मा दाव से सन्तासजणिओ विआरो वड्ढदु । [त्वरतां त्वरतामार्यपुत्र एनां समाश्वासयितुम् । मा तावदस्याः सन्त्रासजनितो विकारो वर्धताम् ।]

राजा—अहमेनां सञ्ज्ञापयामि। (सत्वरं परिक्रामति ।)

विदूषकः (आत्मगतम्)—साहु रे पिङ्गलवाणर साहु । सुट्ठु परित्तादो तुए सङ्कडादो सपक्खो । [साधु रे पिङ्गलवानर साधु। सुष्ठु परित्रातस्त्वया सङ्कटात् सपक्षः ।]

(निष्क्रान्तः सवयस्यो राजा इरावती निपुणिका चेटा च ।)

मालविका—हला देविं चिन्तिअ वेवदि मे हिअअं । ण जाणे अदो वरं किं अणुहोदव्वं हविस्सादित्ति । [हला देवीं चिन्तयित्वा वेपते मे हृदयम् । न जाने अतः परं किमनुभवितव्यं भविष्यतीति ।]

(नेपथ्ये)

अच्छरिअं अच्छरिअं । अपुण्णे एव्व पञ्चरत्ते दोहलस्स मुउलेहिं सण्णद्धो तवणीआसोओ । जाव देवीए णिवेदेमि । [आश्चर्यमाश्च-

Vidūṣaka. Lady, if I were to read but one syllable of policy, I shall forget the Gāyatrī.

King. (*To himself*) How on earth may I get out of this sad pickle !

(*Entering*)

Jayasenā. *(Excitedly)* King,princess Vasulakṣmī while running after her ball was terribly frightened by the ape Pingalaka; and now although reclining in the lap of the queen is trembling like a spray in the breeze and does not regain consciousness in the least.

King. Alas ! How very timid are children !

Irāvatī. (*In consternation*) Let my husband hasten to console her. Let not the illness produced by the fright be aggravated.

King. I will soon bring her to consciousness. (*Moves about quickly.*)

Vidūṣaka. Bravo ! Pingala ape, bravo ! You have indeed saved your side.

(*Exeunt king, the Vidūṣaka, Irāvatī and the female door-keeper.*)

Mālavikā. Friend, I am all in a flutter as I think of the queen. I do not know what I shall have to endure next.

(Behind the scenes.)

A Marvel ! A Marvel ! Even before five nights have passed from the time of the Dohada ceremony, the

9

र्यम् । अपूर्ण एव पञ्चरात्रे दोहदस्य मुकुलैः सन्नद्धस्तपनीयाशोकः । यावद्देव्यै निवेदयामि ।]

(उभे श्रुत्वा प्रहृष्टे भवतः ।)

बकुलावलिका—समस्ससदु पिअसही । सच्चपडिण्णा देवी । [समाश्वसितु प्रियसखी । सत्यप्रतिज्ञा देवी ।]

मालविका—तेण हि पमदवणपालिआए पिट्ठदो होम्म । [तेन हि प्रमदवनपालिकायाः पृष्ठतो भवावः ।]

बकुलावलिका—तहा । [तथा ।]

(इति निष्क्रान्ताः सर्वे ।)

॥ इति चतुर्थोऽङ्कः ॥

---

golden Aśoka tree is covered over with buds. So I will inform the queen.

(Both are delighted on hearing this.)

Bakulāvalikā. Cheer up, my friend, the queen will be true to her word.

Mālavikā. Well then, let us follow the keeper of the pleasure-garden close at her heels.

Bakulāvalikā. All right. (*Exeunt.*)

Here ends the Fourth Act.

पञ्चमोऽङ्कः ।

(ततः प्रविशत्युद्यानपालिका ।)

उद्यानपालिका—उवक्खित्तो मए किदसक्कारविहिणो तवणीआसोअस्स वेदिआबन्धो । जाव अणुचिट्ठिदणिओअं अत्ताणं देवीए णिवेदेमि । (परिक्रम्य) अहो देव्वस्स अणुकम्पणिज्जा मालविआ । जं तस्सि तह चण्डीकिदा देवी इमिणा असोअकुसुमउत्तंतेण पसादसुमुही भविस्सदि । कहिं णु खु देवी भवे । (विलोक्य) अम्मो एसो देवीए परिजणब्भंदरो किं वि जदुमुद्दालंछिदं चीवरबन्धं करे गेह्णिअ चउस्सालादो कुज्जो सारसओ णिक्कमदि । पुच्छिस्सं दाव णं । [उपक्षिप्तो मया कृतसत्कारविधेस्तपनीयाशोकस्य वेदिकाबन्धः । यावदनुष्ठितनियोगमात्मानं देव्यै निवेदयामि । अहो दैवस्यानुकम्पनीया मालविका । यत् तस्यां तथा चण्डीकृता देवी अनेनाशोककुसुमवृत्तान्तेन प्रसादसुमुखी भविष्यति । कुत्र नु खलु देवी भवेत् । अम्मो एष देव्याः परिजनाभ्यन्तरः किमपि जतुमुद्रालाञ्छितं चीवरबन्धं करे गृहीत्वा चतुःशालात् कुब्जः सारसको निष्क्रामति । प्रक्ष्यामि तावदेनम् ।]

(ततः प्रविशति यथानिर्दिष्टः कुब्जः ।)

उद्यानपालिका—(उपसृत्य)—सारसअ कहिं पत्थिदोसि । [सारसक कुत्र प्रस्थितोऽसि ।]

सारसकः—महुअरिए वेअपारआणं बम्हणाणं णिच्चदक्खिणा दादव्वा । ता अज्जपुरोहिदस्स हत्थं पावइस्सं । [मधुकरिके वेदपारगाणां ब्राह्मणानां नित्यदक्षिणा दातव्या । तदार्यपुरोहितस्य हस्तं प्रापयिष्यामि ।]

मधुकरिका—किंणिमित्तं । [किन्निमित्तम् ।]

सारसकः— जदप्पहुदि सुदं सेणावइणा जण्णतुरअरक्खणे णिउत्तो भट्टिदारओ वसुमित्तोत्ति तदापहुदि तस्स आउसो णिमित्तं अट्ठा-

ACT V.

(*Enter the female keeper of the garden.*)

The keeper. I have got constructed an alter round the gold Aśoka-tree which has been duly honoured. So I will inform the queen that I have executed her order. (*Moving about.*) Ah! Fate should really take pity on Mālavikā, so that although the queen is highly incensed against her, yet she might be inclined to favour her on account of this incident of the Aśoka putting forth flowers. Where is the queen? (*Observing*) Ah! the hunchback Sārasaka, one of the servants of the queen, is just issuing out of the quadrangle with a cloth-covered box sealed with a lac seal. I will ask him.

(*Enter the hunch-back as described.*)

The keeper. (*Approaching*) Sārasaka, where are you going?

Sārasaka. Madhukarikā, the Brahmins versed in the sacred lore are to be given their daily dole. So I will put (it) into the hands of the revered priest.

Madhukarikā. What for?

Sārasaka. Ever since the queen learnt that prince Vasumitra was appointed by the general to guard the sacrificial horse, she has been bestowing on those who

दससुवण्णप्पमाणं दक्खिणं देवी दक्खिणीएहिं पडिग्गाहेदि । [यदाप्रभृति श्रुतं सेनापतिना यज्ञतुरगरक्षणे नियुक्तो भर्तृदारको वसुमित्र इति तदाप्रभृति तस्यायुषो निमित्तमष्टादशसुवर्णप्रमाणां दक्षिणां देवी दक्षिणीयैः प्रतिग्राहयति ।]

मधुकरिका—जुज्जइ । अह कहिं देवी । किं वा अणुचिट्ठदि । [युज्यते । अथ कुत्र देवी । किं वानुतिष्ठति ।]

सारसकः—मङ्गलघरए आसणत्था विअब्भविसआदो भादुणा वीरसेणेण पेसिदं लिपिअरेहिं वाचीअमाणं लेहं सुणादि । [मङ्गलगृहे आसनस्था विदर्भविषयात् भ्रात्रा वीरसेनेन प्रेषितं लिपिकारैर्वाच्यमानं लेखं शृणोति ।]

मधुकरिका—को उण विअब्भराअवुत्तन्तो । [कः पुनर्विदर्भराजवृत्तान्तः ।]

सारसकः—वसीकिदो किल वीरसेणप्पमुहेहिं भट्टिणो विअअदण्डेहिं विअब्भणाहो । मोइदो अ से दाआदो माहवसेणो । तेण महासाराइं रअणवाहणाइं सिप्पआरिआभूइट्ठं परिअणं अ उवाअणीकरिअ भट्टिणो सआसं पेसिदो दूदो सुवो किल भट्टारं पेक्खिस्सदि । [वशीकृतः किल वीरसेनप्रमुखैर्भर्तुर्विजयदण्डैर्विदर्भनाथः । मोचितश्चास्य दायादो माधवसेनः । तेन महासाराणि रत्नवाहनानि शिल्पदारिकाभूयिष्ठं परिजनं चोपायनीकृत्य भर्तुः सकाशं प्रेषितो दूतः श्वः किल भर्तारं द्रक्ष्यति ।]

मधुकरिका—गच्छ अणुचिट्ठ अत्तणो णिओअं । अहं वि देविं पेक्खिस्सं । [गच्छ अनुतिष्ठ आत्मनो नियोगम् । अहमपि देवीं द्रक्ष्यामि ।]

(इति निष्क्रान्तौ ।)

प्रवेशकः ।

(ततः प्रविशति प्रतीहारी ।)

प्रतीहारी—आणत्तम्हि देवीए असोअसक्कारव्वावुदाए—त्रिण्णत्तेहि

are worthy of the dole, eighteen golden pieces in order to secure him (long) life.

Madhukarikā. That is as it should be. Where is the queen ? How is she engaged ?

Sārasaka. Sitting in the holy house, she is listening to a letter sent by her brother Vīrasena from the country of the Vidarbhas, read out to her by the scribes.

Madhukarikā. What could be the news from the king of the Vidarbhas ?

Sārasaka. It is reported that the victorious army of our king led by Vīrasena and others has subjugated the king of the Vidarbhas, and his relative Mādhavasena is set free. He has sent many presents of very valuable jewelled vehicles, and some attendants, mostly maidens accomplished in the arts ; and has dispatched a messenger who is to see his majesty tomorrow.

Madhukarikā. Go, attend to your business ; I for my part will see the queen.

(Exeunt.)

Here ends the introductory scene.

(Enter the female door-keeper.)

Door-keeper—the queen who is engaged in doing honour to the Aśoka tree has given me this order : tell my lord I desire to witness for myself in the company of my lord the Asoka tree in its glory of flowers. So I

अज्जउत्तं । इच्छामि अज्जउत्तेण सह असोअरुक्खस्स पसूणलच्छिं पच्चक्खीकरेदुंत्ति । ता जाव धम्मासणगदं देवं पडिवालेमि ।
[आज्ञप्तास्मि देव्या अशोकसत्कारव्यापृतया—विज्ञापयाम्यार्यपुत्रम् । इच्छाम्यार्यपुत्रेण सहाशोकवृक्षस्य प्रसूनलक्ष्मीं प्रत्यक्षीकर्तुम् ' इति । तद्यावद्धर्मासनगतं देवं प्रतिपालयामि ।]

(इति परिक्रामति ।)

(नेपथ्ये) **वैतालिकौ**—दिष्ट्या दण्डेनैवारिशिरःसु वर्तते देवः ।

प्रथमः—**परभृतकलव्याहारेषु त्वमात्तरतिर्मधुं**
नयसि विदिशातीरोद्यानेष्वनङ्ग इवाङ्गवान् ।
विजयकरिणामालानाङ्गैरुपोढबलस्य ते
वरद वरदारोधोवृक्षैः सहावनतो रिपुः ॥ १॥

द्वितीयः—**विरचितपदं वीरप्रीत्या सुरोपम सूरिभि-**
श्चरितमुभयोर्मध्येकृत्य स्थितं क्रथकैशिकान् ।
तव हृतवतो दण्डानीकैर्विदर्भपतेः श्रियं
परिघगुरुभिर्दोर्भिः शौरेः प्रसह्य च रुक्मिणीम् ॥२॥

प्रतीहारी—एसो जअसद्दसूइदप्पत्थाणो भट्टा इदो एव्व आअच्छदि। अहंवि दाव इमस्स पमुहादो किंवि ओसरिअ एदं मुहालिन्दतोरणं समस्सिदा होमि । [एष जयशब्दसूचितप्रस्थानो भर्ता इत एवागच्छति। अहमपि तावदस्य प्रमुखात्किमप्यपसृत्य एतन्मुखालिन्दतोरणं समाश्रिता भवामि ।] (एकान्ते स्थिता ।)

(ततः प्रविशति सवयस्यो राजा ।)

राजा—

कान्तां विचिन्त्य सुलभेतरसम्प्रयोगां
श्रुत्वा विदर्भपतिमानमितं बलैश्च ।
धाराभिरातप इवाभिहतं सरोजं
दुःखायते च हृदयं सुखमश्नुते च ॥ ३ ॥

will now await the king who has been occupying the judgment-seat.

(Moves about.)

(Behind the scenes.)

Two Bards—Hail to our king who by the mere strength of his army tramples the heads of his enemies.

First Bard—In the gardens on the banks of
the Vidiśā, vocal with the sweet warblings of
the cuckoo, delighted, you spend the spring like
the god of love assuming a body ; while your
power ever waxing, O giver of boons, the enemies
have been bent down together with the trees
on the banks of the Varadā, which are used as
the tying posts for your victorious elephants.(1)

Second bard—O god-like (king), the acts of
these two, sung in verse by the wise out of their
love for heroes, have been well known all over
the Kratha-kaiśikas—of you who by means of
your forces took away the glory of the king of
the Vidarbhas, and of Śrikrsna who by his
arms as puissant as iron has forcibly carried
away Rukmiṇī. (2)

Door-keeper. The king is coming here, his setting forth being announced by the shouts of victory ; I will now step aside from his direct path and stand under the arch of the main terrace. *(Stands aside.)*

(Enter king with his companion.)

King. As I think how difficult it is to secure
my beloved and as I hear of the subjugation
of the king of the Vidarbhas by my forces,
my heart feels both happy and sad, like a lotus
in the sun when it is struck by the streams (of
a rain shower.) (3)

विदूषकः—जह अहं पेक्खामि तह एकन्तसुहिदो भवं भविस्सदि। [यथाहं पश्यामि तथैकान्तसुखितो भवान् भविष्यति।]

राजा—कथमिव।

विदूषकः—अज्ज किल देवीए धारिणीए पण्डिदकोसिई भणिदा। भअवदि जइ तुमं पसाहणगव्वं वहेसि ता दंसेहि मालविआए सरीरे वेदब्भं विवाहणेवत्थं ति। ताए वि सविसेसालंकिदा मालविआ। तत्तहोदी कदावि पूरेइ भवदो मणोरहं। [अद्य खलु देव्या धारिण्या पण्डितकौशिकी भणिता। 'भगवति यदि त्वं प्रसाधनगर्वं वहसि तद्दर्शय मालविकायाः शरीरे वैदर्भं विवाहनेपथ्यम्' इति। तयापि सविशेषालङ्कृता मालविका। तत्रभवती कदाचित् पूरयति भवतो मनोरथम्।]

राजा—सखे मदपेक्षानुवृत्या निवृत्तेर्ष्याया धारिण्याः पूर्वचरितैः सम्भाव्यमेतत्।

प्रतीहारी (उपगम्य)—जेदु भट्टा। देवी विण्णवेदि—तवणीआसोअस्स कुसुमसोहादंसणेण मह आरम्भो सफलीकरीअदु त्ति। [जयतु भर्ता। देवी विज्ञापयति—'तपनीयाशोकस्य कुसुमशोभादर्शनेन ममारम्भः सफलीक्रियताम्' इति।]

राजा—ननु तत्रैव देवी।

प्रतीहारी—अह इं। जहारुहसम्माणसुहिदं अन्देउरं विसज्जिअ मालविआपुरोएण अत्तणो परिअणेण सह देवं पडिवालेदि। [अथ किम्। यथार्हसम्मानसुखितं अन्तःपुरं विसृज्य मालविकापुरोगेणात्मनः परिजनेन सह देवं प्रतिपालयति।]

राजा (सहर्षम्। विदूषकं विलोक्य।)—जयसेने गच्छाग्रतः।

प्रतीहारी—इदो इदो देवो। [इत इतो देवः।]

(सर्वे परिक्रामन्ति।)

विदूषकः (विलोक्य)—भो वअस्स किंचि परिवुत्तजोव्वणो विअ

Vidūṣaka. As I see it, you will surely be blessed with perfect happiness.

King. How do you mean ?

Vidūṣaka. To day queen Dhāriṇī said to the learned Kausikī : Revered lady, if you pride yourself upon your skill in decorating, then put on Mālavikā's person the wedding-attire used by the people of the Vidarbha country ; and she too got Mālavikā splendidly decked. It is, therefore, likely that her highness grants you your desire.

King. Friend, this is quite possible, to judge from the former actions of Dhāriṇī who has always followed my inclinations and has been utterly free from jealousy.

Door-keeper. *(Approaching)* Victory to the king! The queen makes this request : please to make my undertaking fruitful by coming to witness the beauty of the gold Aśoka-tree in flowers.

King. Surely the queen is there, is she not ?

Door-keeper. Yes. After dismissing the ladies of the harem who are pleased by being honoured according to their deserts, she is waiting for my lord with her own attendants headed by Mālavikā.

King. *(Joyfully looking at the Vidūṣaka)* Jayasenā, do you go ahead

Door-keeper. This way, this way, king.

(All move about.)

Vidūṣaka. *(Observing)* My friend, in this Pramada-

२६ वसन्तो पमदवणे लक्खीअदि । [भो वयस्य किंचित्परिवृत्तयौवन इव वसन्तः प्रमदवने लक्ष्यते ।]

राजा—यथाह भवान् ।

अग्रे विकीर्णकुरबकफलजालविभिद्यमानसहकारम् ।
परिणामाभिमुखमृतोरुत्सुकयति यौवनं चेतः ॥ ४ ॥

विदूषकः (परिक्रम्य)—अहो अअं सो दिण्णणेवत्थो विअ
३ कुसुमत्थबएहिं तवणीआसोओ । ओलोएदु भवं । [अहो अयं स दत्तनेपथ्य इव कुसुमस्तबकैस्तपनीयाशोकः अवलोकयतु भवान् ।]

राजा—स्थाने खल्वयं प्रसवमन्थरोऽभूत् । यदयमिदानीमनन्य-
६ साधारणां शोभां उद्वहति । पश्य

सर्वाशोकतरूणां प्रथमं सूचितवसन्तविभवानाम् ।
निर्वृत्तदोहदेऽस्मिन्सङ्क्रान्तानीव कुसुमानि ॥ ५ ॥

विदूषकः—भो विस्सद्धो होहि । अम्हेसु सण्णिहिदेसु वि धारिणी पस्सपरिवट्टिणिं मालविअं अणुमण्णेदि । [भो विश्रब्धो
३ भव । अस्मासु सन्निहितेष्वपि धारिणी पार्श्वपरिवर्तिनीं मालविका-मनुमन्यते ।]

राजा (सहर्षम्)—पश्य सखे

मामियमभ्युत्तिष्ठति देवी विनयादुपस्थिता प्रियया ।
विस्मृतहस्तकमलया नरेन्द्रलक्ष्म्या वसुमतीव ॥ ६ ॥

(ततः प्रविशति देवी मालविका परिव्राजिका विभवतश्च परिवारः ।)

मालविका (आत्मगतम्)—जाणामि णिमित्तं कोदुआलङ्का-
३ रस्स । तह वि भिसिणीपत्तगदं सलिलं विअ वेवइ मे हिअअं । दक्खिणेदरं वि णअणं बहुसो फुरइ । [जानामि निमित्तं कौतु-कालङ्कारस्य । तथापि बिसिनीपत्रगतं सलिलमिव वेपते मे हृदयम् ।
६ दक्षिणेतरदपि नयनं बहुशः स्फुरति ।]

vana-garden here, spring seems to be somewhat past his youth.

King. It is even as you say.

Here before (us) the youth of spring now attaining its ripeness, with the Kurabakà flowers scattered, and the mango tree bursting with fruit, fills the mind with longing. (4)

Vidūṣaka. *(Moving about)* O, this gold Aśoka-tree appears to be attired in a vesture of clūstering flowers. Look, your highness.

King. It was quite proper that it was tardy to blossom. For now it stands matchless in its loveliness. See,

it appears as if the flowers of all other Aśoka-trees that first exhibited the wealth of spring, have been transferred to this tree, now that its longing is fulfilled. (5)

Vidūṣaka. Be quite at ease; for even when we are near, Dhāriṇī allows Mālavikā to attend her.

King. (*With joy*) See. my friend,

the queen rises to greet me respectfully, attended by my beloved, like the Earth waited upon by royal Glory who has forgotten to hold a flower in her hand. (6)

(Then enter The queen, Mālavikā, Parivrājikā and the attendants at a respectful distance.)

Mālavikā. *(To herself)* I know the reason of this nuptial attire ; and yet, how my heart quivers like water on a lotus-leaf ! And my left eye, too, is throbbing frequently.

विदूषकः—भो! वअस्स किं वि वेवाहिअणेवत्थेण सविसेसं खु सोहदि तत्तहोदी मालविआ। [भो वयस्य किमपि वैवाहिकनेपथ्येन
९ सविशेषं खलु शोभते तत्रभवती मालविका।]

राजा—पश्याम्याभरणालङ्कृतामेनाम्। यैषा

अनतिलम्बिदुकूलनिवासिनी
लघुभिराभरणैः प्रतिभाति मे।
उडुगणैरुदयोन्मुखचन्द्रिका
गतहिमैरिव चैत्रविभावरी॥ ७॥

धारिणी—(उपेत्य) जेदु अज्जउत्तो। [जयत्वार्यपुत्रः।]

विदूषकः—वड्ढदु होदी। [वर्धतां भवती।]

३ **परिव्राजिका**—विजयतां देवः।

राजा—भगवति अभिवादये।

परिव्राजिका—अभिमतसिद्धिरस्तु।

६ **धारिणी** (सस्मितम्)—अज्जउत्त, एसो दे अम्हेहिं तरुणीअणसहाअस्स असोओ सङ्केदघरअं सङ्कप्पिदो। [आर्यपुत्र, एष
तेऽस्माभिस्तरुणीजनसहायस्याशोकः सङ्केतगृहं सङ्कल्पितः।]

९ **विदूषकः**—भो आराहिओसि। [भो आराधितोऽसि।]

राजा—(सव्रीडमशोकमभितः परिक्रामन्।)

नायं देव्या भाजनत्वं न नेषः
सत्काराणामीदृशानामशोकः।
यः सावज्ञो माधवश्रीनियोगे
पुष्पैः शंसत्यादरं यत्प्रयत्ने॥ ८॥

विदूषकः—भो विस्सद्धो भविअ इमं जोव्वणवदिं पेक्ख। [भो
विश्रब्धो भूत्वेमां यौवनवतीं पश्य।]

३ **धारिणी**—कं। [काम्।]

Vidūṣaka. My friend, the lady Mālavikā looks so lovely in that nuptial dress.

King. I see her decked in those ornaments–she who

wearing a short silk dress and with scanty ornaments, appears to me like a night in the month of Caitra when moonlight is imminent, with the clusters of stars free from mists. (7)

Dhāriṇī. (*advancing*) Victory to my lord !

Vidūṣaka. May your highness be prosperous !

Parivrājikā. May the king be victorious !

King. Revered lady, I salute thee !

Parivrājikā. May you attain the object you desire !

Dhāriṇī. *(Smiling)* my noble lord, here have we turned this Aśoka-tree into a trysting bower for you to enjoy the company of young ladies.

Vidūṣaka. Come, friend, a great favour has been conferred upon you.

King. *(Bashfully walking round the Aśoka-tree.)*

This Aśoka-tree really deserves to be made the recipient of such favours inasmuch as it disregarded the command of the goddess of vernal beauty and evinced its respect for your exertions by bursting into flowers. (8)

Vidūṣaka. Come, be confident, and look at this blooming young—

Dhāriṇī. Whom do you mean ?

विदूषकः—तवणीआसोअस्स कुसुमसोहं । [तपनीयाशोकस्य कुसुमशोभाम् ।]

(सर्वे उपविशन्ति ।)

६**राजा** (मालविकां विलोक्यात्मगतम् ।)—कष्टं खलु ममाद्य सान्निधिविप्रयोगः ।

अहं रथाङ्गनामेव प्रिया सहचरीव मे ।
अननुज्ञातसम्पर्का धारिणी रजनीव नौ ॥ ९ ॥

(ततः प्रविशति कञ्चुकी ।)

कञ्चुकी—जयतु देवः । अमात्यो विज्ञापयति 'तस्मिन्विदर्भ-
३राजोपायने द्वे शिल्पदारिके मार्गपरिश्रमादलसशरीरे इति कृत्वा न प्रवेशिते । सम्प्रति देवोपस्थानयोग्ये । तत्राज्ञां देवो दातुमर्हति ' इति ।

६**राजा**—प्रवेशय ते ।

कञ्चुकी—यदाज्ञापयति देवः । (इति निष्क्रम्य ताभ्यां सह पुनः प्रविश्य ।) इत इतो भवत्यौ ।

९**प्रथमा** (जनान्तिकम्)—हला रआणिए, अपुव्वं वि एदं राउअलं पविसन्तीए पसीददि मे अब्भन्तरगदो अप्पा । [हला रजनिके अपूर्वमप्येतद्राजकुलं प्रविशन्त्याः प्रसीदति ममाभ्यन्तरगत आत्मा ।]

१२**द्वितीया**—जोसाणिए मह वि एव्वं । अत्थि खु लोअवाओ ।
आआमि सुहं वा दुक्खं वा हिअअं समत्थीकरेदित्ति । [ज्योत्स्निके ममाप्येवम् । अस्ति खलु लोकवादः । आगामि सुखं वा दुःखं
१५ वा हृदयं समर्थीकरोतीति ।]

प्रथमा—सो दाणिं सच्चो होदु । [स इदानीं सत्यो भवतु ।]

कञ्चुकी—एष देव्या सह देवस्तिष्ठति । उपसर्पतं भवत्यौ ।

Vidūsaka. Beauty of the flowers of the golden Aśoka.

(All sit down.)

King. *(Looking at Mālavikā, to himself)* Alas! I am at the present moment separated though near.

I am like the Cakravāka bird, and my beloved like his mate. while Dhāriṇī who does not permit our union, is like the night. (9)

(Then enter a chamberlain.)

Chamberlain. Victory to the king. The minister says that in that present sent by the king of Vidarbha were included two accomplished maidens who, as they were fatigued with the journey, were not then presented. Now they are in a fit state to appear before the king. Let the king, therefore, direct in regard to this matter.

King. Introduce them.

Chamberlain. As the king commands. (*He goes out and then reappears along with them.*) This way, this way, ladies.

First. *(Aside)* Ah, Rajanikā, although I am stepping into this palace quite unknown to me before, yet my inner self is filled with delight.

Second. Jyotsnikā ! I have exactly the same feeling. You know indeed the well known proverb : the state of the heart foretells approaching happiness or misery.

First. May it come true on the present occasion.

Chamberlain. Here are the king and the queen; may you advance, ladies.

(उभे उपसर्पतः । मालविका परिव्राजिका च चेट्यौ दृष्ट्वा परस्परमवलोकयतः ।)

उभे (प्रणिपत्य)—जेदु भट्टा । जेदु भट्टिणी । [जयतु भर्ता । जयतु भट्टिनी ।]

राजा—निषीदतम् ।

(उभे उपविष्टे ।)

राजा—कस्यां कलायामभियोगो भवत्योः ।

उभे—भट्टा सङ्गीदए अब्भंतरम्ह । [भर्तः सङ्गीते अभ्यन्तरे स्वः ।]

राजा—देवि गृह्यतामनयोरन्यतरा ।

देवी—मालविए इदो पेक्ख । कदरा दे सङ्गीदसहाइणी रुच्चइ । [मालविके इतः पश्य । कतरा ते सङ्गीतसहायिनी रोचते ।]

उभे—(मालविकां विलोक्य)—अम्मो भट्टिदारिआ । जेदु भट्टिदारिआ । [अम्मो भर्तृदारिका । जयतु भर्तृदारिका ।]

(तया सह बाष्पं विसृजतः ।)

(सर्वे सविस्मयमालोकयन्ति ।)

राजा—के भवत्यौ । का वेयम् ।

प्रथमा—देव इअं अम्हाणं भट्टिदारिआ । [देव इयमस्माकं भर्तृदारिका ।]

राजा—कथमिव ।

उभे—सुणादु भट्टा । जो सो भट्टिणा विअअदण्डेहिं विअब्भणाहं वसीकरिअ बन्धणादो मोइदो कुमारो माहवसेणो णाम तस्स इअं कणीअसी भइणी मालविआ णाम । [शृणोतु भर्ता । योऽसौ भर्त्रा विजयदण्डैर्विदर्भनाथं वशीकृत्य बन्धनान्मोचितः कुमारो माधवसेनो नाम तस्येयं कनीयसी भगिनी मालविका नाम ।]

धारिणी—कहं राअदारिआ इअं । चन्दणं खु मए पादुआपरि-

(Both advance, Mālavikā and the Parivrājikā exchange glances on seeing these two attendants.)

Both. *(Prostrating themselves)* Victory to the king! Victory to the queen!

King. Sit down.

(Both sit down.)

King. Ladies, which art have you practised?

Both. We are well versed in music, your majesty.

King. Queen, take one of these ladies.

Queen. Look here, Mālavikā. Which would you like to have to accompany you in singing?

Both. *(Seeing Mālavikā)* Ah! The princess! *(Prostrating before her)* Victory to our princess! *(They weep with her.)*

(All look on in bewilderment.)

King. Who are you, ladies? And who is this?

First. King, this is our princess.

King. What do you mean?

Both. Listen, king! This is Mālavikā the younger sister of prince Mādhavasena who was rescued from prison by you by conquering the king of Vidarbha with your victorious army.

Dhārinī. She is a princess! How have I been de-

होएण दूसिदं । [कथं राजदारिकेयम् । चन्दनं खलु मया पादुकापरिभोगेण दूषितम् ।]

राजा——अथात्रभवती कथमित्थंभूता ।

मालविका (निःश्वस्यात्मगतम् ।)——विहिणो णिओएण । [विधेर्नियोगेन ।]

द्वितीया——सुणादु भट्टा । दाआदवसं गदे अम्हाणं भट्टिदारए माहवसेणे तस्स अमच्चेण अज्जसुमदिणा अम्हारिसं परिअणं उज्झिअ गूढं अवणीदा एसा । [शृणोतु भर्ता । दायादवशं गतेऽस्माकं भर्तृदारके माधवसेने तस्यामात्येनार्यसुमतिना अस्मादृशं परिजनं उज्झित्वा गूढमपनीतैषा ।]

राजा——श्रुतपूर्वं मयैतावत् । ततस्ततः ।

उभे——एत्तिअं एव्व आणीमो । अदो वरं ण आणीमो । [एतावदेव जानीवः । अतः परं न जानीवः ।]

परिव्राजिका——अतः परमहं मन्दभागिनी कथयिष्यामि ।

उभे——भट्टिदारिए अज्जकोसिईए विअ सरसञ्जोओ पडिभादि । [भर्तृदारिके आर्यकौशिक्या इव स्वरसंयोगः प्रतिभाति ।]

मालविका——अह इं । [अथ किम् ।]

उभे——जदिवेसधारिणी अज्जकोसिई दुक्खेण विभावीअदि । भअवदि वन्दामो । [यतिवेषधारिणी आर्यकौशिकी दुःखेन विभाव्यते । भगवति वन्दावहे ।]

परिव्राजिका——स्वस्ति भवतीभ्याम् ।

राजा——कथमाप्तवर्गोऽयं भवत्याः ।

परिव्राजिका——एवमेतत् ।

विदूषकः——तेणहि कहेदु दाणिं भअवदी अत्तहोदीए उत्तन्तसेसं । [तेन हि कथयत्विदानीं भगवती अत्रभवत्या वृत्तान्तशेषम् ।]

परिव्राजिका (सवैक्लव्यम्)——श्रूयतां तावत् । माधवसेनसचिवं

filing sandalwood by using it as a slipper!

King. Well, then, how was this lady reduced to this state?

Mālavikā. *(Sighing, to herself)* By the decree of fate.

Second Maiden. Listen, your majesty. When our prince Mādhavasena was captured by his kinsmen, his minister, the noble Sumati, secretly carried her away, leaving behind attendants like us.

King. I have heard this before. What happened next?

Both. This is all we know. We do not know what happened afterwards

Parivrājikā. I will now relate, wretched woman that I am, what happened next.

Both. Princess, we seem to hear the voice of the noble Kauśikī.

Mālavikā. Surely.

Both. It is difficult to recognize the noble Kauśikī in the garb of an ascetic. Revered lady, we salute you.

Parivrājikā. Blessings on you!

King. What, are these your kinsfolk?

Parivrājikā. Yes, it is so.

Vidūsaka. Please, revered lady, relate to us the rest of her story.

Parivrājikā. *(Painfully)* Listen then. Know that

६२सुमतिं ममाग्रजमवेष्ठ ।

राजा—उपलब्धम् । ततस्ततः ।

परिव्राजिका—स इमां तथागतभ्रातृकां मया सार्धमपवाह्य भव-
७२त्सम्बन्धाकाङ्क्षया पथिकसार्थं विदिशागामिनमनुप्रविष्टः ।

राजा—ततस्ततः ।

परिव्राजिका—ततश्च

तूणीरपट्टपरिणद्धभुजान्तराल-
मापार्ष्णिलम्बिशिखिबर्हकलापधारि ।
कोदण्डपाणि निनदत्प्रतिरोधकाना-
मापातदुष्प्रसहमाविरभूदनीकम् ॥ १० ॥

(मालविका भयं रूपयति ।)

विदूषकः—भोदि मा भआहि । अदिक्कन्तं खु भअवदी कहेदि ।
३[भवति मा भैषीः । अतिक्रान्तं खलु भगवती कथयति ।]

राजा—ततस्ततः ।

परिव्राजिका—ततो मुहूर्तं बद्धयुद्धास्ते पराङ्मुखीकृताः सार्थवाह-
६योद्धारः तस्करैः ।

राजा—भगवति अतः परमिदानीं कष्टं श्रोतव्यम् ।

परिव्राजिका—ततः स मत्सोदर्यः

इमां परीप्सुर्दुर्जातेः पराभिभवकातराम् ।
भर्तृप्रियः प्रियैर्भर्तुरानृण्यमसुभिर्गतः ॥ ११ ॥

प्रथमा—हा हदो सुमदी । [हा हतः सुमतिः ।]

द्वितीया—अदो खु भट्टिदारिआए एआरिसी समवत्था संवुत्ता ।
३ [अतः खलु भर्तृदारिकाया एतादृशी समवस्था संवृत्ता ।]

(परिव्राजिका बाष्पं विकिरति ।)

Mādhavasena's minister, Sumati, is my elder brother.

King. We understand ; pray, go on.

Parivrājikā. He carried off along with myself, this lady whose brother was reduced to such a state, and desiring to marry her to your majesty joined a caravan that was going to the Vidiśā country.

King. What next ?

Parivrājikā. And then

there appeared a host of yelling bandits, armed with bows, whose breasts were crossed by the quiver-straps, and who wore tufts of peacock-tails hanging down to their heels, and whose on-slaught was so irresistible. (10)

(Mālavikā gesticulates fright.)

Vidūṣaka. Lady, do not be afraid; for the revered lady is relating something that is past.

King. What happened next ?

Parivrājikā. Then the warriors employed by the leader of the caravan joined battle for a moment with the robbers, but were soon put to flight.

King. Revered lady, the sequel to this, which we have now to hear, must be painful.

Parivrājikā. Then my brother

endeavouring to save from the ruffians this lady who was afraid of violence at their hands —my brother who loved his king so well—paid with his dear life his debt to his king. (11)

First maiden. Alas ! Sumati is killed !

Second maiden. That is how our princess is reduced to this state.

(The Parivrājikā sheds tears.)

राजा—भगवति तनुभृतामीदृशी लोकयात्रा । न शोच्यस्तत्रभवान् सफलीकृतभर्तृपिण्डः । ततः ।

परिव्राजिका—ततो मोहं गताहं यावत्संज्ञामुपलभे तावदियं दुर्लभदर्शना संवृत्ता ।

राजा—महत् खलु कृच्छ्रमनुभूतं भगवत्या ।

परिव्राजिका—ततो भ्रातुः शरीरमग्निसात्कृत्वा पुनर्नवीकृतवैधव्य-दुःखया मया त्वदीयं देशमवतीर्य इमे काषाये गृहीते ।

राजा—युक्तम् । सज्जनस्यैष पन्थाः । ततस्ततः ।

परिव्राजिका—सेयमाटविकेभ्यो वीरसेनं वीरसेनाद्देवीं गता देवीगृहे लब्धप्रवेशया मया पुनर्दृष्टेत्येतदवसानं कथायाः ।

मालविका (आत्मगतम्)—किं णु खु संपदं भट्टा भणादि । [किं नु खलु साम्प्रतं भर्ता भणति ।]

राजा—अहो परिभवोपहारिणो विनिपाताः । कुतः ।

प्रेष्यभावेन नामेयं देवीशब्दक्षमा सती ।
स्नानीयवस्त्रक्रियया पत्रोर्णं वोपयुज्यते ॥ १२ ॥

धारिणी—भअवदि तुए अहिजणवदिं मालविअं अणाचक्खन्तीए असम्पदं किदं । [भगवति त्वयाभिजनवतीं मालविकामनाचक्षाणया असाम्प्रतं कृतम् ।]

परिव्राजिका—शान्तं पापं शान्तं पापम् । कारणेनैव खलु मया नैभृत्यमवलम्बितम् ।

धारिणी—किं विअ कारणं । [किमिव कारणम् ।]

राजा—यदि वक्तव्यं कथ्यताम् ।

King. Revered lady, that is the lot of mortals. You must not lament for your noble brother who showed he had not eaten his master's salt in vain. Well, what next?

Parivrājikā. Then I fainted, and by the time I had recovered myself this lady was nowhere to be seen.

King. The revered lady has indeed passed through a severe calamity.

Parivrājikā. Then I burned the body of my brother, and with the sorrow of my widowhood renewed I came to your country and assumed these two red garments.

King. Quite proper; this is the way of life that pious men adopt. What happened next?

Parivrājikā. This lady came from the power of the foresters into that of Vīrasena, who sent her on to the queen; and so was again seen by me when I obtained admission into the queen's palace. This is the end of my story.

Mālavikā. *(To herself)* I wonder what the King will say now.

King. Alas! How indignities are heaped on those that suffer calamities. For

> this lady having a right to the title of queen
> has been treated by us as a slave, as a silken
> garment is used for the purposes of a bathing-
> cloth. (12)

Dhārinī. Revered lady, you did wrong in not telling me that Mālavikā was of noble birth.

Parivrājikā. Heaven forbid! I had indeed a very good reason for adopting secrecy.

Dhāriṇī. What is the reason like?

King. If it is proper to tell, then do tell us.

परिव्राजिका—श्रूयताम् । इयं पितरि जीवति केनापि देवयात्रागतेन सिद्धादेशेन साधुना मत्समक्षमादिष्टा । ‘ संवत्सरमात्रं प्रेष्यभावमनुभूय ततः सदृशभर्तृगामिनी भविष्यति ’ इति । तमेनमवश्यंभाविनमादेशमस्यास्त्वत्पादशुश्रूषया परिणमन्तमवेक्ष्य कालप्रतीक्षया मया साधु कृतमिति पश्यामि ।

राजा—युक्तोपेक्षा ।

कञ्चुकी (प्रविश्य)—देव कथान्तरेणान्तरितमिदममात्यो विज्ञापयति । ‘ विदर्भगतमनुष्ठेयमवधारितमस्माभिः । देवस्य तावदभिप्रायं श्रोतुमिच्छामि ’ इति ।

राजा—मौद्गल्य तत्रभवतोर्भ्रात्रोर्यज्ञसेनमाधवसेनयोर्द्वैराज्यमवस्थापयितुकामोऽस्मि ।

तौ पृथग्वरदाकूले शिष्टामुत्तरदक्षिणे ।
नक्तंदिवं विभज्योभौ शीतोष्णकिरणाविव ॥ १३ ॥

कञ्चुकी—देव एवममात्यपरिषदे विज्ञापयामि ।

(राजा अङ्गुल्यानुमन्यते । निष्क्रान्तः कञ्चुकी ।)

प्रथमा (जनान्तिकम्)—भट्टिदारिए दिट्ठिआ भट्टिदारओ अद्धरज्जे पदिट्ठं गमिस्सदि । [भर्तृदारिके दिष्ट्या भर्तृदारकोऽर्धराज्ये प्रतिष्ठां गमिष्यति ।]

मालविका—एत्तिअं दाव बहुमन्तव्वं जं जीवितसंसआदो मुत्तो ।
[एतावत्तावद्बहु मन्तव्यं यज्जीवितसंशयान्मुक्तः ।]

कञ्चुकी (प्रविश्य)—विजयतां देवः । अमात्यो विज्ञापयति । अहो कल्याणी देवस्य बुद्धिः । मन्त्रिपरिषदोऽप्येवमेव दर्शनम् । कुतः

द्विधा विभक्तां श्रियमुद्वहन्तौ
धुरं रथाश्वाविव सङ्ग्रहीतुः ।
तौ स्थास्यतस्ते नृपती निदेशे
परस्परावग्रहनिर्विकारौ ॥ १४ ॥

Parivrājikā. Listen. This lady, while her father was still living, was told in my presence by an infallible and saintly seer, at a fair held in honour of a deity, that she would have to endure the position of a slave for just a year, and would then get a husband of equal rank. Seeing that the inevitable prophecy was being fulfilled by her continuing to serve your feet, I waited for the appointed time and I think I acted rightly.

King. It was quite proper to wait patiently.

(Entering) A chamberlain. King, the minister sends the following message which I could not deliver before, as another matter had cropped up in the meanwhile: we have considered what ought to be done with reference to Vidarbha. But I would like to know the view of the king.

King. Maudgalya, I wish to appoint the two brothers Yajnasena and Mādhavasena as joint rulers:

let them rule separately the north and south banks of the Varadā like the Sun and the Moon that divide between them and rule the night and day. (13)

Chamberlain. King, I will communicate this your view to the council of ministers.

(The King shows his assent by a movement of his finger. Exit Chamberlain.)

First maiden. *(aside)* fortunately the prince will be established in half of the Kingdom.

Mālavikā. Even this I ought to consider as a great thing that he has been rescued from peril of his life.

(*Entering*) The chamberlain. Victory to the King! The minister says 'How auspicious the King's view! The council of ministers too hold the same view; for

bearing up their fortune divided between them, like the horses of a chariot the yoke put upon them by the charioteer, these two kings will be ruled by you, not being distracted by mutual conflict. (14)

राजा—तेन हि मन्त्रिपरिषदं ब्रूहि । सेनापतये वीरसेनाय लिख्यतामेवं क्रियतामिति ।

कञ्चुकी—यदाज्ञापयति देवः । (इति निष्क्रम्य सप्राभृतकं लेखं गृहीत्वा पुनः प्रविश्य ।) अनुष्ठिता प्रभोराज्ञा । अयं पुनरिदानीं देवस्य सेनापतेः पुष्पमित्रस्य सकाशात्सप्राभृतको लेखः प्राप्तः । प्रत्यक्षीकरोत्विमं देवः ।

(राजा सहसोत्थाय प्राभृतकं सोपचारं परिगृह्य शिरसि कृत्वा परिजनायार्पयति। लेखं च नाट्येन उद्वेष्टयति ।)

धारिणी—अम्महे तदोमुहं एव्व मे हिअअं । सुणिस्सं दाव गुरुअणकुसलाणन्तरं पुत्तस्स वसुमित्तस्स उत्तन्तं । अदिभारे खु सेणावइणा णिउत्तो मे पुत्तओ [अम्महे ततोमुखमेव मे हृदयम् । श्रोष्यामि तावद् गुरुजनकुशलानन्तरं पुत्रस्य वसुमित्रस्य वृत्तान्तम् । अतिभारे खलु सेनापतिना नियुक्तो मे पुत्रकः ।]

राजा—(उपविश्य वाचयति ।) स्वस्ति । यज्ञशरणात्सेनापतिः पुष्पमित्रो वैदिशस्थं पुत्रमायुष्मन्तमग्निमित्रं स्नेहात्परिष्वज्यानुदर्शयति । विदितमस्तु । योऽसौ राजसूयज्ञदीक्षितेन मया राजपुत्रशतपरिवृतं गोप्तारं वसुमित्रमादिश्य संवत्सरोपावर्तनीयो निरर्गलस्तुरगो विसृष्टः स सिन्धोर्दक्षिणे रोधसि चरन्नश्वानीकेन यवनानां प्रार्थितः । तत उभयोः सेनयोर्महानासीत्सम्मर्दः ।

(धारिणी विषादं रूपयति ।)

राजा—कथमीदृशं संवृत्तम् । (शेषं पुनर्वाचयति ।)

ततः परान्पराजित्य वसुमित्रेण धन्विना ।
प्रसह्य ह्रियमाणो मे वाजिराजो निवर्तितः ॥ १५ ॥

King. Tell the council then that written orders to the effect should be sent to Vīrasena, the commander-in-chief.

Chamberlain. As the king commands. *(Goes out and re-enters with a letter accompanied by a present)* The king's order is carried out. But this letter along with a present has arrived from the commander-in-chief, king Puṣpamitra ; let the king look at it.

(The king rises quickly, puts the present respectfully upon his head and then hands it to the attendants ; he then makes as if he opens the letter.)

Dhāriṇī. Ha, how my heart is eager to learn the contents of the letter ! I would learn, after the news of the health of my father-in-law, how my son Vasumitra has been doing. Surely the commander has put a very heavy duty on my son.

King. *(Sits down and reads)* May fortune attend thee! From the sacrificial enclosure, the commander-in-chief Puṣpamitra sends this meṣage to his long-lived son Agnimitra who is in the Vidiśā country, affectionately embracing him : be it known to thee : I, having been consecrated for the Rājasūya sacrifice, let loose a horse, free from all restraint, which was to be brought back at the end of a year, and appointed Vasumitra as its defender, girt round by a hundred princes ; the same horse while wandering on the right bank of the Indus. was claimed by a cavalry squadron of the Yavanas. Thereafter ensued a fierce: struggle between the two armies.

(Dhāriṇī wears an expression of despondency.)

King. How could it be so ? *(Reads the rest of the letter.)*

And then Vasumitra, the mighty bowman, having repulsed his foemen, brought back my excellent horse which was being forcibly carried off by them. (15)

धारिणी--इमिणा दाणिं अस्ससइ मे हिअअं। [अनेनेदानीमाश्वसिति मे हृदयम्।]

३**राजा** (लेखशेषं वाचयति।) सोहमिदानीमंशुमतेव सगरः पौत्रेण प्रत्याहृताश्वो यक्ष्ये। तदिदानीमकालहीनं विगतरोषचेतसा भवता वधूजनेन सह यज्ञसेवनायागन्तव्यमिति।

६**राजा**—अनुगृहीतोऽस्मि।

परिव्राजिका--दिष्टया पुत्रविजयेन दम्पती वर्धेते। (देवीं विलोक्य।)

भर्त्रासि वीरपत्नीनां श्लाघ्यायां स्थापिता धुरि।
वीरसूरिति शब्दोऽयं तनयात्त्वामुपस्थितः ॥ १६ ॥

विदूषकः—होदि परितुट्ठोम्हि पिदरं अणुगदो वच्छोत्ति। [भवति परितुष्टोऽस्मि पितरमनुगतो वत्स इति।]

३**राजा**—मौद्गल्य कलभेन खलु यूथपतिरनुकृतः।

कञ्चुकी--

नैतावता वीरविजृम्भितेन
चित्तस्य नो विस्मयमादधाति।
यस्याप्रधृष्यः प्रभवस्त्वमुच्चै-
र्वन्हेरपां दग्धुरिवोरुजन्मा ॥ १७ ॥

राजा—मौद्गल्य यज्ञसेनश्यालमुररीकृत्य मुच्यन्तां सर्वे बन्धनस्थाः।

कञ्चुकी—यदाज्ञापयति देवः। [इति निष्क्रान्तः]

३**धारिणी**—जअसेणे गच्छ इरावदीपमुहाणं अन्देउराणं पुत्तस्स विअअउत्तन्तं णिवेदेहि। [जयसेने गच्छ इरावतीप्रमुखानामन्तःपुराणां पुत्रस्य विजयवृत्तान्तं निवेदय।]

६**प्रतीहारी**—तह। [तथा।] (इति प्रस्थिता।)

धारिणी—एहि दाव। [एहि तावत्।]

प्रतीहारी—(प्रतिनिवृत्य) इअम्हि [इयमस्मि।]

Dhāriṇī. Now, that relieves my heart.

King. (*Reads the rest of the letter.*) So that now I will offer a sacrifice, having had my horse brought back to me by my grandson, even as Anśumat brought back the horse to Sagara. So, now, dismissing anger from your mind, you must forthwith come with my daughter-in-law to witness the sacrifice.

King. I am indeed favoured.

Parivrājikā. I congratulate the couple on the victory of their son. (*Looking at the queen*)

By your husband you have been established in the commendable position of the foremost of the wives of heroes; but it is your son that gives you the title of the mother of heroes. (16)

Vidūsaka. Your highness, I am well pleased that the son takes after his father.

King. Maudgalya, indeed, the young elephant has imitated the leader of the herd.

Chamberlain.

Not even by such great display of valour does he produce astonishment in our minds, whose irresistible and lofty source you are as (the sage) Aurva is of the fire that consumes water. (17)

King. Maudgalyā, let all prisoners including the brother-in-law of Yajnasena, be set at liberty.

Chamberlain. As the king commands. *(Exit)*

Dhāriṇī. Jayasenā, go and give the news of my son's victory to Irāvatī and other ladies of the harem.

Door-keeper. As the queen orders. (*She sets off*)

Dhāriṇī. Come here a moment.

Door-keeper. (*Turning back*) Here I am

धारिणी--(जनान्तिकम्) जं मए असोअदोहलणिओए पडिण्णादं मालविआए एतं से अहिअणं अ णिवेदिअ मह वअणेण इरावदिं अणुणेहि। तुए हं सच्चादो ण परिब्भंसइदव्वात्ति। [यन्मयाशोकदोहदनियोगे प्रतिज्ञातं मालविकायै तदस्या अभिजनं च निवेद्य मम वचनेनेरावतीमनुनय—त्वयाहं सत्यान्न परिभ्रंशयितव्येति।]

प्रतीहारी—जं भट्टिणी आणवेदि। (इति निष्क्रम्य पुनः प्रविश्य।) भट्टिणि पुत्तविअएण अविभत्तपरितोसाणं अन्देउराणं आभरणाणं रअणमञ्जूसम्हि संवुत्ता। [यद्भट्टिन्याज्ञापयति। भट्टिनि पुत्रविजयेनाविभक्तपारितोषाणामन्तःपुराणामाभरणानां रत्नमञ्जूषास्मि संवृत्ता।]

धारिणी--किं एत्थ अच्छरिअं। णं साहारणो ताणं मह अ एसो अब्भुदओ। [किमत्राश्चर्यम्। ननु साधारणस्तासां मम चैषोऽभ्युदयः।]

प्रतीहारी (जनान्तिकम्)—भट्टिणि इरावदी विण्णवेदि। सारस खु देवीए पहवंतीए तुह वअणं पुढमसङ्कप्पिदं ण जुज्जइ अण्णहा कादुं [भट्टिनि इरावती विज्ञापयति। सदृशं खलु देव्याः प्रभवन्त्यास्तव वचनं प्रथमसङ्कल्पितं न युज्यतेऽन्यथाकर्तुमिति।]

धारिणी—भअवई तुए अणुण्णादा इच्छामि अज्जसुमदिणा पुढमसंभाविदं अज्जउत्तस्स मालविअं पडिवादेदुं। [भगवति त्वयानुज्ञाता इच्छाम्यार्यसुमतिना प्रथमसंभावितामार्यपुत्रस्य मालविकां प्रतिपादायितुम्।]

परिव्राजिका--इदानीमपि त्वमेवास्याः प्रभवासि।

धारिणी--(मालविकां हस्ते गृहीत्वा।) अज्जउत्तो इइं पिअणिवेदणाणुरूवं पारितोसिअं पाडिच्छदु। [आर्यपुत्र इदं प्रियनिवेदनानुरूपं पारितोषिकं प्रतीच्छतु।]

(राजा सव्रीडं जोषमास्ते।)

धारिणी--(सस्मितम्) किं ओहिरेदि मं अज्जउत्तो। [किमवधीरयति मामार्यपुत्रः।]

Dhāriṇī. (*Aside*) Tell Irāvatī from me what promise I made to Mālavikā at the time I appointed her to perform the ceremony of fulfilling the longing of the Aśoka, and tell her also of her noble birth, and entreat her that she should not cause me to deviate from truth.

Door-keeper. As the queen commands. (*Going out and again returning*) Queen, look, I have indeed become a jewelled casket to hold the ornaments (presented to me) by the ladies of the harem who have been uniformly gratified at the triumph of your son.

Dhārinī. What is there to astonish us in this ? For this triumph is as much theirs as mine.

Door-keeper. (*Aside*) Queen, Irāvatī says ; quite befitting is the promise which,all powerful that you are. you have already made and it should not be changed.

Dhārinī. Revered lady, with your consent I desire to bestow Mālavikā on my husband, for whom she was originally destined by the noble Sumati.

Parivrājikā. Now, too, you have full power over her.

Dhārinī. (*Taking hold of Mālavikā's hand.*) Let my husband accept this present as a fitting reward for the good news he has brought me.

(*The king remains silent and abashed.*)

Dhārinī. (*Smilingly*) Would my husband now repulse me ?

विदूषकः——होदि एसो लोअव्ववहारो सव्वो वि णववरो लज्जा-
३६ दुरो होदित्ति [भवति एष लोकव्यवहारः सर्वोऽपि नववरो लज्जा-
तुरो भवतीति ।]

(राजा विदूषकमवेक्षते ।)

३९ **विदूषकः**——अहवा देवीए किददेवीसद्दं मालविअं अत्तभवं पडिग्ग-
हीदुं इच्छदि [अथवा देव्या कृतदेवीशब्दां मालविकामत्रभवान्
प्रतिग्रहीतुमिच्छति ।]

४२ **धारिणी**——एदाए राअदारिआए अहिअणेण एव्व दिण्णो
देवीसद्दो । किं पुणरुत्तेण । [एतस्या राजदारिकाया अभिजनेनैव
दत्तोऽस्यै देवीशब्दः । किं पुनरुक्तेन ।]

४५ **परिव्राजिका**——मा मैवम् ।

अप्याकरसमुत्पन्ना मणिजातिरसंस्कृता ।
जातरूपेण कल्याणि न हि संयोगमर्हति ॥ १८ ॥

धारिणी——मरिसेदु भअवदी । अब्भुदअकहाए जं मए ण लक्खिदं ।
जअसेणे गच्छ । तुमं दाव कोसेअपत्तोण्णं से सिग्घं उवहर । [मर्ष-
३ यतु भगवती । अभ्युदयकथया यन्मया न लक्षितम् । जयसेने गच्छ ।
त्वं तावत्कौशेयपत्रोर्णमस्यै शीघ्रमुपहर ।]

प्रतीहारी——जं भट्टिणी आणवेदि । (इति निष्क्रम्य पत्रोर्णं गृहीत्वा
६ पुनः प्रविश्य ।) देवि एदं । [यद्भट्टिन्याज्ञापयति । देवि एतत् ।]

धारिणी——(मालविकामवगुण्ठ्य) दाणिं अज्जउत्तो पडिच्छदु ।
[इदानीमार्यपुत्रः प्रतीच्छतु ।]

९ **राजा**——देवि त्वच्छासनादप्रत्युत्तरा वयम् ।

परिव्राजिका——हन्त प्रतिगृहीता ।

विदूषकः——अहो देवीए अणुऊलदा । [अहो देव्या अनुकूलता ।]

१२ (धारिणी परिजनमवलोकयति ।)

परिजनः (मालविकामुपेत्य)——जेदु भट्टिणी । [जयतु भट्टिनी ।]

Vidūsaka. Lady, it is commonly observed that every new bridegroom is overcome with bashfulness.

(*The king looks at the Vidūṣaka.*)

Vidūṣaka. Or perhaps his highness would accept her after the queen will have honoured her with the title of Queen.

Dhāriṇī. Her very royal birth itself entitles her to that honour. Where is the use of repetition ?

Parivrājikā. Nay, not so.

Even though sprung from a mine, yet a jewel,
O noble lady, is not worthy of union with gold
until it is polished. (18)

Dhāriṇī. Pardon me, revered lady, that I should have forgotten, owing to the news of the victory ; go, Jayasenā, and bring her quick a silken veil.

Door-keeper. As the queen commands. (*She goes out and returns with a silken veil.*) Here it is, queen.

Dhāriṇī. (*Investing Mālavikā with the veil.*) Let my husband now receive her.

King. Queen, your order leaves me no reply to make.

Parivrājikā. O joy ! She is accepted.

Vidūsaka. Dear me, how very gracious is the queen.

(*Dhāriṇī looks at her attendants.*)

Attendants. (*Advancing towards Mālavikā.*) Victory to the queen !

(धारिणी परिव्राजिकां निर्वर्णयति ।)

परिव्राजिका——नैतच्चित्रं त्वयि । कुतः ।

प्रतिपक्षेणापि पतिं सेवन्ते भर्तृवत्सलाः साध्व्यः ।
अन्यसरितां शतानि हि समुद्रगाः प्रापयन्त्यब्धिम् ॥१९॥

निपुणिका (प्रविश्य)——जेदु भट्टा । इरावदी विण्णवेदि जहा हि उवआरादिक्कमेण किदावराहाए ण मए भट्टिणो अणुऊलं आअरिदं । सम्पदं पुण्णमणोरहेण भट्टिणा अहं वि पसादमेत्तेण वि सम्भावइदव्वा ति । [जयतु भर्ता । इरावती विज्ञापयति । यथा हि उपचारातिक्रमेण कृतापराधया न मया भर्तुरनुकूलमाचरितम् । साम्प्रतं पूर्णमनोरथेन भर्त्रा अहमपि प्रसादमात्रेण संभावयितव्या इति]

धारिणी——णिउणिए अवस्सं ताए सन्देसं सेविदुं अज्जउत्तो जाणिस्सदि । [निपुणिके अवश्यं तस्याः सन्देशं सेवितुमार्यपुत्रो ज्ञास्यति ।]

निपुणिका——जं देवी आणवेदि । [यद्देव्याज्ञापयति ।] (इति निष्क्रान्ता ।)

परिव्राजिका——देव अहममुना भवत्संबन्धेन चरितार्थं माधवसेनं सभाजयितुमिच्छामि यदि मे तव प्रसादः ।

धारिणी——भअवदि ण जुत्तं अम्हे परिच्चत्तुं । [भगवति न युक्तमस्मान् परित्यक्तुम् ।]

राजा——भगवति मदीयेषु लेखेषु तत्रभवते त्वामुद्दिश्य सभाजनाक्षराणि पातयिष्यामि ।

परिव्राजिका——युवयोः स्नेहेन परवानयं जनः ।

धारिणी——आणवेदु अज्जउत्तो किं भूओ वि पिअं अणुचिट्ठामि । [आज्ञापयत्वार्यपुत्रः किं भूयोऽपि प्रियमनुतिष्ठामि ।]

राजा——किमतः परमपि प्रियमस्ति । तथापीदमस्तु ।

(Dhāriṇī looks towards the Parivrājikā.)

Parivrājikā. That is not surprising in you; for good women, who are devoted to their husbands, serve them even by making rivals to themselves, as rivers take hundreds of streams along with them to the sea. (19)

(Entering)

Nipuṇikā. Victory to the King! Irāvatī makes the following request: I have offended my lord by failing to show him courtesy and acted contrary to his wishes. But now that my lord has obtained his wish, he should honour me only by showing me his favour.

Dhāriṇī. Nipuṇikā, my husband will surely see his way to grant her request.

Nipuṇikā. As the queen commands. (*Exit.*)

Parivrājikā. King, I now desire to pay my respects to Mādhavasena, who has obtained his object by becoming your relation, if you favour me.

Dhāriṇī. Revered lady, it is not proper for you to leave us.

King. Revered lady, I will send in my letters to him your complimentary messages.

Parivrājikā. Your kindness makes me your dependent.

Dhāriṇī. Let my husband command what further service I can render him.

King. What could be dearer than this? But let this also be mine—

(भरतवाक्यम् ।)

त्वं मे प्रसादसुमुखी भव चण्डि नित्य-
मेतावदेव मृगये प्रतिपक्षहेतोः ।
आशास्यमीतिविगमप्रभृति प्रजानां
सम्पत्स्यते न खलु गोप्तरि नाग्निमित्रे ॥ २० ॥

[इति निष्क्रान्ताः सर्वे ।]

॥ इति पञ्चमोऽङ्कः ॥

———

(*Benediction*)

Do thou, Oh angry one, ever look upon me with a propitious countenance; so much do I desire in the interest of thy rival. For as long as Agnimitra is the protector, there will not be a blessing such as the removal of any calamity, which my subjects will not secure. (20)

(*Exeunt Omnes*)

Here Ends the Fifth Act.

MĀLAVIKĀGNIMITRA.

NOTES.

ACT I.

From the Nāṭyaśastra we learn that before the commencement of a drama, an elaborate series of preliminaries (पूर्वरङ्ग) had to be performed, consisting chiefly of the प्रत्याहार which would announce the beginning of the performance, the अवतरण when the musicians enter and take their places, the आरम्भ when the chorus try their voices, and the आश्रवण when the musicians try their instruments, and so on up to Nāndī. All these preliminaries are performed by the सूत्रधार who then leaves the stage, and his place is immediately taken by another similar person called स्थापक who introduces the play to the audience. This elaborate practice was, however, given up later on, and we find that the सूत्रधार alone performed both the functions of the preliminaries and of the prologue. (Vide विश्वनाथ's साहित्यदर्पण.). Cf. पूर्वरङ्गं विधायादौ सूत्रधारे विनिर्गते। प्रविश्य तद्वदपरः काव्यमास्थापयेन्नटः। सूचयेद्वस्तु बीजं वा मुखं पात्रमथापि वा॥ दश. III २--३.

I. 1. In this benedictory verse, god Śiva is first praised in terms of apparent contradiction, and then is invoked to favour the audience with the inward vision of spiritual knowledge, which would remove all darkness of ignorance and make them see the Right Path clearly. He is, for instance, the Lord of this universe, established in absolute supremacy, and yet what he wears is just an elephant-hide! Lesser beings than Him, enjoying inferior glory of kingship are seen to be strutting about in fine robes and splendid costumes and thus offer a great contrast to this wearer of elephant-skin, the supreme Lord of this Universe. He stands foremost of all sages who have removed their minds from all sense-pleasures and therefore would avoid all contact with women and yet in Him we find woman forming the counter-part, the complement of his body! He is manifested in this world in eight forms with which He supports the Universe; for this however, He feels within Him not the slightest tinge of vanity! The only explanation for this contradiction is that He is not to be judged by the existing standards with which we judge men, since He is far too divine and spiritual to be weighed in human balance.

एकैश्वर्ये...बहुफले-Fixed or established in absolute (एक) supermacy, calculated to yield a great many rewards or blessings to the devotees (प्रणत). ऐश्वर्य or supremacy is endowed by the possession of eight-fold supernatural powers, known as Siddhis. They are :—अणिमा लघिमा प्राप्तिः प्राकाम्यं महिमा तथा । ईशित्वं च वशित्वं च तथा कामावसायिता ॥ (1) अणिमा, the power of assuming a minute form of the size of an atom, (2) लघिमा, the power of reducing the weight of the body to the minimum, (3) प्राप्तिः the power of getting everything, (4) प्राकाम्यं, irresistible strength of will, (5) महिमा, the power of magnifying the body, (6) ईशित्वं Lordship, Majesty, (7) वशित्वं, power of curbing the senses, and (8) कामावसायिता–power of satisfying one's desires. प्रणत...फले–प्रणतानां (भक्तानां) बहूनि फलानि यस्मात्-तास्मिन्°फले ऐश्वर्ये ।. कृत्तिवासाः–कृत्तिः (the skin, hide) वासः यस्य सः–Having the elephant-skin as his garment, god Śiva is frequently represented as being fond of wearing an elephant-skin. Cf. नृत्तारम्भे हर पशुपतेरार्द्रनागाजिनेच्छाम् । मे॰ I. 38. Also, वधूदुकूलं कलहंसलक्षणं गजाजिनं शोणितबिन्दुवर्षि च । and विभूषणोद्भासि पिनद्धभोगि वा गजाजिनालंबि दुकूलधारि वा ॥ कुमा॰ V, 67, 78. There is another reading एकश्वर्यस्थितोऽपि प्रणतबहुफलः, which too is not bad. It would mean, 'established in i. e. possessed of *one* sovereignty and yet conferring *many* blessings etc.' the contrast being in एकैश्वर्य and बहुफल.

कान्ता...देहः–कान्तया संमिश्रः देहः यस्य सः । He who has his beloved viz. Pārvatī blended within his body. God Śiva is often represented in his form of अर्धनारी-नटेश्वर, wherein his better half is not put off from his body, but forms a literally fitting complement of it ! य अविषयः...यतीनाम्. Thus he stands in ascetic excellence far ahead (पुरस्तात्) of all these Yogins or sages who have completely detached their minds from all objects of the senses.

अविषयमनसाम्––न विद्यन्ते विषयाः शब्दादयो येषां तानि अविषयाणि मनांसि येषां—whose minds are dissociated from the sense-objects. The reading परस्तात is also good. It means 'beyond, higher than.' अष्टाभि...नाभिमानः-The eight forms of god Śiva through which he manifests himself for supporting this universe are-earth, water, fire, air, ether, the sun, the moon and the sacrificer. They are referred to in the Nāndī of Śākuntalam, या सृष्टिः स्रष्टुराद्या etc. Also कुमा० VI. 26 विदितं वो यथा स्वार्था न मे काश्चित प्रवृत्तयः । ननु मूर्तिभिरष्टाभिरित्थंभूतोऽस्मि सूचितः ॥ where Śiva himself speaks of his eight forms solely intended for the weal of the world. He has, therefore, the epithet of अष्टमूर्ति. Even with such a big task which he achieves, He has not the slightest feeling of pride (अभिमान), feeling which is too commonly met with among men who would accomplish comparatively trivial and insignificant purposes. सन्मार्गा...मीशः-May that Lord (ईश) remove your mental outlook of utter ignorance or illusion with the light of wisdom, and enable you to see the right path (सन्मार्ग) of liberation. तामसीं वृत्तिं = तमःसंबन्धिनीं वृत्तिम् । तमस् according to the सांख्य philosophy, is one of the three Guṇas viz. सत्त्व, रजस् and तमस्. सत्त्व is explained as virtue, purity, goodness; रजस् is explained as dust, mist, passion or movement ; and तमस् means darkness or ignorance and is of endless variety, such as disgust, misery, sloth, drowsiness, intoxication, etc. A state of mind in which तमस् preponderates is therefore opposed to virtue, purity and knowledge, and hence it must be done away with, before true vision dawns in the mind.

I. 1. 1. नान्द्यन्ते. 'At the end of the Nāndī or benediction.' The verse, explained above, constitutes the

Nāndī, which is defined thus आशीर्नमस्क्रियारूपः श्लोकः काव्यार्थ-सूचकः i. e 'a verse or verses of the form of a salutation or a benediction and suggestive of the story of the drama.' It is called नांदी because by the praise which it contains it is a source of delight to the gods. Cf. नन्दन्ति देवता यस्यां तस्मान्नान्दीति कीर्तिता। Its another characteristic of suggesting the story of the drama has led commentators into ingenious attempts to find out fantastic allusions to the main elements or incidents of the drama. Our commentator काटयवेम also suggests that epithets like प्रणतबहुफल, एकैश्वर्य etc. refer to a king, while the expression कान्तासंमिश्रदेह may allude to the long cherished union with the object of his love, and the word मार्ग in सन्मार्गालोकनाय points to a particular kind of acting. Cf. अत्र प्रणतबहुफलैकैश्वर्यस्थित्या कान्तासंमिश्रणेन जगद्धरणेन ईश्वर इत्यनेन च लोकोत्तरः कश्चिद् राजाऽस्मिन् नाटके वर्ण्यत इति सूच्यते। सन्मार्गालोकनाय इत्यनेन अत्र कश्चिद् मार्गाभिनयः प्रतिपाद्यत इति सूच्यते। मार्गो नाम नाट्यविशेषः।

सूत्रधारः—The principal stage-manager who arranges the cast of characters, instructs them in their different rules, and is thus responsible for the successful performance of the drama "The threads of which he holds in his hands, as it were." According to मातृगुप्ताचार्य. he must have the following accomplishments:—

चतुरातोद्यनिष्णातोऽनेकभाषासमावृतः। नानाभाषणतत्त्वज्ञो नीतिशास्त्रार्थ-तत्त्ववित्॥ नानागतिप्रचारज्ञो रसभावविशारदः। नाट्यप्रयोगनिपुणो नानाशिल्प-कलान्वितः॥ छन्दोविधानतत्त्वज्ञः सर्वशास्त्रविचक्षणः। तत्तद्गीतानुगलयकलातालावधारणः॥ अवधानप्रयोक्ता च योक्तॄणामुपदेशकः। एवंगुणगणोपेतः सूत्रधारोऽभिधीयते॥

I. 1. 2. मारिषः—A principal actor in the drama, the same as पारिषार्श्विक who serves as an assistant to the सूत्रधार, and therefore addresses him as भाव i. e. sir, your honour. Ordinarily it means " A learned or venerable man." नेपथ्याभिमुखम् Towards the curtain. The word नेपथ्य is used in a variety of meanings. It means (1) Dress or costume, particularly that of an actor, and is used in this sense in our drama Cf. विरलनेपथ्ययोः पात्रयोः प्रवेशोऽस्तु। Act I. (2) The tiring room where the actors dress themselves, (which is always behind the curtain) Cf. यदि नेपथ्यविधानमवसितमितस्तावदागम्यताम्। शा० I.

I. 1. 5. परिषद्–An assembly, the audience. कालिदास ...वस्तु (नाटकं) कालिदासेन प्रथितं वस्तु यस्य तद्–whose story has been woven into the plot (of this drama) by Kālidāsa. The word वस्तु means the story or the subject-matter of the play. मालविकाग्निमित्रम्–मालविकाग्निमित्रौ अधिकृत्य कृतं नाटकम्। A drama composed with reference to मालविका (the heroine) and अग्निमित्र (the hero); compare the expression मालतीमाधवम्.

वसन्तोत्सवः–The festivities that hailed the advent of spring were formerly celebrated on the full-moon day of the month of Caitra. They were marked with great hilarity and boisterousness, men and women equally taking part in these celebrations. For these descriptions see रत्नावली Act I. On such occasions, dramatic performances were also exhibited in competitive tests, and merit was rewarded by means of prizes. These festivities now take place on the full-moon day of the month of Phālguna, and are identified with Holi celebrations. सङ्गीतकम्–Music; triple symphony, singing being accompanied by instrumental music and dancing. Cf नृत्तं गीतं तथा वाद्यं त्रयं संगीतकं स्मृतम् ।

I. 1. 8. प्रथित etc. The पारिपार्श्विक strikes a discordant note of difference, when he says that compared to the work of famous writers like भास, सौमिल्ल and कविपुत्र, the work of a modern playwright will not catch the people's imagination. People generally have a tendency to praise things of the past, while deprecating the present ones. A budding writer, therefore, of the present age, not yet known to the people by his writings, has few chances of securing the people's approval in face of the works of the well-known dramatists of the past. About सौमिल्ल and कविपुत्र we have very little information. Regarding भास, however, there has been lately a keen controversy as to whether he should be looked upon as the author of those thirteen plays published in Trivandrum Series by T. Ganapati Shastri.

I. 1. 9. वर्तमानकवि–A living poet; a poet belonging to the present age. क्रिया–work, composition, writing. Cf. शृणुत मनोभिरवहितैः क्रियामिमां कालिदासस्य । विक्र० I. 2. विवेकविश्रान्तम्–Thoughtless, unreasonable, literally–' from which reason has retired. ' विवेकः विश्रान्तः यस्मिन् कर्मणि ।

I. 2. The Sūtradhāra repudiates the पारिपार्श्विक's suggestion that the audience may not favour the work of कालिदास, because he happens to be their contemporary. The people assembled here are all good critics and know how to judge of the merits of the play, after a thorough examination of its features, good or bad. They will thus, independently and with a clear, unbiased mind, examine this work, and in it they will not be swayed away by the convictions of others. In their eyes, therefore, just as age is no favourable feature of a work, similarly its modernity also is no demerit or a disqualification. Cf. तं सन्तः श्रोतुमर्हन्ति सदसद्व्यक्तिहेतवः । etc. रघु० I. 10. अवद्यम्–Fit to be condemned, censurable पर...बुद्धिः–परस्य प्रत्ययेन नेया बुद्धिर्यस्य–whose judgment is guided by the convictions of others.

I. 2. 1. आर्यमिश्राः–Respected or revered sir. मिश्र is an honorific suffix, always used in the plural. It is addressed to the सूत्रधार and not to the audience as suggested by some. पारिपार्श्विक here accepts the authoritative judgment of his superior, in a matter that had made him anxious regarding the success of the play they were going to enact.

I. 3. The सूत्रधार asks him to expedite and make a beginning for the drama, because he is very much eager to execute the order of the spectators, received by him already with a bowed head (शिरसा). And he compares his eagerness to that of the queen's maid-servant, who appears to be so keen on doing her service (सेवादक्ष) and is coming thither. Very cleverly has the poet linked up the prologue with the interlude of the main action, having introduced the character that comes on the scene immediately.

Here ends the प्रस्तावना or the Prologue called also आमुख. which generally consists of an introductory dialogue between the सूत्रधार and नटी or one of the actors. After giving an account of the author and his qualifications. it introduces the incidents of the drama. Cf. सूत्रधारो नटीं ब्रूते मार्षं वाथ विदूषकम् । स्वकार्यं प्रस्तुताक्षेपि चित्रोक्त्या यत्तदामुखम् । प्रस्तावना वा ॥. दश० III 8. Also नटी विदूषको वापि पारिपार्श्वक एव वा । सूत्रधारेण सहिताः संलापं यत्र कुर्वते ॥ चित्रैर्वाक्यैः स्वकार्योत्थैः प्रस्तुताक्षेपिभिर्मिथः । आमुखं तत्तु विज्ञेयं नाम्ना प्रस्तावनापि वा ॥ Of the प्रस्तावना, there are three varieties, according to दशरूपक (or five according to साहित्यदर्पण) of which प्रयोगातिशय or Particular Presentation is one in which a character is introduced by a remark of the stage-manager. एषोऽयमित्युपक्षेपात् सूत्रधारप्रयोगतः । पात्रप्रवेशो यत्रैष प्रयोगातिशयो मतः ॥ ३ ॥ Thus the प्रस्तावना of our drama also is of the प्रयोगातिशय type.

Next is a विष्कंभक or an interlude in which we have a conversation first between the two maids of queen Dhāriṇī and then between one of them and गणदास, the teacher of dancing. It tells us that a certain beautiful girl by name मालविका was sent as a present to the queen धारिणी by her brother वीरसेन; that she was given in the charge of the teacher गणदास for being trained in the art of dancing; that by chance she was observed in a picture by the king who was greatly impressed by her charms; and that hence the jealous queen is scrupulously guarding her from the king's observation. Incidentally it refers to a ring with the seal of a serpent engraved on it, which plays an important part in Act IV.

I. 3. 7. अचिर,...चलितं. The चलित dance in which instruction was given recently. The Prakrit पउत्त can also be translated in Sanskrit by the word प्रवृत्त, and then the expression अचिरप्रवृत्तोपदेश would mean 'lessons in which had commenced recently.' चलित, read also as छलित in some editions, is a variety of dancing in which the dancer, while acting the part of another, gives expression thereby to her own sentiments. Cf. तदेतच्चलितं नाम साक्षाद् यदभिनीयते। व्यपदिश्य परावृत्तं स्वाभिप्रायप्रकाशकम् ॥ अन्तरेण–About, with regard to ; it always governs the Accusative. कीदृशी मालविका–how मालविका fares ; how far मालविका has progressed. संगीतशाला. The concert-hall.

I. 3. 13. कुतस्ते...धीरता–' Why this seriousness or gravity ', धीरता means a serious mood of mind when the person is lost to all sense of what is passing around. Cf. भो वयस्य, धीरं गच्छ। मा तत्रभवती धारिणी विसंवादयिष्यति। and also धैर्यावलंबिनमपि त्वरयति मां मुरजवाद्यरागोऽयम्। I. 22. हृदय, मोत्ताम्य। आर्यपुत्रस्य वचनमवधार्य धीरं तावद् भव। शा० V.

I. 3. 18. शिल्पिन्–A goldsmith, an artisan. नागमुद्रासनाथं–Possessed of a serpent-seal. The word सनाथ originally meaning "with a lord or protector" retains only the sense of ' with '. त्वयोपगतया लतासनाथ इवायं केसरवृक्षकः प्रतिभाति। शा० I. स्निग्धं निध्यायन्ती–Observing closely or intently. तवोपालम्भे पतितास्मि. I fell under your reproof; I exposed myself to a taunt from you.

I. 3. 22. स्थाने–" It is but proper ". सज्जति दृष्टिः–The eyes get fixed or rivetted. उद्भिन्न...केसरेण. The ring with its up-shooting rays appearing like filaments. कुसुमितः-कुसुमं संजातमस्य - Full of blossoms ; flowered ; the derivative is obtained by the addition of the termination इतच् in the sense of तदस्य संजातम् । अग्रहस्तः–हस्तस्याग्रम् or अग्रश्चासौ हस्तश्च । The extremity of the hand; the palm. The idea of the sentence is that the rays which have shot forth from the ring, and which appear like the filaments of a blossom, have made it appear that the palm of the hand has flowered as it were.

I. 3. 30. ईदृशेन...तापि–Even when she was kept away by such an engagement. If in the queen's attendance, it would have been easy for the king to see her. She was, however removed from the queen by her present employment as a student of dancing in the charge of गणदास, and yet the king sees her! The reading किल instead of कथम् is certainly preferable. दृष्टा किलैषा भर्त्रा–' It is rumoured that she was observed by the king etc.' Then the reply with the particle of assent, आम् 'yes' fits in very well. I. 3. 31. पार्श्वगतः-By the side. स जनः 'That person,' refers to मालविका. I. 3. 36. चित्रशाला—A picture-hall. प्रत्यग्र...चित्ररेखा–The drawing of the picture shining with freshly-laid lours. The word रेखा means ' sketch or drawing .' Cf तथापि तस्या लावण्यं रेखया किंचिदन्वितम् । शा० VI. 14. I. 3. 41. उपचार–The customary obeisance or homage. Cf. गुरुपरितापानि न ते गात्राण्युपचारमर्हन्ति । शा० III. 18. आसन्नपरिचारिणी–standing close (to her).

I. 3. 45. अपूर्वा–Extraordinary, uncommon V. L. अपूर्वरूपा–' of uncommon charms' is certainly better. I.

3. 48. आकृतिविशेष–A distinguished form ; a form possessed of extraordinary loveliness. आदरः पदं करोति–Respect finds access, enters. I. 3. 51. अवधारितवचनः—Whose words were ignored or connived at. शङ्कितः—Suspicious. निर्बन्धुम्–To importune, to ask again and again. Cf. निर्बन्धपृष्टः स जगाद सर्वं स्तुवन्ति पौराश्चरितं त्वदीयम् । रघु० XIV. 32. आवुत्तः–A sister's husband ; brother-in-law. आवुत्तो भगिनीपतिः । अमर० I.3.55. सदृशं बालभावस्य–Quite proper or suited to her child-like nature. वसुलक्ष्मी, a mere child, was not expected to know why her jealous sister, Queen धारिणी, was refusing to reply to the King's question. I. 3. 58. सविशेषम्–With special effort. दर्शन...रक्ष्यते–she is being safely kept away from the king's sight who has already taken a fancy for her, merely by observing her picture. The Queen is, therefore, guarding her from his sight to avoid further complications. I. 3. 60. नियोग–Errand, task. I. 3. 68. कामम्–Granted, admitting. सर्वस्य...बहुमता–Every one thinks highly of the lore (कुलविद्या) which he has inherited. The profession of the family is always highly valued, and one would always have nothing but praise for it in preference to all others. In ancient days in India, trades and professions were handed down amongst families from one generation to another, and no body, therefore, even thought of giving up his legacy for which he had all respect and feelings of sanctity.

I. 3. 69. न पुन...गौरवम्. Gaṇadāsa says that he, too, has a high regard for the art of dancing and dramaturgy, not merely because it happens to be his hereditary lore, but because of its intrinsic value and utility. His respect and admiration for this science is not false and undeserving, but is fully justified by the high merits of the science.

I. 4. The verse describes the merits of Nāṭya, its divine association and its great utility as the highest form of recreation for diverse people. देवानां...चाक्षुषम् Construe–मुनय इदं (नाट्यं) देवानां कान्तं चाक्षुषं क्रतुमामनन्ति । Wise men look upon the Nāṭya as a sacrifice which is pleasing to the eyes of the gods. Every human activity should have, besides its secular purpose, a religious purpose also. All sciences and lores have been associated with the final spiritual goal of man, knowledge thereof being conducive to it. Similarly, this science of dancing and histrionics has also a religious element in it. It is a form of worship of the Gods, a veritable sacrifice, more charming and delightful to their eyes than a real sacrifice where the sight of poor innocent animals being butchered is certainly disgusting. चाक्षुषं–चक्षुरनुभाव्यम्–Visual, optical, to be experienced by the eye. कान्त–Delightful, pleasing. Mr. Pandit observes that " the epithets कान्त and चाक्षुष 'lovely and agreeable for the eye to see' doubtless are intended to imply that the क्रतु proper was neither कान्त nor चाक्षुष, and refer us to a time when animal sacrifice had come to be regarded with disfavour, as being horrid and disagreeable to the eye ; a time, that is to say, when Buddhistic ideas of the Vedic sacrifice predominated." The idea of looking upon नाट्य

as a form of sacrifice has its origin in the belief that this science has been evolved out of the essential portions of the four Vedas, which teach sacrifice. Cf. अत्र नाटयस्य क्रतुत्वनिरूपणं चतुर्वेदसारनाटयवेदविहितकर्मत्वादिति मन्तव्यम्।तस्य चतुर्वेदसारत्वं भारतीये प्रतिपादितम् । सर्वशास्त्रार्थसंपन्नं सर्वशिल्पप्रदर्शनम् । नाटय-संज्ञामिमं वेदं सेतिहासं करोम्यहम् ॥ एवं संकल्प्य भगवान् सर्वान् वेदाननुस्मरन् । नाटयवेदं ततश्चक्रे चतुर्वेदाङ्गसंभवम् ॥ जग्राह पाठ्यमृग्वेदात् साम्नः संगीतमेव च । यजुर्वेदादभिनयं रसानाथवर्णादपि ॥ वेदोपवेदसंबद्धो नाटयवेदो महात्मना । एवं भगवता सृष्टो ब्रह्मणा ललितात्मना ॥ रुद्रेणेद...द्विधा. This line speaks of the sacred association of नाटय with god Śiva, the primordial dancer. The dual manifestation of the God, with the male part combined with the female one (already referred to in I. 1) represents the two-fold aspect of dancing viz. लास्य 'the graceful dancing' and ताण्डव 'the rough and violent form of dancing' of which God Śiva is very much fond. He has thus divided नाटय into two parts in his own person which is blended with that of Umā or Pārvatī. उमा...व्यतिकरे (स्वाङ्गे) उमया कृतः व्यतिकरः संबन्धः यस्य तस्मिन्–His own body which is united with that of Pārvatī. The word व्यतिकर means 'Union'. Cf. उद्दण्डताण्डवमुदञ्चितलास्यलीलां । कर्तुं स्वयं युगपदेव समुत्सुकात्मा । यः कामिनीकलितकम्रतरार्धकायः । सोऽयं विभाति विभुरादिनटः पुराणः ॥ from संगीतविद्याविनोद. त्रैगुण्यो...दृश्यते–People behave, actuated by various motives and sentiments, good or bad, sinful or otherwise. All these tendencies of the mind are a result of the three-fold division of the Sattva, Rajas and Tamas, elements or portions of which enter into the mental and physical constitution of man and shape his thought, action and speech. Life is thus varied, on account of these various feelings and passions prompting man to act. नानारसम्–characterised by various sentiments. रसs are nine, including शान्त. शृङ्गारहास्यकरुणरौद्रवीरभयानकाः। बीभत्साद्भुतंसञ्ज्ञौ चेत्यष्टौ नाट्ये रसाः स्मृताः। निर्वेदः स्थायिभावोऽस्ति शान्तोऽपि नवमो रसः ॥

नाट्यं...समाराधनम्. Yet even in this diversity of life and difference of tastes which people betray, the Nāṭya or the dramatic representation is found invariably to be the one form of recreation in which all people take delight and find pleasure. Drama is a picture of life and therefore all people of diverse tastes find this as a highly delightful entertainment which appeals to their heart. भिन्नरुचि–भिन्ना रुचिर्यस्य–Possessed of different tastes. Cf. नासौ न काम्यो न च वेद सम्यग् द्रष्टुं न सा भिन्नरुचिर्हि लोकः। रघु० VI. 30.

I. 4. 5. नातिक्लेशयति. Does not trouble you much. A dull pupil is always a source of great worry and trouble to the teacher who is required to explain a lot before the lesson he teaches penetrates his brain.

I. 4. 6. परमनिपुणा. Highly efficient or skilful. The skill is manifested in the practical aspect of dancing, the theory of which is first taught and then the pupil is required to exhibit the theoretical lessons in actual dancing, where graceful and perfect movement would count for efficiency. मेधाविनी. Intelligent; quick to understand ; clever. किं बहुना. Why say more? In short.

I. 5. भाविकं. A graceful movement or gesture, calculated to express a certain feeling or sentiment (भाव)

He means to say "In acting (प्रयोगविषये) whatever movement, which brings out the sentiment within, I teach to her, she does it to perfection; nay, she improves upon it; and thus it appears that she teaches me in return as to how best it should be done. My lessons fall far short of the actual exhibition on her part, and I feel that I learn much from her in that art." विशेषकरणात–By improving upon (the lesson taught to her). I. 5. 3 अतिक्रामन्ती–Surpassing, excelling. इरावती is one of the wives of king अग्निमित्र. She was also taking lessons in dancing from the teacher. कृतार्था–Successful; one who has accomplished her object. Teacher's satisfaction is an index of the high success of the pupil. I. 5. 6 तद्विधा...त्वान्–Since persons of this sort (तद्विध) are difficult to meet with or hard to secure. तद्विधानाम्–सा विधा प्रकारः यासां–ताः तद्विधाः तासाम् । पात्रम्–A worthy person, a gem. cf. पात्रविशेषन्यस्तं गुणान्तरं व्रजति शिल्पमाधातुः । I. 6. I. 5. 11. वर्णावरः–वर्णेन अवरः–Inferior in caste; born of a mother inferior in caste viz. वैश्य or शूद्र. अन्तपालदुर्ग–A fortress guarding the frontier of the kingdom. V. L. अन्तपालदुर्ग-स्थापितः–Appointed; kept in command. Some Mss. read मंदाकिनीतीरे in the place of नर्मदाकूले. We cannot accept that reading, however, as मंदाकिनी i. e. the river Ganges was far away from the विदर्भ country which lay close to अग्निमित्र's territory. I. 5. 12 शिल्पाधिकारे योग्या–Fit to receive instruction in fine arts. शिल्प means a fine art or accomplishment. They are 64 in number and include the arts of music, dancing and acting. उपायनं प्रेषिता–was sent as a gift or present.

I. 5. 14. आकृति...प्रत्ययात्. Being convinced of the fact that she has an excellent form, I imagine that she has elements in her which are not at all inferior-(अनून) i. e She comes of a high stock or family, the blood of nobility is in her. वस्तु literally means 'element, or stuff.' This is a common idea with Sanskrit poets. Cf. न तादृशा आकृतिविशेषा गुणविरोधिनो भवन्ति । शा० IV. यदुच्यते पार्वति पापवृत्तये न रूपमित्यव्यभिचारि तद्वचः । कुमा० V. 36. यत्राकृतिस्तत्र गुणा वसन्ति । a सुभाषित. भिद्येत वा सद्वृत्तमीदृशस्य निर्माणस्य । उत्तर० IV. न ह्याकृतिः सुसदृशं विजहाति रूपम् । मृच्छ० IX. The reading आकृतिविनयप्रत्ययात् 'Judged by her fair exterior and modesty' is also good. I. 6. Construe आधातुः शिल्पं पात्रविशेषे न्यस्तं समुद्रशुक्तौ पयोदस्य जलं मुक्ताफलतामिव गुणान्तरं व्रजति । The teacher's (आधातुः) skill imparted to a worthier pupil attains greater excellence (गुणान्तरम्). A good pupil would always show to a greater advantage the teaching of his master, which would thus shine brighter than it did before. It is like the drop of ,water from a cloud falling in a sea-shell in the ocean and transforming itself into a lustrous pearl. It is a belief that the water-drops of a shower getting into sea-shells during the स्वाति नक्षत्र turn into pearls. Cf. स्वात्यां सागरशुक्तिमध्यपतितं सन्मौक्तिकं जायते । नीति०. I. 6. 3. पञ्चाङ्गाभिनय The five-fold acting. The commentator अभिराम notes the five varieties of acting which are:-नृत्त, कैवार, धर्मर,वागड and गीत. Some take it to mean'the five-limb movement' or actingin which the five parts of the body viz, the mind, eye, eye-brow, hands and feet, are employed. दीर्घिका...गवाक्षगता-sitting at the window, commanding the view, of the tank.

दीर्घिका–An artificial tank or lake. गवाक्ष–A round air-hole or window, looking like a bull's eye. (गोरक्षीव). प्रवातमासेवमाना–Enjoying the fresh air or the breeze. लब्धक्षणः–लब्धः क्षणः येन सः–Having got leisure. क्षण means ' leisure'. The Marathi word सण meaning ' a holiday ' comes from this word.

विष्कम्भकः–It is an explanatory scene, so called from its concisely expressing (√ वि + स्कम्भ्) into a short space those subordinate parts of the plot, not enacted before the audience, but a knowledge of which is quite essential to the comprehending of the action in the remainder of the play. Cf. वृत्तवर्तिष्यमाणानां कथांशानां निदर्शकः। संक्षिप्तार्थस्तु विष्कम्भो मध्यपात्रप्रयोजितः ॥ दश० I. 116. It is thus a monologue performed by one person, or a dialogue performed by two or more, of the same or different classes, according as it is शुद्ध or संकीर्ण. Cf. एकानेककृतः शुद्धः संकीर्णो नीचमध्यमैः ॥ or मध्येन मध्यमाभ्यां वा पात्राभ्यां संप्रयोजितः। शुद्धः स्यात् स तु संकीर्णो नीचमध्यमकल्पितः ॥ Thus we see that only the middling characters can enact a विष्कम्भक, and again it may be soliloquy by one character, as in प्रियदर्शिका, or a dialogue by two or three, as in विक्रमोर्वशीय or in our drama. It may occur at the beginning of any of the acts, even the first, just after the प्रस्तावना. Cf. आदौ विष्कम्भकं कुर्यादङ्कं वा कार्ययुक्तितः। अपेक्षितं परित्यज्य नीरसं वस्तुविस्तरम्। यदा संदर्शयेच्छेषं कुर्याद्विष्कम्भकं तदा ॥ दश० III. 28–29.

The main scene of the Act opens now, with the king discussing with his minister वाहतक the political situation created by the letter of his neighbour, the king of the country of विदर्भ. Relations between अग्निमित्र and this king had latterly become very strained. अग्निमित्र had already put in prison the brother-in-law of this king. Prince माधवसेन, the cousin of the king of विदर्भ had promised a matrimonial alliance with अग्निमित्र, by offering his own sister to him in marriage, and it was for this purpose that he was going over to अग्निमित्र with his wife and sister. He was however seized on the way by the frontier-guard, and in the scuffle that ensued, the sister of माधवसेन, the proposed bride of अग्निमित्र, was lost. अग्निमित्र, therefore, demanded the release of his friend and ally माधवसेन, along with his wife and sister. To this demand of his, the king of विदर्भ has sent the present reply, in which he first asks him not to interfere with his private affairs since माधवसेन was his uncle's son. If, however, taking his side अग्निमित्र would demand his release, then he would meet his wishes on one condition viz. that अग्निमित्र on his part must set free his brother-in-law, the minister of मौर्य, who has been kept in prison by him. This has greatly upset अग्निमित्र, who, as we see, dispatches his forces under the command of the general वीरसेन against the विदर्भ king, and we hear of the result of this campaign in the last act of the drama.

I. 6. 11. एकान्त...परिजनः-With his attendants standing in a corner or at a distance. I. 6. 12. प्रतिपद्यते-Proposes to do ; says in reply. अग्निमित्र had demanded in his former letter the release of माधवसेन. The letter which the minister वाहतक had in his hand was a reply to his letter. He, therefore, wants to know what the विदर्भ king intends to do, in order to meet his demand. वैदर्भः-Lit. belonging to विदर्भ; the king of the विदर्भ country, the same as modern Berar. I. 6. 14. आत्मविनाशम्-His own ruin. He means to say that his reply is so offensive that it would provoke अग्निमित्र to declare war against him and in that case nothing short of destruction would be his lot. निर्देश-The specific reply ; the dispatch actually committed to writing. I. 6. 17. भवतः...मोचयितव्यः- This is a portion of अग्निमित्र's letter, reproduced for the purpose of giving a definite reply to the demand contained in it. पितृव्यपुत्रः Uncle's son, cousin. प्रातिश्रुतसंबन्धः- प्रतिश्रुतः संबन्धः येन सः-who has promised an alliance. अवस्कद्य गृहीतः—Having been attacked, he was captured or taken prisoner. मदपेक्षया-Out of regard for me i. e. अग्निमित्र; if you care for my friendly relations with you. सकलत्रसोदर्यः- कलत्रेण सोदर्यया च सहितः-Along with his wife and sister. सोदर्या—समानं उदरं यस्याः सा-Born from the same womb, sister.

I. 6. 19. न वो न विदितं-Not that it is not know to you ; you know it full well. Two negatives give an affirmative sense. द्वौ नञौ प्रकृतार्थं गमयतः । तुल्याभिजनेषु... रीदृक्-Towards relatives of a common extraction, who are therefore likely to put forth their claim for the kingdom, this is the way how kings behave. The विदर्भ king is trying to justify his action of seizing and imprisoning his cousin माधवसेन, who by this relationship was likely to prove a menace to his own position and authority. If, therefore, he has captured him and put him in prison, there is nothing wrong about it. In fact, this is how kings are seen to behave towards their relations, who wanted to thereaten their kingship. The reading तुल्याभिजनेषु भूमेरिव: राज्ञां प्रवृत्तिः is accepted by Mr. Pandit who understands it to mean the 'conduct of kings towards kings who belong to the same family should be like that of the earth i. e. one of perfect impartiality." What is meant possibly is since both अग्निमित्र and the विदर्भ king enjoy an equal status as kings (तुल्याभिजन), अग्निमित्र should not try to heckle him and bring him to book for certain things which he i. e. the विदर्भ king has done in his own interest. Like the earth tolerant of everything, a king ought to be patient and impartial. He should stand aloof and should not try to meddle with the other king's affairs. I. 6. 20 अतोऽत्र... इति–' Therefore, you i. e. अग्निमित्र should remain neutral in this affair between me and माधवसेन.' It is a dispute between two brothers, and an outsider like अग्निमित्र should not interfere. The विदर्भ king censures mildly the conduct of अग्निमित्र in taking the side of माधवसेन as against him. मध्यस्थ:–Indifferent, neutral. मध्ये तिष्ठति सः । ग्रहणविप्लव. The confusion at the time of the capture. अथा...आभिसंधि:–' Now if you must secure the freedom of माधवसेन, then hear my condition.' माधवसेन would be released by me, only on one condition of mine i. e. of the विदर्भ king. Note the sense of the particle अथ ' If '. अभिसंधिः—condition ; terms.

I. 7. The verse sets forth the terms of the विदर्भ king. ' The release of माधवसेन is dependent upon the release of my brother-in-law, the minister of the मौर्य king.' मौर्यसचिव–According to some it is a proper name. If that is not correct and he was the minister of the मौर्य king of पाटलिपुत्र, it seems probable that he was imprisoned by अग्निमित्र to prevent him from exciting the people to rebel against his (अग्निमित्र's) father पुष्पमित्र, who had murdered the last of the Maurvas, बृहद्रथ, and usurped his tnrone in his son's favour. The imprisonment of माधवसेन, the intended brother-in-law of अग्निमित्र, by his cousin the king of विदर्भ, was only a retaliation for his brother-in-law's imprisonment by अग्निमित्र.: संयत–Imprisoned. श्यालः—A brother-in-law; cf. the word साला. मोक्ता–First Future 1st per. sing. 'I shall release.' I. 7.1. कार्यविनिमयः—Exchange of services. अनात्मज्ञः–आत्मानं न जानात्यसौ–One who knows not one's own self, i. e. a fool. प्रकृत्यमित्रः–-A natural enemy. By the very disposition of his territory which is adjacent to me, he is my natural enemy. Cf. राजा आत्मद्रव्यप्रकृतिसंपन्नो नयस्याधिष्ठानं विजिगीषुः। तस्य समन्ततो मण्डलीभूता भूम्यन्तरा अरिप्रकृतिः। ......भूम्यनन्तरं प्रकृत्यामित्रः तुल्याभिजनस्सहजः। कौ० अ० VI. 2. A prince, according to Kauṭilya, is a विजिगीषु, and must always cherish the ambition of becoming a supreme monarch. The first king to subdue would be his neighbour, and that king, therefore, by the very situation of his kingdom is a source of trouble and hence an enemy to the विजिगीषु. प्रतिकूलचारी–Behaving in opposition to me. यातव्यपक्षे स्थित–Standing in the position of an enemy who deserves to be attacked (यातव्य). Ordinarily, though a neighbour, and therefore likely to be a danger to अग्नि-

मित्र, he need not have been attacked. But now, since relations of hostility have developed by reason of his having gone against him (प्रतिकूलचारी), he i. e. वैदर्भ king must be assailed and subjugated. पूर्वसंकल्पितं वीरसेनप्रमुखं दण्डचक्रम्. The forces or an army headed i. e. commanded by वीरसेन, already kept in readiness. उन्मूलनाय–For the purpose of uprooting or extirpating him. I. 7. 6. शास्त्रदृष्टमाह–The minister says what the king has proposed is strictly in conformity with what the science of politics teaches. Treatises like the कौटिलीय अर्थशास्त्र were in the curriculum of princes.

I. 8. The minister explains further what the political science would lay down on this point. It says definitely that an enemy newly installed on the throne does not enjoy the confidence of his subjects and is there unstable like a tree newly planted ; and hence he could be easily uprooted. अचि...राज्यः–अचिरं अधिष्ठितं राज्यं येन सः–who has newly acquired the kingdom. प्रकृति...त्वात्. By reason of his not being firmly established among the subjects (प्रकृति) ; with reference to the tree, it would mean 'Not having struck deep root in the soil (प्रकृति)'. नव...शिथिलः तरुः––A tree that is unstable or loose, having been freshly planted. समुद्धर्तुं सुकरः––Very easy to uproot.

I. 8. 1. तन्त्रकार–The writers on the science of politics. The sentence अवितथं...वचनम् should be taken in the imperative sense, or the sense of the future, supplying भविष्यति as the predicate, which the commentator काटयवेम

does. समुद्योज्यताम्-Let (the general) be made ready to act. I. 8. 4. यथाव्यापारम्-In accordance with the service which they were rendering to the king.

विदूषक-A jester, fun-making, merry fellow, who enjoys the intimacy of the king, because of his constant attendance on him to keep him lively with his jokes. Very often, we find, however, that besides this function, he greatly helps the king in his love-intrigues, by devising methods to bring about the union of the lovers, as is the case in our drama, or in रत्नावली and प्रियदर्शिका. He comes now to inform the king of his success in a plan to give the king an opportunity to see मालविका. I. 8. 6 यदृच्छा...कृतिः--यदृच्छया दृष्टा प्रतिकृतिर्यस्याः सा-whose portrait was seen accidentally (यदृच्छया). I. 8. 11 अपरः कार्यान्तरसचिवः--Another counsellor helping in a different branch of affairs viz. those of love, (while वाहतक was an advisor in politics). In the third Act he is called कामतन्त्रसचिव. The title नर्मसचिव also 'a minister of fun' is very often given to विदूषक. I. 8. 14 उपेय...दर्शने-उपेयस्य-साध्यस्य मालविकासाक्षाद्दर्शनस्य-उपायदर्शने-साधनज्ञाने In visualising a remedy to bring about the desired object viz. the sight of मालविका. प्रज्ञाचक्षुः—The eye of wisdom or imagination. कच्चित्-Note the use of the particle which means ' I hope'. I. 8. 15 प्रयोगसिद्धिं पृच्छ. What of merely thinking ? I have progressed much further."Rather ask me about the success of the enterprise. " I. 8. 17 कर्णे-विदूषक was too shrewd to speak of his plans openly. The audience thus are left in the dark about it, though their curiosity in th matter is very soon satisfied.

I. 8. 18 निपुणमुपक्रान्तम्–you have commenced cleverly. दुर...रम्भे–In this venture where success is so difficult to attain. दुरधिगमा सिद्धिर्यस्मिन् स आरम्भः । आशंसामहे. We hope for (success). Cf. मनोरथाय नाशंसे किं बाहो स्पन्दसे वृथा । शा० VII.

I. 9. With all the resources at his disposal, a man, howsoever powerful, cannot dispense with the help of a friend in the attainment of an object that is beset with difficulties (सप्रतिबन्ध). He is like a lamp in darkness when one cannot see an object, though endowed with eyes, unless the light of the lamp helps him. The figure of speech is दृष्टान्त, complete in all details. अल... विकथ्य–The particle अलम् meaning 'enough' is always used with a gerund or a noun in the instrumental case. वि+कत्थ्–To brag, boast-अधरोत्तरव्यक्तिः–A decision as to who is inferior (अधर) and who is superior (उत्तर).

I. 9. 3 त्वत्सुनीति...भिन्नम्–The tree of your fine intrigue has put forth a blossom. The two teachers quarrelling clearly show that your plan has succeeded.फलमपि...द्रक्ष्यसि. This blossom is a precursor of the fruit which also you will soon see. The reward will be the sight of मालविका, which the king will soon get as a result of this quarrel.

I. 10. परस्पर...यतौ–Striving to gain victory over the other. There is another reading परस्परजयैषिणौ–Desiring to get victory etc. साक्षाद्...शरीरिणौ. The two dramatic sentiments, as it were, in bodily form (शरीरिणौ). They were teachers of acting in which the inner sentiment is fully brought out. The poet means that here they represent the two sentiments, as it were, in bodily form.

I. 10, 4. दुरासदो राजमहिमा-The king's greatness or majesty fills one with awe which makes it difficult for one to approch him.

I. 11. हरदत्त explains his feelings at the sight of the king. He feels a flutter of excitement in his heart as he approaches the king even though he is familiar with him, and the king is always accessible to him. Every moment, the king changes as it were and appears new to his eyes, like the restless ocean which is never the same at any moment. नच...गम्यः-construe:—न परिचितः इति न, अगम्य इति न Not that I am not acquainted or familiar with him i.e. I am familiar with him, nor that he is unapproachable i. e. he is approachable. Instead of अगम्य, Some read अरम्य. चकितं-Tremblingly,with a flutter of fear in the heart. सलिल...मक्ष्णोः--The ocean changes its aspect every moment, without losing its freshness and grandeur ; the same is the case with this king who, too, maintains his dignified majesty and charm, even though he appears to be changing every moment. An object of beauty is thus defined by माघ-क्षणे क्षणे यन्नवतामुपैति तदेव रूपं रमणीयतायाः । Cf. तां तामवस्थां प्रतिपद्यमानं स्थितं दश व्याप्य दिशो महिम्ना। विष्णोरिवास्यानवधारणीयमीदृक्तया रूपमियत्तया वा ॥ रघु० XIII. 5. भीमकान्तैर्नृपगुणैः स बभूवोपजीविनाम् । अधृष्यश्चाभिगम्यश्च यादोरत्नैरिवार्णवः ॥ रघु० I. 16. महत् पुरुषाकारं ज्योतिः--This great lustre in human form. The king is all splendour that has assumed a human form. Cf. तेजसः सपदि राशिरुत्थितः प्रादुरास किल वाहिनीमुखे । यः प्रमृज्य नयनानि सैनिकैर्लक्षणीयपुरुषाकृतिश्चिरात् ॥ रघु० XI. 63.

I. 12. गण्दास says that by the flood of majestic splendour he feels he has been pushed back as it were, even though he is trying to approach the king in the company of his attendant, after having been duly admitted into his presence by the door-keepers. °प्रवेशः-नियुक्तैः पुरुषैः अनुमतः प्रवेशः यस्य सः-whose entrance was permitted by men appointed at the door. सिंहा...चरः-सिंहासनस्य आन्तिके चरत्यसौ-An attendant moving about near the throne. विनि...दृष्टिपातैः-which repel the gaze; which dazzle the eyes. वाक्यादृते-even though no verbal order forbidding to enter was given out; without any words of prohibition. I. 12. 3. The king himself orders the seats for the two teachers. This only shows the high regard that he has for them. युगपत्-At one and the same time; simultaneous. I. 12. 6. तीर्थः-A sacred preceptor; a venerable teacher. दत्तप्रयोगश्चास्मि-And I have also given practical lessons in the art of dancing. परिगृहीतः-Favoured, patronised. I. 12. 9. सोऽहम्-I, possessed of such qualifications viz. a pupil of no ordinary teacher, having good experience of teaching the theory and the art, and in addition enjoying the patronage of Your Majesty. प्रधानपुरुष-Prominent courtiers, principal personalities. आधिक्षिप्तः-was insulted. मयि परिवादकरः-began abusing me. परिवाद means 'censure, abuse.' पल्वल-a puddle. विमृशतु-should examine. विशेषज्ञः प्राश्निकः-A discerning judge; a critical examiner who would understand the difference in merit of the two. I. 12. 14. समर्थं प्रतिज्ञातम्-very well suggested; a fair proposal that. I. 12. 15. प्रथमः कल्पः-A capital idea; an excellent (प्रथम) alternative. Cf. उदारः कल्पः । शा० V. I. 12. 16. पक्षपात-Partiality, favouritism. If the king alone would decide and if it happens that the decision is given in favour of हरदत्त, the king's man, the Queen favouring गणदास would naturally suspect it to be a case of partiality. न्याय्यो व्यवहारः-The conduct of the examination would be just and fair. न्याय्यः न्यायादनपेतः Not deviating from justice. I. 12. 20. प्रस्ताव-the present dispute; the matter under dispute. I. 12. 22. परिव्राजिका-A female ascetic. I. 12. 24. संरम्भ-struggle, contest. कथं प्रेक्षसे-what do you anticipate to be the result ? Who will win ? I. 12. 27. स्वप...कया- स्वपक्षस्यावसादः—तस्य शङ्का ।. Apprehension or fear about the defeat of your side or party. अवसाद literally means ' sinking, dropping down, losing.' न परिहीयते प्रतिद्वन्द्विनः-is not inferior to his opponent. Cf. ओजस्वितया न परिहीयते शच्याः । विक्रमो० III. I. 12. 30. ०राज...हरति-The fact that he is patronised by the king brings him into prominence or gives him a great advantage or superiority (प्रधानत्व). I. 12. 31. राज्ञी...भवती-just remember that you too are the recipient (भाजन) of the title of ' the Queen." If the king's patronage brings हरदत्त to the forefront, गणदास also will not be lagging behind, since he has been favoured by you, the Queen.

I. 13. If the fire receiving the lustre from the sun, exhibits the greatest refulgence at night, the moon too acquires greatness, being favoured by the night. हरदत्त favoured by the King is compared to अनल being nourished with his lustre by the sun while गणदास, patronised by the

Queen, resembles the moon as favoured by the night. If therefore the moon is eqally brilliant as the fire, there is no reason to fear गणदास will suffer in the contest. It is a belief that the sun reposes his lustre in the fire at the end of the day. Cf. दिनान्ते निहितं तेजः सवित्रेव हुताशनः । रघु० iv. 1. Commenting upon this, मल्लिनाथ observes, 'सौरं तेजः सायमग्निं संक्रमते'। 'आदित्यो वा अस्तं यन्नग्निमनुप्रविशति' 'अग्निं वा आदित्यः सायं प्रविशति' इत्यादि श्रुतिः प्रमाणम् ।. I. 13. 2. अविहा or better still अविधा is an interjection meaning 'help, help,' used in calling for help in danger. पीठमर्दिका– 'A lady who assists the heroine in securing her lover'. पीठमर्द refers to the man who assists the hero in his love-affairs. Cf. पीठमर्दो नाम कामपुरुषार्थसहायो नायकसमीपवर्ती पुरुषः। Com. of अभिराम. We shall see how greatly this परिव्राजिका like कामन्दकी in the मालतीमाधव was instrumental in brining about the union of the king and मालविका. An ascetic woman, she is greatly cultured and wise, speaking the Sanskrit language. दशरूप assigns a definite place to such woman as a companion or a help-mate of the heroine, styling her as लिङ्गिनी, and the qualifications she should have are:— शास्त्रेषु निष्ठा सहजश्च बोधः प्रागल्भ्यमभ्यस्तगुणा च वाणी। कालानुरोधः प्रतिभानवत्त्वमेते गुणाः कामदुघाः क्रियासु ॥

I. 14. The Queen wearing auspicious ornaments and accompanied by the ascetic कौशिकी appears like the triad or the collection of the three Vedas embodied, coupled with the spiritual lore. मङ्गलालंकृता–मङ्गलं शोभनं यथा तथा अलंकृता. "Decorated with such dress and ornaments as she must wear as the wife of a living husband; Cf.

सितांशुका मङ्गलमात्रभूषणा." विक्रमो॰ III.12 (S.P. Pandit). त्रयी–The three Vedas are ऋग्वेद, यजुर्वेद and सामवेद. अध्यात्मविद्या–The Upaniṣadic lore or teaching. The knowledge of आत्मन् or ब्रह्मन् i. e. the Supreme soul. विग्रहवती Possessed of a bodily form (विग्रह).

I. 15, The परिव्राजिका gives the king a blessing. May he be lord for hundred years, of the Queen धारिणी and of भूतधारिणी i. e. the earth, the supporter of the creation. Two epithets are used to describe both the Queen and the Earth. महासारप्रसव - 1 The Queen who has given birth to a heroic son; महासारः (lit. of great strength, powerful) प्रसवः संतानो यस्याः सा । . 2 The earth yielding abundant crops (प्रसव) owing to plenty of showers (आसार). सदृक्षमा– Possessed of equal forgiveness or patience. As Pandit observes " The epithets are intended to flatter the Queen, and the blessing that the king may have none but Dhārinī and the Earth for his consorts is doubtless meant to remove from Dhārṇī's mind the remotest suspicion that she (the Parivrājikā) was or was going to be an abettor of the king's intrigue." It might as well be taken as a hint to the Queen to be broad-minded and forgive the momentary breaches of the marital bond on the part of the king! For a similar idea Cf. परिग्रहबहुत्वेऽपि द्वे प्रतिष्ठे कुलस्य मे समुद्रवसना चोर्वी सखी च युवयोरियम् ॥. शा॰ III. 16. I. 15. 4. पर...संघर्षः--A conflict between the two teachers as to which of them has superior knowledge (विज्ञान). प्राश्निकपदम्–The position of a judge or an examiner. I. 15.

6. उपालम्भः-a taunt. पत्तने...परीक्षा-" The town being near, would you have a jewel tested in a village ? " She means that when the king, so well-versed in all arts, is available, it is foolish to ask her, an ignorant lady, to be the judge. The king represents the town, while she represents the village Cf. ता पिंअवअस्सस्स देवीए पुरदो पाढिस्सम् । जदो ण कत्थूरिआ कुग्गामे वणे वा विक्किणीअदि, ण सुवण्ण कसवट्टिअं विणा सिलापट्टए कसीअदि। कर्पूर॰ I. I. 15.9. मध्यस्था-Impartial, disinterested. गुणदोषौ परिच्छेत्तुम्-To measure or gauge our merit and demerit. I. 15. 12 विवादः--Dispute, discussion. The king proposes forthwith a theoretical discussion to test the knowledge of the teachers. He knew full well what the plan was, and yet he says this to avoid rousing any suspicion in the mind of the queen. I. 15. 13. प्रयोग...शास्त्रम . The dramatic science is preeminently a practical science. A theoretical discussion, therefore, will not do. वाग्व्यवहार-A verbal disputation ; a wrangling in words. I. 15. 17. यदि मां etc. This clearly shows that the queen has begun to smell the plot. I. 15. 18. न मां...मर्हति. " The queen should be pleased not to allow me to suffer defeat from one who is only my equal in learning. हरदत्त is in no way superior to me, and yet if I am not given a chance by the queen to prove my merit, हरदत्त who is at best my equal in learning (समानविद्य) would certainly assume airs of superiority and insult me. The queen should therefore allow me to enter into the contest." The reading ' न मां अभिनयविद्यातः परिभवनीयं मन्तुमर्हसि' is given by Mr. Pandit who interprets it thus:-

'I pray you not to think that I may be beaten in the art of dancing.' I. 15. 19. उरभ्रसंपात-A fight of two rams. The विदूषक likens their contest to a ram-fight which must be staged by them, if they want to deserve the wages they get ! I. 15. 21. कलहप्रियः—कलहः प्रियः यस्य सः One who likes quarrels, fond of squabbles. I. 15. 23. विदूषक protests against the queen's allegation saying in spite of his efforts to the contrary the two teachers will fight to a finish. The instance he gives is that of an elephant-fight which would never stop until one of the two is thoroughly vanquished. अन्योन्यकलहित. Quarrelling with each other. कलहित-कलहः संजातः अस्य सः कलहितः । उपशमः- Silence, peace. I. 15. 24. स्वाङ्ग...नय-The graceful acting exhibited in their own person. I. 15.27. तदि...प्रत्याययितव्यम्- 'What more should they exhibit to convince us of their merit ? ' ' What further have these (teachers) to satisfy us about ?' Notice again the attitude of the king who shows as if he is so solicitious to cut short the whole dispute now, without any further tests, what the परिव्राजिका has seen of their acting being taken as sufficient exhibition of their art. ' In reality, of course, the king only pretends to be indifferent and makes the परिव्राजिका say what is necessary to judge between the two disputants.' I. 15. 28. वक्तुकामा-वक्तुं कामो यस्याः सा. Desiring to speak out. I. 16. The परिव्राजिका explains why she cannot rest satisfied with the performance of the two teachers alone, but she must see how their pupils also acquit themselves before she decides in the matter. श्लिष्टा...संस्था The individual performance of some in the dramatic art is very well done. i. e. some excel as actors when they act personally, but are not able to teach others how to act well. **श्लिष्टा.** Done properly. Some read शिष्टा-' Excellent '. क्रिया-Acting, performance. आत्मसंस्था-आत्मनि संस्था यस्याः सा-Restricted to one's own self individual, personal. संक्रान्ति...युक्ता-while others distinguish themselves in transferring their art to their pupils. Some show superior skill in imparting (संक्रान्ति) that skill to another. यस्यो...एव. He certainly is the best teacher who combines in himself both the merits viz. personal acting and imparting it to his pupil. He deserves to be placed at the head (धुरि) of all teachers. धुरि lit. at the yoke. 'Just as the most powerful bull (पुंगव) is chosen from a herd of bulls to be put to the yoke i. e. chosen for the place of honour, so such a teacher should be put in front of or given the first place among all teachers.' I. 16. 3. पिण्डितार्थः--The sum and substance, the essence. I. 16. 6. मन्दमेधा-Dull-witted. मलिनयति-Discredits or brings disgrace. I. 16. 9 देवि...यते. The king shows as if he agrees with the queen's objection. I.16.10. विनेतु...यति. Gaṇadāsa, on the other hand, answers the queen's objection. No doubt, a bad pupil discredits the teacher for no fault of his. But can he not make a proper choice of his material? Acceptance of such a pupil of inferior stuff betrays a want or dullness of the teacher's intelligence. अद्रव्यं-A bad material, an inferior stuff i. e. a bad pupil. बुद्धिलाघवम् Inferiority of intelligence. The sentence is interpreted by some in another way. " The improvement (परिग्रह)

of a dull pupil shows the superior talent (लाघवं=कौशल्य) of the teacher (विनेतुः), " The word परिग्रह cannot, however, be taken in the sense of 'Improvement.' What गणदास means is that there is no harm in judging the merits of the teachers by the performance of their pupils. If the pupil selected happens to be inferior, that should reflect on the teacher, since he could have acted wisely in making a selection.

I. 16. 14 कथमिदानीम्–" what to do now? ". The queen is chafing inwardly to find that all her attempts to frustrate the plot of विदूषक are being foiled by her own protege गणदास. उत्साहकारणं मनोरथं–The king's desire to see मालविका, if fulfilled, will only inflame his passion, or will encourage him for further endeavour. विरम... रम्भात्-Stop this vain effort. It is useless to proceed in the matter and arrange a demonstration in acting. To the teacher, it does no good, since his position is not going to be harmed in any way.

I. 16. 19. विदूषक tries to provoke him further, when he saw the Queen was dissuading him. संगीतापदेशेन–Under the pretext of music. सर......मोदकानि–The sweet balls offered as presents to the Goddess of Learning (by the inmates of the harem). सुलभनिग्रह. Where defeat is easy. निग्रह–Defeat, vanquishing; in Nyāya philosophy, it means 'a flaw in argument or a fault in syllogism by which a disputant is put down in argument.' विदूषक sarcastically says to him that गणदास should do well not to carry the dispute further, as the Queen has suggested. It would only endanger his present comfortable position, where now he can at least enjoy the delicious presents of his pupils. As the chances of his defeat are greater, he would then lose everything ! I. 16. 21. अवसरप्राप्तम्-which the occasion demands.

I. 17. गणदास is greatly provoked at the sordid picture which विदूषक has drawn of him, and he, therefore, strongly protests against his insinuations. लब्धा... निन्दाम्-of a man whoputs up with insults, shrinking from a contest for fear of losing the position which he has secured. लब्धास्पदः-लब्धं आस्पदं येन सः-one who has obtained a position. तितिक्षमाण-suffering, tolerating. यस्या... वदन्ति-The knowledge of such a man wanting in the dignity of learning serves only as a means of livelihood to him. He demeans himself and his knowledge which he prostitutes for the sake of eking out the bare means of subsistence. He is thus a huckster, a trafficker in knowledge, a Bania dealing in the commodity of learning—a position which, गणदास says, he can never tolerate. I. 17. 3. आचिरोपनीता-Lately initiated, recently given over to you for instruction. The Queen turns to another objection now. The pupil is raw, having been very lately put under his charge, and has had no time to assimiliate the instruction properly. It is therefore unfair and unjust (अन्याय्य) to ask गणदास to give a demonstration. (प्रदर्शन). I. 17. 4. अत...निर्बन्धः-And that is exactly the reason why I insist on having a practical demonstration. The fact that the pupil is new is a point in my favour, and hence my insistence (निर्बन्धः). I. 17. 6. The Queen releases her final shaft. 'Well then, let the परिव्राजिका alone view the exhibition of both. The other audience is not needed." This completely upsets the plan of the विदूषक and the king who feel that everything is lost now. परिव्राजिका, however, comes to the rescue and saves the situation. I. 17. 8. नैत...दोषाय-' It is unfair to throw the whole responsibility of decision on me alone. I admit I am a judge, but I must have some one to consult before taking any definite decision. Even an omniscient judge (सर्वज्ञ) may give a wrong judgment, if he does it alone and unaided.' I.17.11. किं...करोषि-'Why do you take me to be asleep, when I am wide awake to all that is passing round.' The Queen feels thoroughly vanquished in her attempt to stop the exhibition. Even her own people have gone against her, and this naturally irritates her. सासूयम्-in anger, in a pet.

1. 18. पराङ्मुखी-पराग् मुखं यस्याः--whose face is turned away. प्रभ...विन्यः--wives no doubt have a full sway over their husbands ; yet for getting angry with them, there must be some reason or justification for it. कारणकोपाः--कारणेन कोपो यासां ताः. परिव्राजिका mildly censures the queen's peevish attitude towards the king for which she says she i. e. the Queen has no reason whatsoever. Women rule their husbands, but there must be some sense in their moods and attitudes. I.18. 4. दिष्टया Fortunately, luckily. कोपव्याजेन under the pretext of resentment. विदूषक takes

this opportunity to provoke Gaṇadāsa still more. Her apparently unjustified anger is a cloak under which, he says, she wants to save him the ignominy of defeat सुशि...भवति. Not every learned man is good or skilful in imparting his knowledge. I. 18. 7. एवं गृह्णाति. This is how people understand or rather misunderstand. They think, for instance, that I am an incapable teacher and am being shielded by the Queen against inpending and certain defeat, by hook or crook !

I. 19. गणदास is greatly enraged at the attitude of the Queen and dealares that if he is not allowed to give a practical demonstration of what he has taught, he would take it that the Qneen has given him up once for all. क्रियासंक्रान्तिः-Skill in imparting the instruction in acting. परित्यक्तः--Deserted, abandoned, given up. I. 19. 1. गति :—Course. alternative. The Queen has to yield at last and give her consent to the exhibition. I. 19. 4- अपदे शंकितोऽस्मि. I had entertained doubts when there was no scope for them (अपदे). कस्मिन् अभिनेयवस्तुनि-In what particular piece of acting. I. 19. 7. यदा...वती. Note how the king refuses to give any suggestion, though he has much to say in the matter. He is thus in a position to say to the Queen later on 'न खलु मनास्विनि मया प्रयुक्तमिदम् । किमपि...स्मि with a shrug of the shoulders, परिव्राजिक. also hesitates to make any suggestion. 'There is som thing hanging heavy on the Queen's mind, which hase made me afraid.' I. 19. 10. विस्रब्धम्. Freely, confidently. प्रभ...जनस्य I shall certainly have power over my servants, who are at my disposal and will act as you order. I. 19. 11. मम चेति ब्रूहि Note the coaxing or the flattering tone of the king. ' You have power over me as well. ' It would also mean ' you have power over my servants also. I. 19. 13. चतु...हरन्ति. The छालित (the same as चलित) depending upon four verse quadrants or lines, is declared to be a very difficult piece to act (दुष्प्रयोज). एकार्थसंश्रयं (प्रयोगं) - The demonstration of one and the same piece of acting. I. 19. 20. वर्गौ The two parties or sides (representing the two teachers). संगीतरचना- Arrangement of all the accessories of music. उत्थापयिष्यति Will make us start to go (to the Concert hall). I. 19. 22. विजयप्रत्यार्थिनी - Opposed to his success. She tries to explain her position as one who opposed the exhibition right from the beginning. Her opposition was not prompted by her desire to see गणदास defeated. There were other motives which, of course, she cannot explain. I. 19. 27. निर्ण...ब्रवीमि. I speak in the capacity or the authority of one who has been called upon to give a judgment. सर्वा...क्तये- For the purpose of revealing to the view (आभिव्यक्ति) the graces of all the limbs. विरलनेपथ्ययोः-विरलं नेपथ्यं ययोः। Wearing thin stage-costumes. Note the shrewd romantic suggstion of the Parivrājikā, who by this wants to enable the king to observe मालविका at the height of her physical charms, so that at the very first sight he may be enamoured of her. I. 19. 32. The Queen levels a taunt at the king, before leaving the place. If he would show such resourcefulness (उपायनिपुणता) or genius in political affairs, as he has betrayed in his love-intrigues, he would certainly achieve wonders.

I. 20. अन्यथा गृहीत्वा–misunderstanding. मनास्विनी A proud lady प्रायः...भागाः—Generally men of equal learning are envious of one anothers fame. Colleagues are jealous of each other. पर...पुरोभागाः–परस्परस्य यशसि–यशोविषये पुरोभागो येषाम्। पुरोभाग–Envy, jealousy, fault-finding (दौषेकदृष्टि) I. 20. 2. हन्त–A particle implying joy or surprise.

I. 21. Construe जीमूत.......भिः उद्ग्रीवैर्मयूरैः अनुरसितस्य पुष्करस्य निर्ह्रादिनी उप...त्था मायूरी मार्जना मनांसि मदयति।. The sound of the drum, resembling the rumble of clouds has attracted the peacocks who look up with upstretched necks and reply the sound with their own notes. Thus reverberating, the sound gladdens the mind. जीमूत... किभिः–जीमूतानां स्तनितं विशङ्कन्ते ते–तैः जीमू...भिः । The peacocks who suspected it to be the thundering (स्तनित) of clouds. The peacocks are greatly delighted and begin to dance and cry at the appearance of the thundering watery clouds in the sky Cf. शुक्लापाङ्गैः सजलनयनैः स्वागतीकृत्य केकाः। प्रत्युद्यातः कथमिव भवान् गन्तुमाशु व्यवस्येत् ॥ मे० I. 22. धौतापाङ्गं हरशशिरुचा पावकेस्तं मयूरं । पश्चादद्रिग्रहणगुरुभिर्गर्जितैर्नर्तयेथाः ॥ मे० I. 44. जीमूतः–जीवनस्य–उदकस्य–मूतः–बन्धः । watery cloud. उद्ग्रीवाः–with upturned necks उद्गता ग्रीवा येषाम् ते. Cf, मनोभिरामाः शृण्वन्तौ रथनेमिस्वनोन्मुखैः। षड्जसंवादिनीः केका द्विधा भिन्नाः शिखण्डिभिः॥ रघु० I. 39. अनुरसितस्य पुष्करस्य–The drum which received in reply or was answered by the notes of peacocks. निर्ह्रादिनी–Reverberating, echoing, resounding. Cf. निर्ह्रादी ते मुरज इव चेत् कन्दरेषु ध्वनिः स्यात्। मे० I. 58. उप...स्वरोत्था–उप-

हितः संयोजितः मध्यमस्वरः मध्यमसंचितस्वरः तस्मादुत्तिष्ठति उदेति–इति तथा। Arising out of i. e. beginning with the middle tone, set to the middle note. The reading उपचितमध्यमस्वरोत्था would mean 'in which the middle has gained in intensity etc.' मायूरी मार्जना–मार्जना means the sound of the drum, and this particular high pitched sound, harmonising with the middle note is dear to the peacocks, for which reason it is called मायूरी. मदयति–Delights, maddens. Note the alliteration of the sound म in the last line. I. 21. 1. सामाजिकाः–members of the audience. I. 21. 3. अविनयः–Indecorum, immodesty. The queen did note how impatient and restless the king was to go to the theatre; and he had the audacity to hasten his wife also to the place where he was expecting to see the object of his love! I. 21. 6. विदूषकं has noted that the queen is watching the king's excitement. Therefore he cautions him to be more patient. धीरं गच्छ–Go with patience, 'put on a grave mood and walk slowly.' विसंवादयिष्यति–will countermand the whole show; will thwart the plans. Mr. Pandit takes it in a different way; 'Lest the queen धारिणी should find you inconsistent with yourself i. e. lest she should discover by your impatience to go to the संगीतशाला, that the innocence you have claimed with regard to the origin of the dispute and the indifference you have shown as to the result of the contest of the two masters of dancing and music was merely assumed and that an intrigue lay at the bottom of the affair."

I. 22. The king says that howsoever he might try

to be calm, the sound of the drum hastens me on, as if it is the sound of my desire (Lit. the rattle of the mind-chariot) descending on the path of fulfilment. धैर्यावलम्बी-Observing patience or a calm attitude. सिद्धिपथः-सिद्धेः पन्थाः-The path of fruition or fulfilment.

ACT II.

The second Act is a continuation of the First, or as it is technically called, an अंकावतार, hinted by persons at the end of the preceding Act, and therefore we have the same characters here and no interludes. Cf. एष उत्तराङ्कस्य पूर्वाङ्कानुसंगतत्वाद् अङ्कावतारः प्रवेशकविष्कम्भकादिशून्यः । प्रथमाङ्के विदू°--तेन हीत्यारभ्य 'अह वा मिअंगसदो ज्जेव उठ्ठावइस्सदीत्युपक्रमे मृदङ्गशब्दश्रवणानन्तरं सर्वाण्येव पात्राणि प्रथमाङ्कप्रक्रान्तानि । पात्रसंक्रान्तदर्शनं द्वितीयाङ्कादावारम्भः।...Marginal note in a Ms, cited by Pandit. कतरस्य—of which of the two. कतर is used while referring to one of the two, and कतम, one of many. Cf. न चैतद् विद्मः कतरन्नो गरीयः । यद् वा जयेम यदि वा नो जयेयुः । भग० II. 6. II. 0. 5. ज्ञानवृद्ध-Old in knowledge, advanced in learning, as opposed to वयोवृद्ध meaning advanced in age. पुरस्कार-Preference, precedence. II.0. 7. स्वानियोगं...कुरु. Occupy your place of duty (नियोग) vacated by you, fill in your post left vacant.

II. 0. 9. शर्मिष्ठायाः कृतिः--The composition of शर्मिष्ठा, the daughter of वृषपर्वन् and the wife of king ययाति who loved her deeply. Cf. ययातेरिव शर्मिष्ठा भर्तुर्बहुमता भव । सुतं त्वमपि

सम्राजं सेव पूरुमवाप्नुहि ॥ शा० IV. 6. लयमध्या–लयेन तालकालेन मध्या मध्यलययुक्ता–Having or to be sung in medium time. लय means 'Time in music'; तालान्तरालवर्ती यः कालोऽसौ लय ईरितः। It is of three kinds, द्रुत, मध्य and विलंबित. Cf. पादन्यासो लयमनुगतः। मा० II. 8. The medium time is selected for love-songs. Cf. अत्र शृङ्गाररसत्वात् लयमध्येत्युक्तम् । तथा चोक्तं भारतीये-शृङ्गारहास्ययोर्मध्यलयः। चतुष्पदा Having four parts, चत्वारि पदानि यस्याः सा। तस्याश्चतुर्थवस्तुकं प्रयोगं–Performance or representation with reference to the fourth theme (वस्तु) or stanza. चतुर्थस्य तुर्यस्य वस्तुनः प्रबन्थस्य प्रयोगं। " We must suppose that the poem (of शार्मिष्ठा) consisted of four stanzas, each embodying a separate theme (वस्तु)"–Pandit.एकमनाः–With a concentrated mind, attentively.

II. 1. The king tells how very eager he feels to have a sight of मालविका. The curtain, still hanging, separates her who is inside the green room (नेपथ्यगृह). His eager eyes have, however, stepped forth, as it were, in their impatience to brush aside this curtain. तिरस्करिणी–The curtain, the screen. व्यवसितम्–Is busy, has set out. II. 1. 3. नयनमधु–The honey of the eyes. The delicious sight of मालविका is as sweet as honey. Cf. इयममृतवार्तिर्नयनयोः ।उत्तर० I. 38, सान्निहिता मक्षिका यस्य तद्–with the wasp hovering near (the honey). The wasp or the bee is none other than Queen धारिणी, who is guarding मालविका, as the bee would, the honey in the bee-hive. अप्रमत्तः watchful, vigilant.

II. 1. 5. आचार्य...सौष्ठवा–आचार्येण प्रत्यवेक्ष्यमाणं अङ्गानां सौष्ठवं यस्याःसा–Whose grace of the limbs was being minutely observed by the teacher. He was anxious for the success of his pupil and therefore he wants to see everything flawless. The word सौष्ठव means 'The elegance of the body. The proportionate and graceful development of the various parts of the body.' Cf. सौष्ठवं नाम अङ्गानां शोभनः अवस्थानविशेषः । यथोक्तम्–अनुच्चनीचचलतां अङ्गानां समपादताम् । कटिकूर्परशीर्षांसकण्ठानां समरूपताम् । रम्यां प्रतीकविश्रान्तिमुरसश्च समुन्नतिम् । अभ्यासोपहितां प्राहुः सौष्ठवं नृत्यवेदिनः ॥ Com. II. 1. 7. न......मधुरता Her loveliness, I am sure, does not fall short of the picture. The king had seen her portrait. विदूषक reminds him of it and says that the king will surely not feel disappointed while observing her in person now. Very often pictures inprove the appearance which in reality is not so good. Such is not the case, however, with मालविका.

II. 2. In his praise of the beauty of मालविका, the king, however, goes to the other extreme. It is the painting that falls short of her real charms. He started with doubts first, regarding her form, which he thought would fail to come up to the mark of the picture, being possibly overdrawn. But now he feels doubtful about the painter's skill, who, possibly, was distracted and hence could not secure enough concentration to do full justice to her. चित्र...हृदयम्–So long as मालविका was to me what I had observed of her only in the picture, I had a misgiving in my heart that her pictured loveliness would fail to have a real existence, i. e. would not be in consonance (विसंवाद) with what she actually is. संप्रति-

लिखिता. Now I must change my opinion ; and I feel that the painter who has drawn her was greatly distracted in his concentration (शिथिलसमाधि). For a similar idea Cf. यद्यत् साधु न चित्रे स्यात् क्रियते तत्तदन्यथा। तथापि तस्याः लावण्यं रेखया किंचिदन्वितम्॥ शा० VI. 14. II. 2. 1. मुक्तसाध्वसा (भव) Leave off all nervousness (साध्वस). सत्त्वस्था. composed, in (your) natural element. (सत्त्वं). II. 2. 2. सर्वस्थानानवद्यता– flawlessness or perfection in every part or limb (स्थान). Pandit reads सर्वावस्थासु अनवद्यता which means "Faultlessness in all conditions." This reading cannot be accepted, as the king refers here to the perfect beauty of the various parts of her body, and not to the different conditions. The next verse makes it clear.

II. 3. दीर्घाक्षं (वदनं)-दीर्घे आक्षिणी यस्य तत् - Having long eyes. शरदिन्दुकान्ति-शरदिन्दोः कान्तिरिव कांतिर्यस्य तत्- Possessed of the loveliness (कान्ति) of the autumnal moon, which regains her lustre, being freed from obscuring clouds. अंसयोः नतौ बाहू- Arms sloping at the shoulders, bent or curved at the shoulders. संक्षिप्तं उरः- Compact bosom. निविडोन्नतस्तनं (उरः)-निबिडौ उन्नतौ च स्तनौ यस्मिन्-Having thick (निबिड), swelling (उन्नत) breasts. पार्श्वे प्रमृष्टे इव- The two sides as if polished; lit. 'as if they were planed off' like boards that are thinned off by the plane and rendered smooth. मध्यः पाणिमितः--The waist was so thin and small that it was measurable (मित), or could be encompassed, by the palm of the hand. Cf. मण्णे मज्झं तिवलिवलिअं डिम्भमुट्ठीअ गेज्झं। कर्पूर० I. 30. मध्येन सा वेदिविलग्नमध्या वलित्रयं चारु बभार बाला।कुमार० I. 39. नितम्बि (जघनं)- नितम्बा-

तिशययुक्तं ।· अरालाङ्गुली–अराला आकुञ्चिता अङ्गुलयःययोः तौ (पादौ)– with curved toes. छन्दो...वपुः– Her body is so framed that it would suit any form of dancing which the dancing teacher may fancy that she should perform. छन्दः-Will, fancy. श्लिष्टं–संगतं–conforming, suited. Cf. ।श्लिष्टा क्रिया कस्यचिदात्मसंस्था । I. 16. For the description of the beauty of मालविका's form, Cf. अङ्गं लावण्णपुण्णं सवणपरिसरे लोअणा हारतारा । वच्छं थोरत्थाणिल्लं तिवलिवलइअं मुट्ठिगेज्झं अ मज्झम् । चक्काआरो निअम्बो तरुणिमसमए किं णु अण्णेण कज्जं । पंचेहिं जेव्व बाल। मअणजअमहावेजअन्तीअ होन्ति । कर्पूर० III. 19. उपवहनं—A preliminary humming of notes of the requir- ed melody. The other reading उपगानं, explained by the commentator as रागलप्ति, means the same thing.

II. 4. A maiden's love for her lover whom she has not yet won is the predominant sentiment of the song. She gives expression to her feelings of despair, hope, anxiety and helplessness, in succession. In the first line, for instance, there is the mood or feeling of despair (निर्वेद) on account of the fact that she realises her lover to be beyond her reach. All at once the corner of her left eye (अपाङ्ग) has begun to throb. Well, the twitching of the left eye in the case of woman is a very good indication of a prospective meeting of the lover. In the second line, therefore, there is the feeling of joy mingled with surprise (हर्षविस्मय). " But then meeting after such a long time, how should he be approached and wooed ? " The difficulty of the situa- tion creates a feeling of anxiety, which is expressed in the third line. The anxiety deepens, as no way out of the difficulty is to be found. A feeling of helplessness (दैन्य) comes over, and the last line gives expression to this sentiment. Thus we find, though the dominating sentiment of the song is love, it gives expression to these various subordinate feelings. Cf. अत्र चतुष्पद्यां क्रमेण पादचतुष्टये निर्वेदः हर्षविस्मयः चिन्ता दैन्यं चेति भावास्तत्तदनुभावैर्मुख-रागादिभिः सम्यक् प्रदर्शिता इत्यनुसंधेयम् ।

II. 4. 1. यथारसमभिनयति-Brings out the emotion through acting. As the two stage directions, one viz. उपवहनं कृत्वा चतुष्पदं वस्तु गायति, preceding the love-song and another viz. यथारसमभिनयति show, मालविका sings the song first and then begins dancing and acting, so as to reveal the emotion of the song. The form of dancing is छलित or चलित in which, while acting the part of another, the dancer gives expression thereby to her own sentiments. परिव्राजिका, the sister of माधवसेन's minister, knew that मालविका was promised in marriage to king अग्निमित्र, and also knew further that she i. e. मालविका loves the king. She has, therefore, selected this particular song of शार्मिष्ठा, that it may serve as an appropriate medium to express her own feelings for the king. The sentiment of the song is, as the Com. says, अयोग-विप्रलंभशृङ्गारः । i. e. love in separation of a maiden who has not yet secured her lover. Cf. अत्र रसस्तु अयोगाविप्रलम्भशृङ्गारः । अप्राप्तिर्विप्रलम्भः स्याद् यूनोर्जाताभिलाषयोः ।...तत्र-संप्राप्तेः प्रागभावो यस्तमयोगं प्रचक्षते ॥ II. 4. 8. द्वारीकृत्य-Making it a medium. (त्वयि) आत्मा उपक्षिप्तः-She has as it wer surrendered herself to you. II. 4. 3. एव-

मावयोर्हृदयम्-Such is the present condition of our hearts; that is how in our hearts we feel for each other.

II. 5. Construe:—'इमं जनं अनुरक्तं विद्धि' इति गेये वचनं स्वाङ्ग......पूर्वकं अभिनयन्त्या (मालविकया) धारिणीसंनिकर्षात् प्रणयगतिमदृष्ट्वा सुकु......व्याजं अहं उक्त इव। इमं जनं—This person. मालविका refers to herself in the third person Cf. अयं जनः कस्य हस्ते समर्पितः। शा० IV. स्वाङ्गनिर्देशपूर्वम्—To be taken as an adverbial compound with अभिनयन्त्या-Acting this expression of the song with proper gestures, pointing to (निर्देश) her own body-हस्तादिभिः प्रकाशयन्त्या। प्रणय...षात्-Finding no other way by which to express her love for me, as the Queen धारिणी was present in person. The presence of धारिणी deprived her of all direct ways of expressing her feelings for me, and, therefore, she had recourse to this indirect and suggestive method of revealing her love. सुकुमारप्रार्थनाव्याजम्-सुकुमारा चासौ प्रार्थना च तस्याः व्याजः यस्मिन् कर्मणि तथा (अहं उक्त इव)-An adverbial compound. She addressed me, as it were, under cover of this gentle plaint or request. The song incorporates a soft request of a maiden to her lover to succour her, helpless as she finds herself to be. This lover of the poem is a different person than the king. The king says that मालविका also finds herself in the same predicament and it appeared that she was pouring her own heart, and that her touching appeal was addressed to me and not to the lover of the poem. The word सुकुमार is taken by some in the sense of 'a youth,' meaning thereby "under the pretext of addressing the youthful lover of the poem." II. 5. 3. विदूषक is trying to detain मालविका, as she was going away after finishing her part. क्रमभेदः-The proper sequence of things to be done. II. 5. 5. उपदेशविशुद्धा-flawless as regard the performance. II. 5. 7. Gaṇadāsa has asked her to stay back, as she was going away. She turns round instantaneously and there stands in a very charming posture, which elicits this remark of appreciation from the king. सर्वा...पुष्यति-Beauty, under all conditions, develops fresh charms. In every posture, the beauty and loveliness of the form is always seen at an advantage. Cf. अहो सर्वास्ववस्थासु रमणीयत्वमाकृतिविशेषाणाम्। शा० VI. किमिव हि मधुराणां मण्डनं नाकृतीनाम् ॥ शा० I.

II. 6. The king describes her standing pose in all the details of the charm. The attractive features that he notes are—(i) The erect upper portion of the body, (ii) The position of the left hand on the hip, while the right is hanging down loosely, and (iii) the eyes cast down in bashfulness at the toe of her foot that is pressing the flowers on the pavement. सन्धि...वलयं (हस्तं) सन्धौ मणिबन्धे स्तिमितः निश्चलः वलयः कङ्कणं यस्य सः। The hand the bracelets of which are motionless or resting on the wrist. कृत्वा__द्वितीयम्-Making the other i. e. the right hand, which resembles (in tenderness) a branch of a श्यामा creeper, hang down loosely (स्नस्तमुक्तम्). The body of a beautiful woman is often likened to a creeper, the hands resembling the delicate branches and tender sprouts the lips. Cf. श्यामास्वङ्गं etc. मे० II. 37. also अधरः

किसलयरागः कोमलविटपानुकारिणौ बाहू ॥ शा० I. 21. स्रस्तमुक्तम्-स्रस्तं शिथिलं यथा भवति तथा मुक्तम्. Hanging down loosely. Some take it to mean "from which the pearls have gone."! पादा...कुट्टिमे-the pavement inlaid with jewels, the flowers on which were being pressed (आलुलित) by the toe of the foot. The right part of the body was relaxed, and she was standing with her eyes cast down, in the natural bashfulness of a girl who would not stare at the audience, all the time trying to play with the flowers scattered on the pavement, with the toe of her right foot. पातिताक्षं स्थितं-the standing posture in which the eyes were cast down. The fourth line should be construed thus :—अस्याः ऋज्वायतार्धं स्थितं नृत्ताद् अतितरां कान्तम् । स्थितम्-the standing posture. A Past Passive Participle is used as a noun, according to Paṇini's Sutra, नपुंसके भावे क्तः । ऋज्वायतार्धम्-in which the upper part of the body (आयतार्धम्-Lit. the long half) is straight or erect. A full view of the body could be had only when she was standing erect, which she could not do during the movements of dancing. अतितरां कान्तम् Is more charming or attractive. II. 6. 1. A sort of a tussle is going on between the Queen and the विदूषक. He wants to detain her on the stage as long as possible, while the Queen would like her to go at once. Hence she remarks to गणदास, that she is surprised to find that the words of a fool like Gautama are taken so seriously by him. II. 6. 3. देवप्रत्ययात्-owing to the confidence which the king has in him. The king's confidence is certainly not misplaced. सूक्ष्मदर्शिता-A subtle insight, acute perception.

II. 7. अमन्दतां एति-Leaves off the dullness of intellect, becomes sharp of intellingence. विपाश्चित्-A wise man. The simile is that of a mud-removing (पंकाच्छिद्) fruit of the कतक tree, which frees the turbid (आविल) water of its mud by contact with its powder or paste (निकष) and secures transparency for it. We should understand निकष to mean 'power or paste of the कतक fruit.' Similarly, argues गणदास, even a fool like विदूषक may have gained in wisdom by his association with the wise king. विवाक्षितं-वक्तुमिष्टम्—What is intended to be spoken. II. 7. 1. साक्षिणी-The witness, a judge, used with reference to परिव्राजिका. He means that the judge should give her opinion first, and then he will point out the flaw noted by him. II. 7. 5. यथादृष्टम्—just as you have observed. An outspoken plain criticism, whether with reference to the flaw or the merit is solicited. II. 7. 6. यथादर्शनम्-In accordance with the rules of the art. The reading यथाशास्त्रम् means the same thing.

II. 8. The परिव्राजिका explains how the exhibition of मालविका fully conforms to the standards of dancing. अङ्गै...वचनैः-by the various parts of her body which had words concealed in them, i. e. which are eloquently expressive. The ideas of the song were very well brought out in acting by means of the silent movements of the various parts of the body, which thus suppressed the actual words of the song within. Cf.

अन्तर्निहितानि अभ्यन्तरस्थापितानि वचनानि पदानि यैस्तैरङ्गैः हस्तादिभिः। अत्र अभ्यासपाटवादङ्गानां स्वत एवान्तर्निहितवचनत्वमुत्प्रेक्षितमिति मन्तव्यम्। लयमनुगतः-Conformed to the time of the song. In perfect time were the movements of the feet. तन्मयत्वं रसेषु-She could be perfectly one with the sentiments of the song, like despair, joy, surprise, etc. She could be perfectly absorbed in these sentiments. शाखा...नयः—The acting was soft and delicate (मृदु), in which the branch-like hand (शाखा) was used as the instrument of expression. शाखायोनिः-शाखा योनिः प्रभवः यस्य सः-Proceeding from the branch-like hand (शाखा). The graceful movements of the hand resemble the movements of a branch of a creeper. Some interpret शाखा to mean 'a measure of the hands in the dance.' Cf. शाखा नाम नृत्तहस्तानां मानप्रचारः। यथोक्तम्-शाखा तु नृत्तहस्तानां या मात्रा चित्रवर्तिने ॥ तद्विकल्पानुवृत्तौ-In the successive exhibition of the different shades in acting. तस्य आभिनयस्य विकल्पः भेदः तस्य अनुवृत्तिः अनुसृतिः। भावो... विषयात्-One emotion seemed to drive away another from the field (विषयात्). What she means is this: Various emotions pertaining to the one sentiment of love had to be acted by her ; at one time, there was despair, and just the next moment there was joy mixed with surprise. That gave place to anxiety, which was followed by despondency or a feeling of helplessness. While acting in a variety of ways to suit these emotions, she could successfully create the proper atmosphere of these varied emotions, which followed one another in quick succession, like the scenes in a movie. Cf. भावः अभिनीयमानः निर्वेदादिः विषयात आश्रयात्। प्रकृतात् स्थायिन इत्यर्थः। भावं पूर्वाभिनीतं

संचारिणं नुदति अपाकरोति । नुदति–Drives away, dispels. Cf. मन्दं मन्दं नुदति पवनश्चानुकूलो यथा त्वाम् । मे॰ I. 10. रागबन्धः स एव–Yet the main sentiment of love remained the same throughout. The various emotions exhibited were but the resultants of love, and therefore this basic sentiment also was fully revealed in acting.

II. 8. 2. स्वपक्षे शिथिलाभिमानाः–Losing the same high regard for my side ; feeling diffident regarding the success of my side. II. 8. 3. अद्य नर्तयितास्मि–To-day, after this success in the performance which has elicited such conpliments from the judge, I feel I deserve the position of a professor in the art of dancing.

II. 9. न श्यामायते–A denominative from the adj. श्याम–Which does not turn black, which maintains its flawless quality. Gold is tested in fire and it turns black, if it is impure. Similarly the instruction of the teacher must stand the scrutiny of the judge, and is declared good only when found flawless by him Cf. तं सन्तः श्रोतुमर्हन्ति सदसद्व्यक्तिहेतवः । हेम्नः संलक्ष्यते ह्यग्नौ विशुद्धिः श्यामिकापि वा ॥ रघु॰ I. 10, आपरितोषाद्विदुषां न साधु मन्ये प्रयोगविज्ञानम् । शा॰ I. 2. II. 9. 2. दिष्ट्या वर्धते भवान्—I congratulate you upon ; lit. you propser with the good luck of etc,. Cf. दिष्ट्या धर्मपत्नीसमागमेन पुत्रमुखदर्शनेन च वर्धते भवान् । शा॰ VII. परीक्षकाराधनेन–having pleased the judges or having satisfied them. II. 9. 3. वृद्धिहेतुः–The cause of good fortune i. e. success. II. 9. 6. प्रथमोपदेशदर्शनं–At the time of the first exhibition of the instruction. He means that the beginning of every function of some consequence must be attended with the worship of a Brahmin, and the same should have been done here. II. 9. 8. अहो प्रयोगाभ्यन्तरः प्रश्नः–"Oh ! what a relevant question ! what a vital point in acting is being referred to ! " She means that his question is quite irrelevant and beside the point, having nothing to do with the present matter in hand viz. the exhibition given. II.9.9. पण्डितंमन्या–One who thinks oneself to be a wise person, a conceited woman. पंडितं आत्मानं मन्यते सा। प्रसन्न...केशपाशैः–With your abundant hair shining white like the clear (प्रसन्न) rays of the moon. पाश after a word signifying 'hair' means ' abundance, mass, quantity.' भीषयसे-Frighten. II. 9. 14. मन्दस्मितम्–a gentle smile. दशरूप mentions six varities of हास, viz. स्मित, हसित, विहसित, उपहसित, अपहासित and अतिहसित, and among these, the first two are to be noted with reference to the उत्तम characters. The मन्दास्मित, in which the teeth are slightly visible, would accordingly correspond to the हसित variety. Cf. स्मितमिह विकासिनयनं किंचिल्लक्ष्यद्विजं तु हसितं स्यात् । मधुरस्वरं विहसितं साशिरःकम्पमिदमुपहसितम् ॥ अपहसितम् सास्राक्षं विक्षिप्ताङ्गं भवत्यतिहसितम् । द्वे द्वे हासिते चैषां ज्येष्ठे मध्येऽधमे क्रमशः ॥ दश० IV. 76-77. II. 9. 15. उपा...विषयः– My eye has perceived its object possessed of the essence of glory or loveliness (उपात्तसार). उपात्त is a Past Passive Participle from उप+आ+दा, meaning ' Has taken out, is possessed of. ' The object of the eye is रूप. Here is an object, the lovely smiling face of मालविका, however, which has the greatest charm about it. Cf. अनवाप्तचक्षुःफलोऽसि । येन त्वया दर्शनीयं न दृष्टम् । शा० II.

II. 10 The king compares the smiling face of मालविका, with its teeth half visible, to an opening lotus whose filaments are partially seen. स्मयमानं-A Present Part. of √स्मि I. A. किंचिदभिव्यक्तदशनशोभि–With the charm of teeth (दशन) slightly revealed. Cf. आलक्ष्यदन्तमुकुलाननिमित्तहासैः । शा० VII. 17. उच्छ्वसत्-Blooming, opening. असमग्रलक्ष्यकेसरं (पंकजं)-असमग्रं असंपूर्णं लक्ष्याः केसराः यस्य तत् । with its filaments not completely visible. The filaments correspond to her small teeth in the simile.

II. 10. 1. महाब्राह्मण-A great Brahmin, said ironically. Cf. भो महाब्राह्मण, काममेतदभिनन्दनीयम् । शा० V. नेपथ्यसङ्गीतकम्- A musical or dramatic performance in regular stage-costume, done in public. This however being a private affair, it was not necessary to observe the preliminary worship of some deity and Brahmins. II. 10. 3. मया.....मिष्टम्-Like the foolish चातक bird, I expected a drink of water from the sky resounding with the rumble of rainless clouds. I thought, such a function commencing, I would be given an offering of sweet things ; it proved to be, however, a vain hope of a silly चातक bird who foolishly expects to get a few drops of water to drink from dry clouds. Cf. अरण्ये मया रुदितमासीत् । शा० II. The चातक bird imagined to be living on rain-drops, is often alluded to by the Poets. Cf. स्वस्त्यस्तु ते निर्गलिताम्बुगर्भं शरद्घनं नार्दति चातकोऽपि ॥ रघु० V. 17. रे रे चातक सावधानमनसा मित्र क्षणं श्रूयताम् । अम्भोदा बहवो हि सन्ति गगने सर्वेऽपि नैतादृशाः ॥ केचिद् वृष्टिभिरार्द्रयन्ति वसुधां गर्जन्ति केचिद् वृथा । यं यं पश्यसि तस्य तस्य पुरतो मा ब्रूहि दीनं वचः ॥ भर्तृ० I. II. 10. 9.

पण्डितपरितोष-प्रत्यया-Depending for their decision on the satisfaction of the learned. विदूषक says that he is incapable of pronouncing any judgment regarding the merits of this teacher or the other one. He depends in this matter on what the learned persons like the परिव्राजिका say, and would then form his own opinion accordingly; Cf. मूढः परप्रत्ययनेयबुद्धिः । I. 1. कटकं-A bracelet. शोभन भणितं-You said it was good, you commended her. II. 10. 3. गुणान्तरमजानन्-When you do not know the merits of the other teacher i. e. हरदत्त ; Without knowing how the pupil of हरदत्त has acquitted herself. The expression गुणान्तरम् may also mean 'The excellence of skill or merit, Cf. पात्रविशेषन्यस्तं गुणान्तरं व्रजति शिल्पमाधातुः । I. 6. Then the sentence would mean 'When you are unable to appreciate the excellence of skill in acting, why should you offer this reward, which is best given by really worthy men.' The Queen does not like the idea of the king's bracelet going into the hands of मालविका as a gift, which, though outwardly a reward, is clearly intended to be the lover's token of his love for the girl. II.10.14. परकीयमिति कृत्वा-A nice retort to the queen. 'Why, where is the harm, says he ; after all, he is not to lose anything. He takes the credit for having given as a reward what belongs to others Cf. the Marathi saying 'हलवायाच्या घरावर तुळशीपत्र.' II.10.16. ननु... शिष्या-She suggests to गणदास to send away his pupil now that she has finished exhibiting her parts. विदूषक's raillery with the obvious intention of detaining मालविका was becoming intolerable to her and hence this hint of hers to गणदास. II. 10. 19. एता...सेवितुम्-I have exhausted my power of ingenuity now; only thus far can my ingenuity help you: I can think of no other way to detain her any longer. II. 10. 20. अलमलं परिच्छेदेन-Do not set any limit to your genius. If you mean, you can still help me to achieve my object. Note the flattering tone of the king.

II. 11. The king explains how sad he feels, when मालविका has disappeared from view. तिरस्करणम्-disappearance, vanishing from sight. भाग्या...अक्ष्णोः-I feel as if the sun of the good luck of my eyes has set. हृद...मिव-The heart's great festivity of joy has come to a close (अवसानं). द्वार...धृतेः-The door of pleasure (धृति) has been closed as it were. धृति also means 'Fortitude, courage,' 'The portals of fortitude have closed as it were.' II.11. 2. आतुरः-troubled with illness or disease. विदूषक means that the king is like a poor patient who has no money to pay to the physician, and yet expects him to bring the medicine for him. The king would not take any trouble himself, afraid of the risks. He wants विदूषक to arrange everything for him with a view to secure मालविका II. 11. 6. अवसितो दर्शनार्थः-when मालविका has been seen, the purpose of the exhibition is finished. दाक्षिण्यम्-outward politeness without any sincerity. Cf. दाक्षिण्येन ददाति वाचमुचितामन्तःपुरेभ्यो यदा। शा० VI. 5. II. 12.9. वैतालिकः-A bard, a minstrel. It is his profession to praise the king, and also to announce the hour of the day, in apt verses. उपारूढः-Developed, grown. मध्याहः-मध्यमहः-the mid-day.

II. 12. He describes how the mid-day heat of the sun affects the various birds. पत्रच्छायासु–in the shade of lotus-leaves. मुकुलितनयनाः हंसाः–the swans have half-closed their eyes; lit. with their eyes in the form of a bud (मुकुल). सौधम्–a great palace, a big mansion. वलभि...वतानि (सौधानि) –वलभिपरिचयस्य द्वेषिणः पारावताः येषु–तानि । The pigeons have come to hate flocking together (परिचय) on the terrace-tops (वलभि). The pigeons flocking on the roofs or terraces of the houses is a common sight. Cf. तां कस्यांचिद् भवनवलभौ सुप्तपारावतायाम् । नीत्वा रात्रिं चिरविलसनात् खिन्नविद्युत्कलत्रः ॥ मे० I. 38. परिचयः–' Accumulating, flocking.' It also means ' Acquaintance, contact or association;' in that case it would mean ' Hating their contact with the roofs.' बिन्दूत्क्षेपान् पिपासुः शिखी–the peacock desires licking (पिपासुः) the splashing water-drops. परिपतति–flies to, dashes to. भ्रान्तिमद् वारियन्त्रम्–A revolving water-wheel, known in Marathi by the word रहाटगाडगें. उस्रैः–by the rays. सप्तसप्तिः–a god having seven horses, i. e. the sun. दीप्यते–blazes, shines brilliantly. त्वमिव नृपगुणैः–Just as you (i. e. the king) shine with the kingly virtues. II. 12. 4. उचितवेलातिक्रमे–if the proper time of taking food is transgressed or allowed to go. चिकित्सकः–A physician. हरदत्त...भणसि–What have you to say to this ? Would you like the king to miss his lunch-time, which would be so bad for his health?' विदूषक thus suggests to him not to insist on his show being exhibited just then. II. 12. 6. नास्ति...त्र–There is no scope left for me to make any other proposal. I have got to bow down to what विदूषक says.' II. 12. 11. मज्जनविधि-The act of bathing, the usual or customary bath. II. 12. 17. न केवलं...विका-As in her personal charm, so in her skill (शिल्प) in dancing, she has no second. अद्वितीया-Matchless, peerless, unrivalled.

II. 13. The king means to say that मालविका is already so beautiful that by her personal charms alone she can strike the heart of one with feelings of love. Now the additional accomplishment of this graceful art has lent her greater power, and she is a deadlier shaft in the hands of Cupid who has steeped it in poison as it were to make it more dreadful. अव्याजसुन्दरी-Artlessly beautiful, naturally charming without any artifical make-up. तां ललितेन विज्ञानेन योजयता-Uniting her with i.e. endowing her with the knowledge of the fine arts. परिकल्पितः-Made ready, devised, prepared. कामस्य बाणः-The shaft of Cupid. A beautiful woman is looked upon, by Sanskrit poets, as a shaft or weapon of the god of love. The verse is a good example of the निदर्शनालंकार.

II. 13. 1. चिन्तयितव्योऽस्मि ते-You have to pay serious thought to my condition. Love has made him its victim and therefore his malady has to be carefully attended to by him. II. 13. 3. विपणिकन्दुः-A cauldron or a frying pan in the market place (विपणि). II. 13. 5. एवमेव...त्वरताम्-Make haste in the cause of your friend, in the same way as you would be doing to pacify your hunger. II. 13. 9. गृहीतक्षणोऽस्मि-I have pledged my word; I have undertaken the venture. 'The phrase has origin in a formula, used in connection with the श्राद्ध ceremony. A Brahmin is duly invited to attend the ceremony, and he uses this expression, when he accepts the invitation गृहीत्वामुकसंज्ञस्यामुकगोत्रस्य चामुके । श्राद्धे तु वैश्वदेवार्थं करणीयः क्षणस्त्वया ॥ इत्येवं श्राद्धकृद् ब्रूयात् तं प्राप्नोतु भवानिति । स वदेत् प्राप्नवानीतीतरस्तं प्रति द्विजः ॥ Cited by Pandit from शौनक॰ 16.—'The person who addresses in the words of the formula (the श्राद्धकृत्) is said *to give* the क्षण and the Brahmin to whom it is addressed, to *take* the क्षण, in the language of ignorant priests. Hence,because the word क्षण is so often used in the formula, so it has come, in the common parlance of Brahmaṇas, who subsist mostly upon occasional dinners at Śrāddhas, and to which class our विदूषक belonged, to signify 'an engagement at a Śrāddha, which, when once begun, must be carried out, on pain of incurring sin.' It may be observed that Vidūṣaka's way of expressing his obligation to accomplish what he has undertaken is perfectly in keeping with his character. क्षण घेणें is still used in Marathi in the sense of 'pledging one's self for the performance of a thing'—Pandit. मेघा...ज्योत्स्नेव-मेघावल्या रुद्धा चासौ ज्योत्स्ना च । Like moonlight obstructed or veiled by the clouds. सूनोपरिचरः-Hovering over the slaughter-house (सूना). आमिषलोलुपः—Greedy of the flesh (आमिष). Like the vulture, you too eagerly want to snatch the object of your love but, are afraid of धारिणी. अनातुरः-Patient, calm, unexcited. तस्मात् ...रोचसे-He means, there are hundred and one difficulties in the way of success for which you have to wait patiently. I would very much like you to exercise patience while you eagerly solicit success in this venture Note the wise counsel of विदूषक to the king.

II. 14. Construe :-सर्वा...हृदयस्य मे वामलोचना सा स्नेहस्यैकायनीभूता । सर्वा...हृदयस्य मम-Of me who have lost all heart in the activities of the ladies of my harem. Thinking of मालविका alone, I have ceased to feel any interest in the harem. वामलोचना—Possessed of lovely (वाम) eyes. स्नेहस्यैकायनीभूता-She has become the sole centre of my affection. एकायनीभूता is a च्वि form (अभूततद्भावे च्विः।). एकायनं One abode, the sole resort.

ACT III.

III. 0. 1. परिचारिका-A female attendant. III. 0. 6. बीजपूरकं-The fruit of citron, known as महाळुंग in Marathi. प्रमदवनपालिका--The female keeper of the प्रमदवन garden. Her name is मधुकरिका, lit. meaning 'a female bee,' while that of परिव्राजिका's attendant is परभृतिका meaning literally 'a cuckoo.' The same names have been given to the two female attendents in the शाकुंतल, where at the beginning of the Sixth Act they are carrying on a lively dialogue in the garden of दुष्यन्त. तपनीयाशोक:-The golden अशोक tree, so called because of its bright yellow blossoms. III. 0. 11. अपि...व्यापार:-The particle अपि, thus used at the beginning of a sentence introduces a question. 'Are you having a happy time while doing your work in the garden'? III. 0. 16. अरिक्तपाणिना-' Without empty hands.' परिव्राजिक

means that she must have some present to offer when she would visit the queen. She cannot do so empty-handed. We have a meeting between the queen and परिव्राजिका in Act IV, but it may not be the same referred to here. Shall we suppose that परिव्राजिका made it a point to see the queen as frequently as she could, with a view to see how the wind was blowing and also to remove the suspicions, if any would be entertained by the queen as regards her hand in the quarrel between the two teachers ? शुश्रूषितुम्-To wait upon, to serve, III. 0. 21. अन्योन्यसंघर्षित-संघर्षित-Mutually quarrelling, disputing with each other. संघर्ष: संजात: अस्य ।. One who has a dispute. Compare a similar expression, अन्योन्यकलहितयो: in Act I. Cf. also अत्रभवतो: परस्परविज्ञानसंघर्षो जातः । Act I. III. 0. 24. आगमिनौ-Possessed of theoretical knowledge (आगम). किंतु ...गणदास:-' But then गणदास has the palm or is adjudged to be the superior of the two, because of the excellent merits (गुणविशेष) of his pupil. मालविका, the pupil of गणदास, showed superior skill to that of the pupil of हरदत्त, and hence गणदास is ranked higher (उन्नमित). This means that the king kept up his promise of witnessing the performance of हरदत्त's pupil next day, and only afterwards was the decision given in favour of गणदास. III. 0. 26. कौलीनं—कुले जातं-Lit. belonging to a family, or arising from a group of people ; a scandal, gossip. Cf. कौलीनभीतेन गृहान्निरस्ता न तेन वैदेहसुता मनस्त: । रघु० XIV. 84. कथं श्रूयते-' How is that (scandal) to be heard ; What is that ? ' III. 0. 30. बलवत् साभिलाष:-greatly enamoured, strongly or deeply attached. Cf. बलवदपि शिक्षितानामात्मन्यप्रत्ययं चेत: । शा०

I. 2. वित्तं रक्षन्--Having regard for the feelings of the queen ; out of consideration for her feelings. आत्मनः प्रभुत्वं न दर्शयति-He does not exhibit the strength of his power or authority (प्रभुत्वं). She means that the king, being so deeply attached to मालविका, could easily have got hold of her through his kingly authority. He does nothing of the kind, however, because he would not like to wound the queen's feelings, who would certainly take such things to heart. अनुभूतमुक्तेव......म्लायमाना-Fading or pale like jasmine wreath, worn (अनुभूत) and cast away (मुक्त). अनुभूतमुक्ता-आदौ अनुभूता पश्चान्मुक्ता-Enjoyed first and then thrown away. She means that मालविका also seems to have been affected by a reciprocal feeling of love, as a result of which she has lost the fresh lustre of her face latterly.

III. 0. 34. शाखावलम्बि-शाखामवलम्बते तत। Hanging on the branch. पेशलतरं-Softer, more tender than this citron fruit. मधुकरिका has been of much service to परिव्राजिका, in securing for her the required present. This service will not go unrewarded. The present of a hard fruit will yield to her a softer reward in the near future. What does she refer to ? Some happy prospect of the king's or the queen's favour ? Or was she to be lucky like मालविका in winning the king's love ? The expression त्वमपि 'you too' favours the latter suggestion. III. 0. 42. चिराय... दोहदनिमित्तं-Regarding the longing (दोहद) of this gold अशोक tree which is delaying (चिरायमाणः) to put forth its blossoms. Sanskrit poets curiously imagine in their romantic fancy that the trees have various cravings or longings like those of a pregnant woman, and only when they are satisfied, they would burst into blossom. We have a beautiful verse which mentions the different cravings of the various trees. स्त्रीणां स्पर्शात् प्रियङ्गुर्विकसति बकुलः शीधुगण्डूषसेकात् । पादाघातादशोकः तिलककुरबकौ वीक्षणालिङ्गनाभ्याम् ॥ मन्दारो नर्मवाक्यात् पटुमृदुहसनाच्चम्पको वक्त्रवातात् । चूतो गीतान्नमेरुर्विकसति च पुरो नर्तनात् कर्णिकारः ॥ According to these conventions, the अशोक tree, when it withholds its flowers, is believed to desire that a young and beautiful woman should be decorated with ornaments, dressed beautifully and should then kick it with her foot which should itself be nicely decorated. This ceremony is called the दोहदपूरण or gratifying the desire of the Aśoka.

प्रवेशकः–This is an explanatory scene serving the same purpose as the विष्कम्भक, only with this difference that the characters taking part in this scene are exclusively of the inferior class speaking the Prakrits. It must come between two Acts; and thus unlike the विष्कंभक, its existence in the first Act is not possible. Cf. तद्वदेवानुदात्तोक्त्या नीचपात्रप्रयोजितः । प्रवेशोऽङ्कद्वयस्यान्तः शेषार्थस्योपसूचकः ॥

The Pravesaka tells us, among other things, that the king is now deeply in love with मालविका who too responds to his feelings in a similar way, and that he will not use his authority to gain his ends, out of respect for the queen's feelings, which thus makes him depend soley on the efforts of विदूषक and his friends. The craving of the Aśoka tree, on par with that of the king is also significantly referred to, as it gives an opportunity to मालविका to satisfiy both. This information is necessary for the audience to follow the action of the main scene which commences now.

III. 0. 47. कामयमानावस्थः-कामयमानस्य इव अवस्था यस्य सः। In the condition of a love-lorn person ; in a love-sick state. III. 1. Constant thinking of the object of his love; viz. मालविका and the acute pangs caused thereby constitute the theme of this beautiful verse. He cannot understand, says he, why his heart, which has its highest bliss i. e. मालविका enshrined within, should suffer so much torment! One suffers for want of the object which one cherishes. The body gets thin, not having obtained the pleasure of her embraces. The eyes may be in tears, because deprived of her sight. But the heart, which has stored within itself the precious treasure of love viz. मालविका, from whom it is never separated—that this heart should suffer great agony is something which is very very strange! क्षामं-Thin, emaciated Cf. मध्ये क्षामा etc. मे० II. सास्रं-अस्रैः सहितं—full of tears. सारङ्गाक्षी-सारङ्गस्य इव अक्षिणी यस्याः सा-Having eyes like those of an antelope (सारंग); gazelle-eyed. प्रसक्ते निर्वाणे-when the highest bliss is so closely connected or associated (with the heart). प्रसक्त-closely adhering to, closely connected. निर्वाणं supreme bliss, highest felicity. Cf. अये लब्धं नेत्रनिर्वाणम् । शा० III. It is also a philosophical term meaning ‘ absolute extinction or annihilation of individual or worldy existence ’ and refers to the final state of liberation or the मोक्ष according to the Buddhist philosophy. The fourth line gives us the notion of apparent contradiction or विरोध. निर्वाण has also the sense of 'the means of extinguishing fire etc.' 'When the heart is equipped with the means of extinguishing the fire within, why should it bear this torment of scorching agony?'. III. 1. 4. परिदेवितं-Lamentation, bewailing. श्राविता-was made to listen, informed. भवता संदिष्टम्-Your massage. Apparently the king has tried through विदूषक to take बकुलावालिका, the queen's maid, into confidence, and he wants her to speak the message of his love to मालविका. III. 1. 10. अनुगृहीतास्मि ...नियोगेन-I feel favoured by this mission entrusted to me. The mission is that of a messenger of love or a go-between. तपस्विनी-The poor pitiable girl, having the sense of the Marathi expression 'गरीब बिचारी or गरीब बापडी.' तपस्वी करुणापात्रम् । हला० नागरक्षित इव निधिः-Like a valuable treasure guarded by a cobra sitting on it. न सुखं...भविष्यति will not be easily secured, cannot be easily obtained. घटयिष्यामि-I shall try to unite or bring about a union. Cf. इत्थं नारीर्घटयितुमलं कामिभिः । शिशु० IX. 87. तप्तेन तप्तमयसा घटनाय योग्यम् ॥ विक्र० II. 16. It has also the sense of 'accomplishing an object or effecting a purpose.' Cf. तटस्थः स्वानर्थान् घटयति च मौनं च भजते । मालती० I. 14. III. 1. 13. संकल्पयोनिः-Born of fancy or thought; whose source (योनि) is thought. It is an epithet of the god of Love; Cf. epithets मनोभव, मनसिज, etc. प्रातिबन्धवत्सु विषयेषु अभिनिवेश्य-Having made one attached towards objects that are fraught with difficulties (प्रातिबन्ध). जनोऽयम्-This person i. e. I. The king refers to himself in the third person. कालान्तरक्षमो न भवति-Is unable to brook any delay; cannot bear any delay

(कालान्तर). Cf. दूरगतमन्मथा अक्षमेयं कालहरणस्य । शा॰ III. The king means that it was the god of love who impelled him to love an inaccessible object like मालविका, and now tortures him so much that he cannot brook any delay in the attainment of his object.

III. 2. The king wonders at the disparity that exists between the tender weapon like the flower and the acute heart-rending agony which it produces. हृदयप्रमाथिनी रुजा–हृदयं प्रमथ्नाति सा–A heart-wrenching agony. विश्वसनीयमायुधम्–A weapon like the flower which is seemingly harmless, which rouses no suspicion as being harmful or dangerous. The god of love has five arrows with which to strike the lovers, and they are:—अरविन्दमशोकं च चूतं च नवमल्लिका । नीलोत्पलं च पञ्चैते पञ्चबाणस्य सायकाः ॥ उन्मादनस्तापनश्च शोषणः स्तम्भनस्तथा । संमोहनश्च कामस्य पञ्चबाणाः प्रकीर्तिताः ॥. The two particles क्व and क्व bring out a great incongruity or disparity between two objects. The king says, for instance, 'Look at these two objects, Cupid's weapons viz. flowers, and the agonising torture they effect. What a great incongruity or inconsistency exists between the two! There should be some proportion between a cause and its effect. Here there is none. The effect is absolutely disproportionate to the cause.' Cf. भगवन् कुसुमायुध, त्वया चन्द्रमसा च विश्वसनीयाभ्यां प्रतिसन्धीयते कामिजनसार्थः । कुतः । तव कुसुमशरत्वं शीतरश्मित्वमिन्दो–। द्वयमिदमयथार्थं दृश्यते मद्विधेषु ॥ विसृजति हिमगर्भैरग्निमिन्दुर्मयूखै--। त्वमपि कुसुमबाणान् वज्रसारीकरोषि ॥ and further कुतस्ते कुसुमायुधस्य सततैक्ष्ण्यमेतत् । शा॰ III. 2. मृदु तीक्ष्णतरम्–" A delicate thing is often most piercing. मन्मथः-Cupid, the god of love-मनो मथ्नाति सः । तदि... त्वयि-In you is illustrated the saying that a tender thing is often the sharpest. III. 2. 3. उपायोपक्षेपः-उपायस्य उपक्षेपः- Devising of the remedy or means. पर्यवस्थापयतु-Compose yourself; be at ease. III. 2. 5. उचितव्यापारविमुखेन चेतसा- with a mind disinclined or averse to the proper duties. क्व दिवसशेषं यापयामि-Where should I pass the rest of the day? √यापय्-The causal of या 'to go.' Cf. क्व नु खलु... श्रमक्लान्तमात्मानं विनोदयामि । शा० III. वसन्ता...कोरकानि-The buds (कोरक) of the red Asoka tree, indicative of the arrival or advent (अवतार) of spring. दोलाधिरोहणं-Sitting on the swing. III. 2. 17. निसर्गनिपुणाः-Instinctively shrewd or clever.Cf. स्त्रीणामशिक्षितपटुत्वममानुषीषु संदृश्यते किमुत याः प्रतिबोधवत्यः । शा० V, 22. स्त्रियो हि नाम खल्वेता निसर्गादेव पण्डिताः । मृच्छ० IV.19. अन्यसंक्रान्तहृदयम्-अन्यस्यां संक्रान्तं हृदयं यस्य whose heart is transferred to another (woman). उपलालयन्तम्-Fondling, coaxing, caressing. कथं...न लक्षयिष्यमि-'How will she not detect?' The king says that his heart is already given over to मालविका, and it will be therefore very difficult for him to conceal his love when in the company of इरावती. In spite of all his fondling and caresses इरावती. with her instinctive shrewdness of a woman, will easily see through and discover his love for another woman. Cf. अन्यसंक्रान्तप्रेमाणो नागरिका अधिकं दक्षिणा भवन्ति। विक्र०III. अन्यसंक्रान्तहृदयोऽपि प्रथमसंभावनामपेक्षते अतिशिथिलसौहार्द इदानीमेषः । शा० VI.

III. 3. The king says that all these considerations to refuse her proper request by giving various plausible excuses would be far better than allow himself to be caught in a compromising situation where he will have to pretend, to keep up an appearance of an ardent lover, even though at heart he has not the slightest attachment for her. उचितः प्रणयः. विहन्तुं वरम्-It is better to decline (विहन्तुं) the request (प्रणय) which is quite proper for this occasion. खण्डनहेतवः दृष्टाः-Many excuses to refuse (खण्डन) the request are seen i. e. are known to me. He means that any number of plausible excuses, such as urgent calls of state affairs, can be invented for the purpose of saying 'No' to the queen इरावती. उपचार...शून्यः-But a formal behaviour of courtesy with these clever women, even though full of greater ardour or fervour (पूर्वाभ्यधिकः) will certainly be found out to be lacking in the sincere feeling of love, (भावशून्य) and therefore it will not do for the present occasion when it is far better to refuse her request. Cf. प्रियवचनशतोऽपि योषितां दयितजनानुनयो रसादृते । प्रविशति हृदयं न तद्विदां मणिरिव कृत्रिमरागयोजितः ॥ विक्र० II. 22. मनस्विनीनां-objective genitive. अन्तःपुरप्रतिष्ठितं दाक्षिण्यं-Your courtesy which is a constant or unfailing feature in your behaviour towards ladies of the harem. एकपदे-All of a sudden. पृष्ठतः कर्तुम्-to keep it back, to throw away. He means that the king was never rude to the ladies who were always sure of his courteous, chivalrous behaviour. It will not do for him, therefore, to shake off his courtesy all at once and disappoint the ladies in their legitimate demands. III. 3. 9. नन्वे... भवन्तम्-The idea underlined is that of a man beckoning a friend of his to come near quickly, with the fingers of his hand. Cf. एष वातेरितपल्लवाङ्गुलीभिस्त्वरयतीव मां केसरवृक्षकः ।

शा० I. III. 3. 11. अभिजात:-Noble, high-born, nobly sympathising. ' On the meaning of this, compare also the following of भर्तृहरि quoted in the कुवलयानन्द:-प्रदानं प्रच्छन्नं गृहमुपगते संभ्रमविधिः । निरुत्सेको लक्ष्म्यामनभिभवगन्धाः परकथाः ॥ प्रियं कृत्वा मौनं सदसि कथनं नाप्युपकृतेः । श्रुतेऽत्यन्तासक्तिः पुरुषमभिजातं कथयति ॥'—Pandit.

III. 4. The king says that like a noble person the Spring who feels so much for him in his present suffering, first inquires of him in gentle soft words, as one would do an ailing friend, as to how far his malady is bearable; and then strokes him gently by way of encouragement. The words of the Spring are the sweet notes of cuckoos who have found their voice at the advent of Spring, while the fragrant southern breeze represents the stroking of his hand. Construe the verse thus :--आमत्तानां कोकिलानां श्रवणसुभगैः कूजितैः मनसिजरुजः सह्यतां सानुक्रोशं पृच्छता इव माधवेन चूत...सुरभिः सांद्रस्पर्शः दक्षिणो मारुतः (दक्षिणः) करतल इव अङ्गे व्यापृतः । श्रवणसुभगैः कूजितैः-The warbling (कूजित) of cuckoos agreeable or charming (सुभग) to the ear. Cf. तच्छ्रुत्वा ते श्रवणसुभगं गर्जितं मानसोत्काः । मे० I 11. सानुक्रोशम्-Compassionately. मनसिरुजः सह्यतां-The endurable nature of love's malady (रुज्). दक्षिणमारुत-The southern breeze coming from the Malaya mountain which teems with the sandal-wood forests. Such breezes are looked upon as one of the charming features of spring. Cf. कुबेरगुप्तां दिशमुष्णरश्मौ गन्तुं प्रवृत्ते समयं विलङ्घ्य । दिग्दक्षिणा गन्धवहं मुखेन व्यलीकनिश्वासमिवोत्ससर्ज । कु० III. 25. ते एहिं मलआणिला विरहिणीणीसाससंपक्किणो । जादा झत्ति सिसुत्तणे वि बहुला

तारुण्णपुण्णा इव ॥ कर्पूर० I. 20. The word दक्षिण has a double meaning, referring to करतल as well, in the sense of 'The palm of the right hand.' चूतप्रसवसुरभि-Fragrant with mango blossoms. सान्द्रस्पर्शः-सान्द्रः स्पर्शः यस्य सः-The word, सान्द्र means ' close, intimate '; it also means ' soft, pleasing' : both the senses will do well here. व्यापृतः-Applied, used for the purpose of stroking. माधवेन-वसन्तेन.-By the Spring. III. 4. 2. निर्वृतिलाभाय. For getting happiness or pleasure. All the Mss. read णिव्वुदिलाहाअ, which apparently seems to be a direct Prakrit translation of the Sanskrit form निर्वृतिलाभाय. We should, however, expect a genitive form °लाहस्स for the Sanskrit Dative, since the Prakrit has lost the dative case.

III. विलोभयितुकामया—With a desire to tempt you. III. 5. The Vernal Beauty (माधवी श्री) is imagined to be a lovely lady who has put on the various face-decorations supplied to her by the spring, and in that she surpasses the other women. A lady's toilet consists of the red lac-dye which she applies to her lips, the various paintings to be drawn on the forehead, cheeks and the bosom, and the reddish-black mark on the forehead in saffron mixed with musk (कस्तूरी). The Vernal Beauty has all these supplied to her by the spring, and she appears to be looking down upon this art of adorning the face, as practised usually by women. विशेषितगुणः ...लक्तकः—the red lac-dye (अलक्तक), applied to the lower lip red like the बिंब fruit seems to have been surpassed (विशेषित). The red colour of the lips is often compared to that of the ripe बिंब fruit. Cf. तन्वी श्यामा शिखरिदशना पक्वबिम्बाधरोष्ठी । मे॰ II. प्रत्या...रुणम्–The कुरबक blossoms exhibit a variety of colours, dark, bright (अवदात) and red. They thus throw into the back-ground (प्रत्याख्यात) the charm of the creeper-like painting on the face or the cheeks. The word विशेषक or more often पत्रविशेषक refers to these creeperlike paintings on the face or the cheeks. Cf. हिमव्यपायाद्विशदाधराणामापाण्डरीभूतमुखच्छवीनाम् । स्वेदोद्गमः किंपुरुषाङ्गनानां चक्रे पदं पत्रविशेषकेषु ॥ कुमा॰ III. 33. For the idea of the कुरबक blossoms serving as such paintings on the face of vernal beauty, Compare, विरचिता मधुनोपवनश्रियामभिनवा इव पत्रविशेषकाः । मधुलिहां मधुदानविशारदाः कुरबका रवकारणतां ययुः ॥ रघु॰ IX. 29. लग्न......नैः तिलकः–By the blossoms of the तिलक tree, with the bees (द्विरेफ) clinging to them like collyrium (अंजन). तिलकक्रियापि आक्रान्ता–The decoration of the saffron mark on the forehead is superseded or excelled. Cf. लग्नद्विरेफाञ्जनभक्तिचित्रं मुखे मधुश्रीस्तिलकं निवेश्य । रागेण बालारुणकोमलेन चूतप्रवालोष्ठमलंचकार ॥ कुमा॰ III. 30. Also अलिभिरञ्जनबिन्दुमनोहरैः कुसुमपङ्क्तिनिपातिभिरङ्कितः । न खलु शोभयति स्म वनस्थलीं न तिलकस्तिलकः प्रमदामिव ॥ रघु॰ IX. 41. सावज्ञेव...योषिताम्-The vernal beauty ridicules as it were (सावज्ञा) the art of adorning (प्रसाधन) the face as practised ordinarily by women (योषितां). III. 5. 2. पर्युत्सुका–In a state of anxious longing, in an excited or agitated condition. Cf. पर्युत्सुकां कथयसि प्रियदर्शनां तां । विक्र॰II. 16. अयि संप्रति देहि दर्शनं स्मर पर्युत्सुक एष माधवः । कुमा॰ IV. 28. III. 5. 14. विभवः–Power, courage. She means that she is denied the relief that she will have, if she will commuicate the whole thing to her affectionate friends. Cf.

स्निग्धजनसंविभक्तं दुःखं सह्यवेदनं भवति । शा० III. III. 5. 15. अप्रतीकारगुरुका वेदना–' The agony which is severe because it has no remedy (प्रतिकार); for it is next to impossible that I shall ever secure the king's love.' कुत्र...प्रस्थितास्मि–मालविका is so much engrossed in her thoughts of love, that she has forgotten where she was to go. गौतमचापलात्–Through the mischief of Gautama i. e. विदूषक. Perhaps it was a part of his plans to see that the Queen sustains a fall from the swing, which he might have specially contrived. This gives an opportunity to मालविका to serve as a substitute for the Queen in fulfilling the cravings of Aśoka, and thereby get a chance to meet the king. Note how very deep-laid are the plans of विदूषक with a view to help the king in his love-affairs! III. 5. 20. अन्तरा निःश्वस्य–A sigh in the middle of her speech and just before what she is going to say gives a diferent construction to the whole sentence. It is tantamount to an expression of doubt as regards the queen's promise, which मालविका thinks, she will never be able to fulfil. " The Queen said to me, that if I succeed in getting the Aśoka to blossom within five nights, she will gratify me by giving me what I cherish most in my heart! And what else is that but the king's love? Will the Queen ever gratify me on that score! It is impossible. The Queen's promise, therefore, is all vain and can never be fulfilled by her." A series of such thoughts is suggested by this stage-direction, which thus lends a beautiful touch to the whole situation. अनुपदम्–Immediately after me पदस्य पश्चात् । चरणालंकारहस्तया-With the ornaments of the feet, such as red lac-dye, anklets, costume and other ornaments of the body. III. 5.25. शीधुपानोद्वेजितस्य मत्स्याण्डिका--Sugar for one who has become helpless under the intoxicating influence of wine (शीधु). ' मत्स्यण्डिका is a kind of fine sugar, so called because it is soft and yellowish-white like sand and is composed of globules like the eggs of fish (मत्स्याण्ड) '. The use of sugar is noted as an antidote against intoxication by liquor. Cf मद्यं पीत्वा यदि वा तत्क्षणमवलेढि शर्करां सघृताम् । मदयति न जातु मद्यं मनागपि प्रथितवीर्यमपि ॥ योगरत्न, cited by Pandit. विदूषक means ' the sight of मालविका will now certainly serve as a cure to your love-malady, under whose influence you have far gone.' III. 5.29. नातिपर्याप्तवेषा-Insufficiently or scantily dressed. नातिपर्याप्तः वेषः यस्याः सा।

III. 6. उच्छ्वसितम्-Revived, taken in a fresh breath, was refreshed. विक्लवं-Afflicted, distressed. तरुन्नतं... सारसात्-The king compares himself to a thirsty (पिपासतः) traveller, who is anxiously looking out for water, and feels revived as it were, when he hears the cry of the cranes which indicates the existence of water some where in the grove of trees. आरसित-Crying.

III. 8. मम जीवितमेतद्-Pointing to मालविका, the king says that his very life embodied in her is coming towards him. नितंबबिम्ब-The word बिम्ब means any round or disc-like surface ; the whole word would mean, therefore, ' Round hips. ' Cf. चक्काआरे रमणफलहे को वि कंचीमरट्टो । जिस्सा

तिस्सा उणवि भणिमो भूसणं दूसणं अ ॥ कर्पू० II. 23. समुन्नतं-swelling, uplifted. अत्यायतं-stretched far, very broad. III. 7. 8. अवस्थान्तरमुपारूढा-She has developed a change in her condition. She has grown pale and wears a few ornaments ; thus she looks like a Kunda creeper in spring with all its leaves ripened and a few blossoms left.

शर......स्थला-शरकाण्ड इव पाण्डु गण्डस्थलं यस्याः सा-whose broad cheeks(गण्डस्थलं) are pale like stalk of a reed(शर).परिमिताभरणा-with measured i. e. few ornaments. माधवपरिणतपत्रा-माधवेन-वसन्तेन परिणतानि पत्राणि यस्याः सा-whose leaves are ripened (परिणत) by spring. The ripened leaves correspond to the pale cheeks and the blossoms to the ornaments. Cf. छविः पाण्डुरा । पत्राणामिव शोषणेन मरुता स्पृष्टा लता माधवी । शा० III. I0. III. 8. 3. सौहार्द-Friendship, The king means that the विदूषक infers her condition to be due to love-sickness, on account of his great attachment for him. A friend looks at every thing with a favourable eye and tries to put a construction suited to his own interest, even in the absence of proper evidence for it. Cf. सर्वः कान्तमात्मीयं पश्यति । शा० II. III. 8. 6. अयं......अशोकः-The Aśoka imitates मालविका in her love-sick condition. Both of them have their delicate longings to be fulfilled and both have not put on the flowery robes (नेपथ्य). प्रच्छायशीतले-rendered cool by the thick shade (प्रच्छाय). Cf. तेन खस्यां प्रच्छायशीतलायां सप्तपर्णवेदिकायां मुहूर्तमुपविश्य परिश्रमविनोदं करोत्वार्यः । शा० I. III. 8. 12. नैता......मन्ये-with this much i. e. simply because she said that she too feels a longing in her heart (उत्कण्ठिता), I cannot assure myself with the thought that your conjecture that she is love-sick is correct. प्रसन्नतर्कः-प्रसन्नः तर्कः यस्य सः-Whose inference is clear or accurate.

III. 6. Vague longings are produced in the heart by the fragrant cool breezes in spring. वोढा-a noun of agency from $\sqrt{}$वह्, by the addition of the termination तृच्; 'One that carries along.' किस......नुगतः-किसलयपुटभेदेभ्यः निर्गतैः सीकरैः अनुगतः। Accompanied by the particles of water issuing from the opening folds of the tender sprouts. अनिमित्तामुत्कण्ठां-Causeless, vague longing. III. 9. 1. लतान्तरितौ-लताभिः अन्तरितौ-Screened or concealed by the creepers. III. 9. 5. ग्राह-A shark, crocodile, The king means that he would risk any thing for the sight of मालविका and if he sees her, he would not care for anybody. We shall, however, see later how this proves to be an idle boast of the king, who is at great pains to conciliate इरावती. III. 9. 8. निरवलम्बात्-Vain, fruitless, the basic object of which is beyond reach. III. 9. 9. विदूषक looks at the king, meaning to say "Look! here is additional evidence for what I conjucture. Don't you feel convinced?" III. 9. 10. स्नेहस्य वामतां-The perversity of love, which never runs a smooth logical straight-forward course.

III. 10. The king tries to bring out the perversity of love. "Here is मालविका in a state of anxious longing, but she has not spoken of the object of her love, for whom she is pining so much. विदूषक has put forth a conjecture with reference to me-a conjecture which does not always arrive at the truth. Very often we see how inferences go wrong. And yet in spite of all this, I am flattering myself with the thought that I am the object of her love and these lamentations are with reference to me and none else. Thus is love perverse, in that reason or no reason, the person clings obstinately to the object of his love and tries to feed himself with baseless conjectures even." For similar idea Cf. एवमात्माभिप्रायसंभावितेष्टजनचित्तवृत्तिः प्रार्थयिता विडम्ब्यते... । सर्वं तत्किल मत्परायणमहो कामी स्वतां पश्यति ॥ शा० II. तत्त्वावबोधैकरसः तत्त्वावबोधे एकरसः यस्य सः-whose chief or essential feature is the ascertainment of the truth. Too much reliance cannot be placed on inference which often is not accurate. रम्भोरु-रम्भा means a plantain tree; the expression means 'a beautiful lady having shapely round and tapering thighs like the interior stem of the plantain tree.' Cf. यास्यत्यूरुः सरसकदलीस्तम्भगौरश्चलत्वम् ॥ मे०II. लक्ष्यम्-Target, object, theme. III. 10. 3. अर्पितमदनसंदेशा-अर्पितः मदनसंदेशः यस्याः सा । To whom the message of love is given or entrusted for being communicated to मालविका. III. 10. 8. दास्याः सुता-The daughter of a slave; a term of abuse. III 10. 16. त्वं...योग्यतया नियुक्ता-You have been appointed by your fitness (योग्यतया). Mr. Pandit interprets it in an different way thus:—" You are now invested with an equality with the Queen (देव्याः योग्यतया); you are now made an equal of धारिणी; or you have been appointed to do a work fit to be done by a queen." III. 10. 20. हृदय...सुखिततया-Do not feel happy, do not flatter yourself with the happy position etc. She means that she cannot forget that she is after all a slave. The present glory is but momentary and, who knows, may serve as the last. मृत्युमण्डनं-The funeral decoration. Married women who die before their husbands or even virgins are decorated before their body is removed to the funeral pyre. She means that the unrequited love wi'l surely cause her death, aud in that case no additional decoration will be necessary for her! III. 10. 30. हला मर्षयेदानीम्-Now pardon me To all appearances मालविका was a maid-servant and therefore on an equal footing with बकुलावालिका. She has no right to claim such services from her and therefore asks her forgiveness for this impropriety on her part.

III, 11. सरसां रागरेखाम्-The wet streak of the paint. प्रथमा...द्रुमस्य-The tree of love was consumed to ashes by God Śiva. It has however revived now, and the lines of the paint appear to be the first sprouts of that tree. मदन or the God of love was burnt by the wrath of Śivā, when he first tried to infuse in his mind feelings of love for पार्वती. The third canto of कुमारसंभव gives a beautiful description of this incident. III. 11. 2. आधिकारः (उपक्षिप्तः) The duty has been assigned. V. L. अलंकारः (उपाक्षिप्तः)-which would mean 'quite a fitting decoration (of the paint and anklets) has been laid on the foot of this lady (तत्रभवत्याः) i. e. मालविका.'

III. 12. The king observes, in his romantic fervour, that she deserves to kick two things with such a beautiful foot—the Asoka tree and her lover who has given her a fresh offence. अग्रपाद-like अग्रहस्त, it would mean 'the fore-part i. e. the toes of the foot.' स्फुरितनखरुचा

with a flashing lustre of the nails. प्रणिहितशिरसम्-with a bowed head, with his head placed at the feet of his mistress. आर्द्रापराधम्-whose offence is wet i. e. fresh or recent. The offence generally consists of infidelity on his part, as he is observed turning his eyes on to another girl ; and the punishment meted out to him is a straight kick from his beloved, which he accepts ungrudgingly, nay, for which he seems to be longing in a way. Cf. एकः सख्यास्तव सह मया वामपादाभिलाषी । मे० II. 8. III. 12. पारयिष्यसि-You will be able (to offend her and get a kick in return). What he means is that very soon मालविका will be enlisted as his beloved with whom he will play the gallant. The sentence is read differently by some thus :—प्रहरिष्यति तत्रभवती त्वामपराद्धम् । 'Very soon she will strike you also, (after she has finished with the Aśoka).' III. 12. 3 सिद्धिदर्शिनः—One who foresees success. Cf. प्रातिगृहीतं ब्राणवच्चह्मनम् ॥ विक्र० II

III. 12. 4. युक्तमदा-In a state of intoxication. The introduction of इरावती in such a condition coupled with her youthful exuberance, explains her insolent behaviour with the king. III. 12. 7. शृणोमि...मण्डनम्--This youthful intoxication is a feature that lends special charm to women. Cf. नयनान्यरुणानि घूर्णयन् वचनानि स्खलयन् पदे पदे। असति त्वयि वारुणीमदः प्रमदानामधुना विडम्बना ॥ कुमा० IV.12. III,12. 10. प्रथमं...संवृत्तः-'Popular sayings or maxims very often have little truth in them. This saying, however, has become true because of you. The state of intoxication has really lent you a peculiar charm.' III. 12. 11. अलं मयि स्नेहेन-Cf.

सौहार्दमेवं पश्यति. । III. 12. 14. अखाण्डितात् प्रणयात्--Because of unfailing love (for my mistress). She means that the king loves her so much that he would never fail to keep this engagement. III. 12. 16 अलं सेवया...भण-Enough of this flattery. (सेवया Lit. servile attitude); speak with an impartial attitude (मध्यस्थता). III. 12. 19 वसन्तोपायनलोलुप-Greedy to receive the gifts of spring. III. 12. 30 परिहासनिमित्तम. To make fun of us; for the sake of joke. III. 12. 36. चूता...दंष्टम्-while searching for the king, निपुणिका has sighted मालविका being decorated by बकुलावलिका. Such a sight was most unpleasant and was very much like the biting of ants (पिपीलिका) for one who is up on the tree to find out a mango-sprout. पिपीलिका' The red ants living on trees. They are known in Konkan by the name of हुमले. The mango-tree is a very favourite abode of them. They configure its leaves into hollow globular nests for them'-Pandit. The sentence could be interpreted in a different way also. The Prakrit expression is दंसिदं which would gererally be translated by the Sanskrit word दार्शितं । the sentence would be-चूताङ्कुरं विचिन्वत्योरावयोः पिपीलिकाभिः दार्शितम् or as some Mss. read पिपीलिकादर्शनम्. It would then mean ' We see the red ants as we are in search of the mango-sprouts. The red ants are a sure indication of the existence of the mango-sprout in the vicinity, as smoke is that of fire. Similarly, since मालविका is here with बकुलावालिका, the king also must be near-by.' King's fondness for मालविका was an open scandal, being talked about by the inmates of the harem. इरावती also knows it, as she says later आशङ्कितस्य तावदन्तं गमिष्यामि ।. III. 12. 42. अभूमिरियं मालविकायाः–' A maid like मालविक cannot have access to this garden meant for the queens. This is therefore not a proper place (अभूमि) for her to be in! Cf. अभूमिरियमविनयस्य । शा॰ VII. We cannot however believe that even maids like मालविका were prohibited from entering into the प्रमदवन. If निपुणिका can come, why not मालविका? In the प्रवेशक at the beginning of this Act, the maid of परिव्राजिका moves about in the garden unrestricted. A better way of interpreting this sentence would be this :– ' This is certainly not the proper role for मालविका to play. Being waited upon by बकुलावलिका who has decorated her feet and dressed her as befits a queen, मालविका is thus transcending all bounds proper to a maid-servant, and playing the part of a queen, which is highly improper tor her (अभूमि)." III. 12. 49. संभावना–Honour. Some Mss. read 'महती खलु मे संभावना ' It is a great honour done to *me* indeed!' said, of course, ironically. इरावती means that the queen धारिणी has shown the greatest disrespect to her in asking her maid-servant to play her role, instead of asking her, the queen's equal, to play that part. In her jealousy, The queen has shown to इरावती great disrespect. III. 12. 57. स्थाने...हृदयम्–She has observed the charming figure of मालविका and then said this sentence. ' It is but proper that my heart is filled with fear. The king certainly will desert me for the sake of such a girl.' III. 12. 60. चरण...विन्यसः–The drawing of the different lines of the red paint on the foot. III. 12. 62. आत्मन... प्रशंसितुम्. I feel so awkward to appreciate your skill, just because you have exhibited that on *my* foot. I am afraid it would appear I am praising my own foot and not your skill.

III. 12. 66. त्वरस्वे...दक्षिणायै–'Be quick now to receive your reward as a teacher. 'बकुलावलिका has made you her teacher in this art; and very soon she would gratify you, her teacher, with the nice present (दक्षिणा) of मालविका ! ' It can be interpreted in another way also, as a remark of विदूषक in answer to the ingenious invention of बकुलावलिका in representing the king to मालविका as her teacher. ' Well then, if that is the case, make haste to repay the obligation by giving him his due reward. Be quick to give your teacher his reward. " III. 12. 67. दिष्ट्या...–सि–' It is so good of you that you have not the slightest conceit; you are prepared to give the credit where it is due. ' This indicates her regard and love for the king. III. 12. 74. सिद्धं मे दौत्यम्– I have succeeded in my mission ! मालविका has clearly indicated how she feels for the king, and the way has been paved now for success in my enterprise as love-messenger. She is a soft soil, and I can hope to get immediate success. ' III. 12. 75. मुखमारुतो लम्भयितव्यः- It ought to be dried by blowing on it the wind from the mouth (मुखमारुत). प्रवातः–प्रकृष्ट वातः यस्मिन् सः—Windy, having a good breeze.

III. 13. The king says that a very nice opportunity has come now to offer his first services of love to मालविका, viz. helping her foot to dry up by blowing on it the wind from the mouth, and he is sorry that he cannot avail himself of it. प्रथमतरः सेवावकाशः—An excellent (प्रथमतर) occasion for doing service. III. 13. 1. अनुशयः-Regret, remorse, grief. चिरं......वितव्यम् You need not be sorry for having lost this opportunity. You will get many such occasions in course of time. III. 13. 4. अरुणशतपत्रम् A red lotus having hundred petals. अंकपरिवर्तिनी-Rolling about on the lap. Note the clever and bold way in which बकुलावलिका works up the mind of मालविका in favour of the king. III. 13. 6. इरावती......प्रवेक्षते-इरावती looks at निपुणिका, with a feeling of surprise at such a bold blessing of बकुलावालिका, and also with a view to indicate that their suspicion proved correct. III. 13. 8. अवचनीयं मन्त्रयसे-You speak absurd things which you ought not to say (अवचनीय). Cf. युवामपेतम् । किमपि हृदये कृत्वा मन्त्रयेथे ।...... also इमामसंबद्धप्रलापिनीं प्रियंवदामार्यायै गौतम्यै निवेदयामि । शा०I. III. 13. 12. प्रिया......तव. We can also take it as a question. 'Do you love me ?' III. 13. 15. गुणे......भर्तुरपि-The king also loves you, drawn towards you by your merits for which he has great attraction (आभिनिवेश). III. 13. 18. एतदेव मयि नास्ति-'I havent that in me i. e. the king's love. Surely I know the king loves me not.' एतत् may also refer to merits. I have'nt that i. e. merit in me. मालविका says this to draw out बकुलावालिका who, she thinks, is expected to know more of the king, being his pupil and thus coming into closer contact with him. III.

13. 20. सत्यं.........दृश्यते-' you have'nt that indeed!'.— this she says a bit ironically. She means ' who would believe that you have not the king's love? It is fully betrayed by the thin and pale limbs of the king.' Cf. ननु भणितमेव कमलनालायमानैरङ्गैः विक्र० II. III. 13. 22. प्रथमगणित- Considered or thought well beforehand. हताशा-Lit. a disappointed creature. It is a term of abuse in the sense of ' Accursed, wretch,' approaching the Marathi expression 'मेली' III. 13. 25. अनु...कुरु-'And now follow the authoritative dictates of the wise in this matter— Love should be tested by love.' If you have any doubts as to what I have said about the king, you can realise that for yourself; if you express your love to him you will soon find that your love is responded by him. III. 13. 27. आत्मनश्छन्देन-From your fancy or imagination. The king's love for me is your own invention and therefore not true. III. 13. 30. बिम्बान्तरितानि अक्षराणि— Words that are being echoed or exactly reproduced (by me). She means that what she has said in this matter is an echo of whatever the king has spoken ; it is not her invention. बकुलावलिका has thus clearly hinted that she speaks under instructions from the king whose message of love she is communicating. III. 13. 33. देवीं ...विश्वसिति—मालविका feels convinced of the king's love, but then there is the insurmountable difficulty of the Queen, which fills her heart with diffidence in any love's enterprise that she would undertake. III. 13. 35. भ्रमर...तंसनीयः- She means that the fear of the queen should not deter मालविका from loving the king. There may be some

risk, but nobody leaves off the pursuit of one's cherished object because of such threatening dangers. भ्रमरसंबाध–' The swarm of bees; or the dread of bees ' अवतंसनीयः–Should be put on as an ear-ornament (अवतंस) Pot. Part. from अवतंसय्–A denom. from अवतंस; Cf. अवतंसयन्ति दयमानाः प्रमदाः शिरीषकुसुमानि । शा० I. 3. III. 38. त्वं...भव ' If any calamity befalls me in this enterprise, at least you will help me through.' मालविका has consented to respond to the king's love, and hence she appeals to her to help her in the perilous situation, if any would develop later. दुर्जातं–Peril, calamity; cf. मम सुरारिसंभवे दुर्जाते महाराज एव शरणमासीत् । विक्र० II. III. 13. 39.विमर्दसुरभि.–Fragrant when crushed (विमर्द). She puns on the word बकुलावलिका i. e. a garland of बकुल flowers which would emit greater fragrance when crushed. Similarly she says that मालविका would find her at her best when she is faced with danger or calamity.

III. 14. The king admires the skilful way in which बकुलावलिका has tried to win over मालविका to her purpose. भाव...प्रस्तुतेन वाक्येन–the words (in the message of love) which बकुलावलिका began to speak (प्रस्तुत), after having ascertained her love for the king (भावज्ञान). प्रत्याख्याने...त्तरेण (वाक्येन)–while pleading she gave proper replies to meet the objections (प्रत्याख्यान) raised by मालविका. स्वे निदेशे स्थापिता thus was मालविका brought round or won over to her (बकुलावलिका) purpose; made firm in her own purpose. स्थाने...धीनाः–It is quite proper that a lover's life is in the hands of his love messenger.

Everything depends on her and the way in which she would manage the affair. The success is assured if the pleading is done skilfully. III. 14. 2कारि...विका- मालविका has already been induced to get access in him i. e. to yearn for him, to love him. She has already been made ready to embark on love's adventure. Cf. काम इदानीं सकामो भवतु येनासत्यसन्धे जने सखी पदं कारिता। शा० IV. III. 14. 5. निर्विकारस्यापि-Even of a person who is unaffected by passion निपुणिका tries to put the whole blame on बकुलावलिका who, says he, is encouraging innocent मालविका in this affair. III. 14. 7. स्थाने...हृदयम् 'My heart was rightly apprehensive. I don't think बकुलावलिका is solely responsible, मालविका also has a hand in the matter.' She is not so innocent; She thus refuses to accept निपुणिका's reading of मालविका. गृहीतार्था-Who has ascertained all facts. III. 14. 11. समाप्तपरिकर्मा-Whose decoration (परिकर्मन्) has finished. परिकर्मन्-Decoration, toilet, dressing. यावदेनं कृताचारपरिकर्माणं प्रेक्षे। शा० II. III. 14. 1L. श्रुतं...दानीम्- 'So now it turns to be the queen's bidding. मालविका is not here of her own accord, but because the Queen धारिणी has sent her on some mission.' 'इरावती has been suspecting that धारिणी herself is at the bottom of the affair, and thinks that she is now satisfied that her suspicions are correct and that she wants to know no more.'—Pandit. III. 14. 17. एष...दृश्यते-This speech is so worded that it refers both to the bunch of sprouts of the Aśoka tree as also to the king. With reference to the king, it would mean 'Here is he, greatly enamoured or flushed with passion (उपारूढराग) and fit to enjoy—(उपभोगक्षमः)

III. 14. 18. किं भर्ता–The trick of बकुलावलिका has succeeded and मालविका who understands her remark with reference to the king, clearly declares her love for the king. III. I4. 23. पर्याप्त...कामिनाम्–This is quite enough (पर्याप्तं) for lovers. A lover is amply satisfied to know that his love is returned by his beloved. The actual union may or may not take place.

III. 15. अनातुरोत्कण्ठितयोः समागमेन–By the union of the two in which one of them is very eager while the other is indifferent (अनातुर). प्रसिध्यतापि–Even if it succeeds. The king means that he would feel no pleasure (रति) in a union in which one of the lovers is panting with love while the other is utterly indifferent. पर...रागयोः-On the other hand, requited mutual love cares not for the bodily union and would not mind even if death ensues through the despair of securing such a union. It is far better to die loving each other though not actually united rather than be wedded to one who is utterly indifferent. 'अकृतार्थेऽपि मनासिजे रतिमुभयप्रार्थना कुरुते' । शा॰ II. 1. समानुरागयोः—Whose love is equal.

III. 16. सदृशाविनिमयात्. Because of this mutal exchange of similar gifts. The Aśoka tree has given her a *red* sprout for an ear-ornament, while she in return gave him a kick of her *red* foot. The exchange of gifts is thus of like objects. आत्मानं वंचितं मन्ये—'Both of them have thus satisfied each other, while I stand looking on. I feel I am deceived in my love for the girl.' Cf. वयं

तत्वान्वेषान्मधुकर हतास्त्वं खलु कृती । शा० I. 20. III. 16.5. निर्गुणः- dull, unappreciative, devoid of the good qualities of a gentleman. कुसुमोद्भेदमन्थरः-Slow to put forth blossoms. III. 17.मुखरं...विणा-मुखरैः नूपरैः आरौति-तच्छीलमस्य-तेन । loudly tinkling with the noisy or jingling anklets. 'ललितं साधारणं दोहदम्-A craving that is in common with that of the gallant lovers, who too cherish a kick from their beloved. ललितकामी is explained by Mr. Pandit as 'a person fond of the graceful actions of young women' स्त्रीविलसित-कामी, विलसनशीलः कामी वा ।. III. 17.1. वचनावसरपूर्वम्-'Creating an opportunity for speaking.' 'I should enter after such an occasion to speak has been created.' III. 17. 6 इदं...हृदयेन'-did anticipate that in my heart, I had already suspected the king to be hovering about on account of his love for this girl.' III. 17.13. त्वया गृहीतार्थया-you who know everything. III, 17.18. कथं...जीविष्यति-'How otherwise should this wretched Brahmin live? It is thus that he makes his living by pampering to the king's tastes and providing him with what he wants'. ब्रह्मबंधुः- A contemptuous term for a Brahmin; an unworthy Brahmin. Cf. the Marathi word भटुरगा. III. 17. 22. एन ...यम् She has not acted independently on his own initiative in this transgression; she depends on another viz. the queen who has ordered her to do this. परवती— Depending on another. जाने तपसो वीर्यं सा बाला परवतीति मे विदितम् । शा० III. 1. भगवन् परवानयं जनः प्रतिकूलाचरितं क्षमस्व मे । रघु० VII. 81.

III. 18. Construe-विलासिनि वामोरु, किसलयमृदोः ते वामस्य

चरणस्य कठिने पादस्कन्धे निहितस्य संप्रति बाधा न? विलासिनी full of graces, charming, sportive. वामोरु-Oh one possessed of lovely thighs. III. 18. 3. अहो...पुत्रः-' How immodest is my lord ! ' The king's appearance on the scene, his raising her by her hands, and then such a question were too much for इरावती who saw in it nothing but his indecent flirting with the girl. There is another good reading नवनीतहृदयः ' Possessed of a heart as soft as butter ; ' in her caustic sarcasm she means, ' What a soft heart my lord has ! It melts like butter at the sight of a tender foot kicking the hard stem of a tree, while totally forgetting the engagement he has given to me '! III. 18. 9. उपपन्नावसरं अर्थित्वम्-My request whose occasion has come.

III. 19. The king means that in his case also, as in that of the Aśoka, the flower of happiness has not bloomed. He too has a craving viz. the nectar of touch. Will she satisfy this longing, since he has no desire left for anything else now ? धृतिपुष्पम्-The flower of pleasure or happiness. न बध्नाति-has not borne. चिरात् प्रभृति-for a long time. अनन्यरुचेः-न विद्यते अन्यस्मिन्-अन्यस्यां वा-रुचिः यस्य सः तस्य-Having a liking for nothing else or for no other woman. III. 19. 4. अयं...फलति च-He i. e. the king will not only flower but will also bear fruit. In the case of the Aśoka there is a doubt as to whether it will put forth even flowers. But if the king is satisfied by you in his craving, he will bear both the flowers and the fruit. As Pandit observes, this is certainly a coarse allusion to the fact that मालविका would bear children to the King and thus reap a greater advantage. ' The coarseness of the allusion is in keeping with the condition of इरावती, who is under the influence of wine.' III. 19. 7. जङ्घाबल-The strength of the legs ; taking to the heels. We must try the strength of our legs and vanish. III.19.10.साधु...न्तम्-' You are carrying on very well ;' she says this, of course, sarcastically,, as one would say in Marathi, वा ! फार छान चालवलंय ! III. 19. 13. के...हस्य-' Insignificant maids that we are, who are we to receive such a favour of love from the king ?' III.19.17. मया...विज्ञाता-I did not realise the deception (वंचना) that was being practised on me,being all the time unsuspicious (अशंकितया) like the deer charmed (रक्तया) by the hunter's song. The deer is believed to be very much fond of the hunter's whistle or music, with which he beguiles the innocent creature into a trap. Cf. व्याधानुसारचकिता हरिणीव यासि । मृच्छ० I. Cf. also the सुभाषितः-यस्य चाप्रियमन्विच्छेत् तस्य कुर्यात् सदा प्रियम् । व्याधा मृगवधं कर्तुं सम्यग्गायन्ति सुस्वरम् । Similarly, says इरावती, that she was being deceived by the king with false promises of love and engagements, while out here he was carrying on his flirtation with another girl. III. 19. 21. प्रतियोजय-Devise, plan. कर्म......भवति - If a thief is caught in the very act of thieving (कर्मगृहीतेन), the only plausible defence that he can submit is that he was there learning the art of cutting or digging holes in the wall (सन्धिच्छेदन). Cf. लोप्त्रेण गृहीतस्य

कुम्भीलकस्यास्ति वा प्रतिवचनम् । विक्र० III. विदूषक means, you have been caught now in the very act of flirting with मालविका, and you have therefore to give some sort of defence that will absolve you from the guilt of infidelity and prove you to be innocent. Like the thief who, caught red-handed, would say that he was only taking an academical interest in the art without any personal motive of actually committing the robbery, can you not also say that you have no personal interest in मालविका whom you chanced to meet and therefore tried to pass away your time in some light-hearted conversation with her? III. 19. 23. अर्थः-Interest. आत्मा विनोदितः-I diverted or amused myself. III. 19. 27. विश्वसनीयोऽसि-'I should cartainly believe you;' she says this of course, ironically. ईदृशं विनोदवस्तुकं-Such a means of amusement viz. मालविका. The repetition of विनोद is for the purpose of giving a sarcastic retort to the king's expression विनोदितः. अन्यथा...क्रियते-Had I known that you had such a nice means of amusing yourself, I would certainly not have done thus, unfortunate that I am: I would never have interrupted your amusement.' III. 19. 31. मा...भणतु-'Do not say anything that would repel his courtesy.' विदूषक means, 'The king is all along behaving with you with the utmost politeness. Remarks like these, however, will only provoke him unnecessarily and would drive off all courtesy from his mind.' उपरोधं-उपरोधकारकं वचनं-words calculated to put a stop to the considerations of courtesy. समा......प्रमाणम्-Mere matter-of-fact talk with the Queen's servant met accidentally can not be looked upon as a serious offence. Is it so? I ask you as the best judge in the matter?' संकथा talk, conversation. III. 19. 38. रशनासंदितचरणा–with her feet fettered or entangled (संदित) by the girdle (रशना). It had dropped down from her waist in her angry excited condition that caused hurried movements. III. 19 39. निरपेक्षता–utter disregard, indifference. III. 19. 40. शठः—A rogue, a cunning lover who affects his love for one lady while secretly loving another–गूढविप्रियकरः ।.

III. 20. परिचयवत्यवधीरणा–It could be interpreted in two different ways ; (i) परिचयवती अवधीरणा–' The usual scorn.' The king says that he has often met with such treatment of utter disregard from her ; it is not a new thing to him or to her. (ii) परिचयवति अवधीरणा–Disregard shown to a person who has been too familiar. ' Familiarily breeds contempt.' It is nothing unusual, therefore, if she behaves thus towards one who stands too intimately related to her. Such is not, however, the case of the girdle, which is prostrate at her feet for the first time. चरण etc. construe—चरणपतितया मेखलयापि याचिता, हे चण्डि, तां (अवधीरणां) न विसृजसि–The girdle is at your feet, pleading for mercy on my behalf. With a male companion, you could be rude ; but not so with your female companion, the girdle (मेखला Fem.). Still, Oh angry one, you do not leave off your scornful attitude. चण्डी–A hot-tempered lady. Cf. चण्डी मामवधूय पादपतितं जातानुतापा यथा । It is also read by some as चण्डितां–'Angry attitude,' to be construed with विसृजसि. III.20. 1. इय...सरति–'This wretched girldle also sides with you.' It too appeared to be working for the king, since it would not allow इरावती to leave the place quickly, but wanted to detain her with the king.

III. 21. इरावती in tears, striking the king with the golden girdle is compared to a row of showering clouds smiting the विन्ध्य peak with lightning. वाष्पासारा to be taken with both इरावती and मेघराजि ; आसार means 'a shower.' अव्यपेक्षाच्युतेन—dropping down unexpectedly or accidentally, चण्डं हन्तुं अभ्युद्यता-Prepared to strike me hard or cruelly (चण्डं). मेघराजि-Row of clouds. III. 21. 1. भूयोऽपि-Again, for a second time. Already before she had raised the girdle to strike him; See the stage-direction इति रशनामादाय राजानं ताडयितुमिच्छति । This was the second time.

III. 22. उद्यतं दण्डं किं संहरासि-Why should you take back (संहरासि) the whip (viz, girdle) raised against me ? वर्धयासि विलसितं-You increase your charms. इरावती, flushed red with anger, and ready to strike the king with the girdle. was a fascinating sight for the king. III. 22. 1. नून...तम्-' This will be now permitted. 'She would not now object to my falling prostrate at her feet, which form of conciliation, she will receive with favour, in her present mood.' III. 22. 4. स्पर्शदोहदं पूरयिष्यत:-which will fulfil your craving for the touch. It is a sarcastic reference to what the king had demanded of मालविका-'स्पर्शामृतेन पूरय दोहदमस्याप्यनन्यरुचेः । III. 19. III. 22. 5. उत्तिष्ठ कृतप्रसादोऽसि-विदूषक says jokingly. ' The favour has been shown to you,' that is she has made her exit, and thus removed the source of disturbance! III. 22. 10. देवै... नियंत्रणा-इरावती served as a great check in his affair with मालविका. Somehow she has departed, and it is therefore a matter for rejoicing. The gods have shown us a great favour in removing this great obstacle in the way of your improper relations (अविनयस्य) with मालविका. Mr. Pandit reads differently thus-दिष्ट्या अस्याविनयस्य अप्रसादिता गता. "It is good that इरावती has erred by going away unreconciled and has thereby furnished the king with an excuse for paying his court to मालविका; if she had not done so, it would have been so very difficult to disregard a loving and unoffending wife as इरावती." Pandit. This also is a good interpretation. Even though the king's motto is–न हि कमलिनीं दृष्ट्वा ग्राहमवेक्षते मतंगजः, he can now pursue the object of his love without feeling the qualms of conscience regarding इरावती, as in her case he had done everything he could reasonably do to reconcile her. She has spurned his prostration and thus lost some moral advantage in her favour, and weakened her case. A feeling of repentence comes over then, and the woman tries to conciliate her lord Cf. अवधूतप्राणिपाताः पश्चात् संतप्यमानमनसोऽपि। निभृतैर्व्यपत्रपन्ते दयितानुनयैर्मनस्विन्यः॥ विक्र० III. 5. For a similar remark of विदूषक Cf. अनुकूलमत्रभवत एतत्। न खल्वक्षिदुःखितः अभिमुखे दीपशिखां सहते। विक्र० II. III. 22. 9. साव...करोति--before she comes back like the planet Mars (अंगारक) retrogressing to his mansion (राशि) in the Zodiac. 'In certain positions planets are said to look towards you and in others to turn away from you. When they have turned their back on you, they are said to be unfavourable, and when they are looking towards you, they are favourable. Mars is the only exception, because when it returns and looks you in the face, it is unfavourable. In the present instance, इरावती who has gone unreconciled and and turned her back upon the king is more favourable to the king's paying his attentions to मालविका, than she would be if she were to return and be reconciled, as that would make it difficult to disregard her.' III. 22. 13. मनसिजवैषम्यम्-The perversity or inconsistency of love.

III. 23. The king means that in his present condition of the mind which has been solely captured by मालविका, इरावती's spurning of his prostration is a definite service rendered to him by her; for even though she loves him, she has departed in anger. He can therefore safely ignore her for the time being. प्रणिपातलङ्घनं-The slighting of the prostration. एवं etc. Construe-मयि प्रणयवती (अपि) एवं कुपिता सा उपेक्षितुं शक्यम् ।. ' It is possible to connive at or neglect her though full of love for me, since she is in such an angry mood.' Cf. किं तु प्राणिपातलंघनादहमस्यां धैर्यमवलम्बिष्ये । विक्र० II. The perversity of love lies in the fact that he feels like ignoring the one who loves him ardently while the one towards whom he is drawn is away at a distance and almost inaccessible to him. The translation has been given with the following reading—एवं प्रणयवती सा नहि शक्यमुपेक्षितुं कुपिता ।

ACT IV.

IV. 1. The king enters in a love-sick state all the time thinking of मालविका and brooding over the possibility of his being able to taste the pleasures of love in his union with her. His love he compares to a tree which first strikes the root, then puts forth a shoot, then blossoms and lastly yields the delicious fruit. Similarly the feeling of love for मालविका was rooted in his heart when he first heard of her and felt interested in her. When he saw her, love appeared to have put forth the shoot of passion. The touch of her hands sent a thrill of horripilation through his body, a veritable blossoming, as it were, of this feeling. Will he be lucky now in tasting the joys of love, as one would the delicious flavour of the fruit ? श्रुतिपथगतां तामाश्रित्य–'Resorting to her who came to my ears i. e. when I merely heard of her, as the tree gets planted in the soil.' मालविका represents the soil. श्रुतिपथगतां तां भूमिं वृक्ष इव ।. आस्था–Interest, attachment. रूढरागप्रवालः–रूढः राग एव प्रवालः यस्य सः. The tree whose sprout of passion was put forth. मुकुलितः–मुकुलानि संजातानि अस्य–with the buds produced on the tree ; for a similar idea in this line, Cf. स्पृष्टः सरोमविक्रियमङ्कुरितं मनसिजेनेव ॥ विक्र० I. 11. व्यक्त...त्वात् With the horripilation (i. e. the hair standing on their ends) becoming manifest (at the touch). कुर्या...फलस्य–Construe–मनसिजतरुः क्लान्तं मां फलस्य रसज्ञं कुर्यात् किम् ? 'I feel now weary (क्लान्त) at heart ; will this tree of love enable me to taste the flavour of its fruit ? रसज्ञः–रसं

जानात्यसौ—Who knows i. e. tastes the flavour. Some read कान्तं for क्लान्तं, meaning 'a lover.'

IV. 1. 6. सरुजचरणत्वात्-Because of her aching feet. IV. 1. 11. यो...काया-मालविका fares now as does a cuckoo seized by a cat, which means she is now ruined once for all. IV. 1. 16. पिङ्गलाक्षी-The queen having eyes, which turn to reddish-brown colour under the influence of wrath. सारभाण्डभूमिगृहे-In an under-ground cellar where all precious valuables or treasures (सारभाण्ड) are stored. It is a veritable death-trap for her. IV. 1. 17. मत्संपर्कम्-My contact; meeting me. IV. 1. 10. विमुखः अस्माकम् Averse to us, opposed or ill-disposed towards us. IV. 1. 23. विहस्त-Lit. Handless, i. e. disabled, incapacited, made powerless. Cf. रामापरित्राणाविहस्तयोधं सेनानिवेशं तुमुलं चकार। रघु० V. 49. सुखप्रच्छिका-सुखं पृच्छतीति-Inquiring after health. IV. 1. 28. किं...जन इति-'Have you lately seen the loved person i. e. the king'? Mr. Pandit who has the same reading, interprets it thus, 'Why have I not seen the beloved one i. e. you, इरावती ?' The Commentator काटयवेम reads differently-किं नु नावलोकितो वल्लभजनः। VI. 1. 29. कुतो...पृच्छसीति-' Why this formal questioning, when you know full well, how far your servant i. e. myself enjoys the king's love'? She means that धारिणी ought to know that the king does no more care for इरावती; her question therefore proceeds from mere formality and possibly smacks of some sarcasm also. Another way in which it is interpreted, "Why this formal courtesy, knowing full well that the title of the 'beloved one' belongs now to your servant i. e. मालविका ?" Mr. Pandit reads- मदो वा उपचारो वा । यत्ते परिजनस्य वल्लभत्वं जानत्यपि पृच्छसीति— ' This is either an affront (मदः lit. arrogance) or an empty form, since you ask the question, knowing that the belovedness belongs to your maid-servant.' IV. 1. 30. निर्भेदाद् ऋते-Without distinct or direct mention. ' without a giving out (निस्) of the name of मालविका.' उपन्यासः-Suggestion,reference. Cf. पावकः खलु एष वचनोपन्यासः । शा० V. IV. 1. 33. अनुबध्यमाना-Being importuned or asked again and again, being pressed. भवतो...कृता-The Queen was made acquainted i. e. informed about (अन्तरेण) your indiscretion (अविनय). IV. 1. 35. दीर्घरोषता—Long-continued, persistent anger. IV. 1. 39. निगलवत्यौ-chained in fetters. अदृष्ट...भवत:-They are enjoying their residence in the nether world where the sun's rays (पाद) are not visible, as if they were two snake-maidens (नागकन्यके). The पाताल or nether world is supposed to be inhabited by the नाग्स or snakes whose maidens are belived to be very beautiful.

IV. 2. विबुद्धचूतसाङ्गिन्यै-Clinging to the full-bloomed (बिबुद्ध) mango-blossom. प्रबलपुरोवातया अकालवृष्ट्या-By an untimely shower preceded by (पुरस्) a strong gale. पुरोवात is understood by some to mean 'the front or the opposing wind.' कोटरं गमिते-are driven to the hollow of a tree (कोटरं) बकुलावालिका, the love-messenger, is compared to a cuckoo whom the Sanskrit poets style as Cupid's messenger;Cf. त्वां कामिनो मदनदूतिमुदाहरन्ति । वि० IV. 11; and मालविका is made to resemble the female bee. The king represents the mango tree while the hollow is the cellar. Thus the metaphor is complete.

IV. 2. 1. उपक्रमस्य गतिः-Scope for some plan or stratgem IV. 2. 5. मम......मोक्तव्या-Prof. Tawney remarks on this, ' It is clear that the head queen exercised in some departments an amount of authority that would have de lighted the soul of Mr. J. S. Mill. ' IV. 2. 12. कर्णे ते कथयामि-A similar devise as in the I Act is introduced here, and the plan speaks highly of the inventive brain of the विदूषक. IV. 2. 16. रक्तचन्दनधारिणा-smeared with the red sandal paste. This application was to serve as an embrocation to the foot. The other reading रक्तचन्दनवारिणा is interpreted as ' an oil of red sandal wood.' IV. 2.22. जयसेना...गच्छ-the king asks विदूषक to take his female attendant जयसेना also into confidence. She has observed the विदूषक whispering some secret in the king's ears and hence this precaution. Her assistance was also necessary for putting into practice the dodge for bringing the Queen's ring to liberate मालविका and her friend बकुलावलिका. IV. 2. 33. उपचारयन्त्रणा-the restraint imposed by the conventional formality; the worry of the etiquette.

IV. 3. अनुचितनूपुरविरहं (चरणं)-अनुचितः नूपुरैः विरहः यस्य-The foot whose separation of the anklets is unusual, unaccustomed to leave off the anklets, which were removed because of the paining foot. कलभाषिणि-Talking in a sweet voice; Cf. मां वा नयाशु कलभाषिणि यत्र कान्ता। विक्र० IV. 11. IV. 3. 4. अस्ति मे विशेषः-There is a definite change for the better. The same expression occurs in शा० III. IV. 3 5. यज्ञोपवीतबद्धाङ्गुष्ठः-with his thumb tied up by the sacred thread.यज्ञोपवीतं-the sacred thread worn over the left shoulder and under the right arm ; originally it was the ceremony of investiture with the sacred thread. the विदूषक resorts to this first aid with a view apparently to stop the circulation of the poison of the snake by which he pretends to be bitten. संभ्रान्तः-Excited,agitated. IV. 3. 11. आचा...णात्-for the purpose of collecting flowers for a customary offering. Such an offering is given to the deities or to great persons when one visits them. Cf. अवाकिरन् बाललताः प्रसूनैराचारलाजैरिव पौरकन्याः । रघु० II. 10. विदूषक had already provided for his pretence when he said just before that he would find some present for the Queen whom he was visiting shortly Cf. अहमपि देवीं द्रष्टुमरिक्तपाणिर्भविष्यामि ।. He refers to it again in this sentence (देवीं द्रक्ष्यामि) with a view to make out that he has risked his life for the Queen who in a way is thus responsible for this disaster. IV. 3 13. जीवितसंशयनिमित्तं-The cause of danger (संशय) to his life. IV. 3. 19 द्वे दन्तपदे-The two marks of its fangs. These were in reality the pricks purposely caused by means of the pointed tips of the केतक plant. Observe how cleverly the विदूषक has arranged for the whole make-up.

IV. 4. दंशच्छेदः-Excision of the bitten part, amputation. क्षतेः रक्तमोक्षणम्-Bleeding the wound, taking off the blood from the wound (क्षतिः). दष्टमात्राणां-Immediately after they are bitten. आयुषः प्रतिपत्तयः-Remedies

(प्रतिपत्ति) to save the life. Cf. प्रतिकारविधानमायुषः सति शेषे हि फलाय अल्पते। रघु० VIII. The remedies have been suggested by परिव्राजिका, because as Mr. Pandit says, धारिणी should not suspect her. For we can suppose that the विदूषक must have settled his plan in consultation with the परिव्राजिका, before she went to the Queen and he came over to see the king. Her presence with the Queen was necessary, as in the first Act, for the purpose of removing any suspicion of her hand in the matter and also to help विदूषक in inducing the Queen to part with her ring. ' It is also intended to give her a character for learning and knowledge of medicine.' The remedies referred to here are found mentioned in the medicine manuals of authors like वाग्भट and others. The वैद्यचंद्रोदय mentions the following in this connection—आदौ तु स्रावयेद् रक्तं छित्वा शस्त्रेण दंशतः। बहिर्वेगीकृते रक्ते विषं तस्माद्विनश्यति ॥. IV. 4. 8. सिमसिमायन्ति—Tingle with pain. This is an onomatopoetic or imitative verb, expressive of a tremulous and aching sensation, probably convulsive. The corresponding Marathi form शिवशिवतात comes from this Prakrit word. IV. 4. 11. अशुभं...विकारेण. The trouble (of the snake-bit) has taken a bad turn, seems to prove fatal. योगक्षेमं वह–Look after the welfare. योग means ' a fresh acquision of things not obtained already '; while क्षेम is 'the preservation of what has been acquired.' योगश्च क्षेमश्च योगक्षेमम्। Cf. तेषां नित्याभियुक्तानां योगक्षेमं वहाम्यहम् । भग० IX. 22. The Prakrit word आविआरेण may be translated into Sanskrit in two ways:-(i) आविचारेण-' without hesitation ' or (ii) अविकारेण-Without any change (in behaviour). IV. 4. 17. चिकित्सते—treats you, cures you. IV. 4. 19. ध्रुव......गौतमः—It is necessary that विदूषक must leave to effect the release of मालविका and बकुलावलिका from the prison. Having, therefore, arranged the plan, either he or the परिव्राजिका must have spoken about it to the king's physician before coming to the garden. IV. 4. 21. वर्षवर-a eunuch, an attendant in the women's apartments. वर्षधर or वर्षधर्ष also means the same thing. IV. 4. 28. यथार्थनाम्नः of one whose name is significant or true to its sense. The name ध्रुवसिद्धि of the surgeon meant 'one who gets a sure success, an infallible doctor.' IV. 4. 32. उद........कल्पयितव्यम्-For performing the magic rite of उदकुम्भविधान, something bearing a serpent-seal (सर्पमुद्रितं) has to be utilised. The उदकुंभविधान rite has been mentioned in works like the भैरवतंत्र as a magic remedy against serpent-bites. A jar is filled with water and certain Mantras are repeated. The enchanted water is then sprinkled over the part bitten by a snake, repeating the same Mantras again. It is assured that the poison of the deadliest serpent is thus counteracted. The reading उदकुंभपिधाने means 'for the purposing of covering the jar.'

IV. 4. 37. कर्मसिद्धौ-When the treatment has proved successful ; कर्म refers to the treatment of the doctor; Cf. संप्रति विषवैद्यानां कर्म ।, प्रातिपात्तिः–' News,information. The same sentence occurs in मुद्रा० IV. Cf. also कियच्चिरेणार्यपुत्रः प्रतिपात्तिं दास्यतीति । शा० VI. It may also be taken as a hint to

जयसेना to tell the king when the plot has succeeded and मालविका has been released. IV. 4. 40 यथा...निर्विषो गौतमः— The परिव्राजिका puts on an air of one who is thoroughly ignorant of the plot and makes this remark which bears these different interpretations. (i) 'As my heart tells me, गौतम is by now cured of the poison, or (ii) गौतम has been bitten by a non-poisonous snake.' To the king she suggests 'the snake-bite is a hoax and गौतम is simply pretending the effects of poison of which he has nothing.' IV. 4. 43. प्रकृतिस्थः-प्रकृतौ तिष्ठति सः- came back to the normal, his usual self or his natural condition. IV. 4. 45. वचनीयात्-From the censure or blame of having been indirectly responsible for the death of the poor Brahmin! IV. 4. 49. एष...विज्ञापयति-This is again another falsehood invented to enable the king to leave धारिणी immediately without rousing her suspicion. Note how the innocent soft-hearted Queen is being successfully duped by a pack of scoundrels around her ! IV. 4. 52. आतपाक्रान्तः-Full of the sun's heat. शीत...प्रशस्ता-A cooling remedy (शीतक्रिया) is to be preferred for this i.e. for your aching foot. The king affects a deep concern for the Queen that she may be lulled into an unsuspicious mental slumber.

IV. 5. एकान्तसाधु-Absolutely good. सन्दिग्धं-doubtful. diffident P, P. of √सम् + दिह्. The king feels doubtful whether विदूषक would succeed in releasing मालविका. IV.5. 1. सर्वमङ्गलकर्माणि-' All auspicious ceremonies,' referring humorously to the very undertakings like the release of मालविका and the bringing about of another meeting between the two. IV. 5. 6. क्षुद्रा–Insignificant, worthless, dull-headed. IV. 5. 13. प्रत्युत्पन्नबुद्धिः–Ready-witted; also प्रत्युत्पन्नमतिः।. IV. 5. 17. दैवचिन्तकः–An astrologer. दैवं चिन्तयति सः।. सोपसर्गम्–Calculated to give trouble, having a malignant influence. सर्व...क्रियताम्–All prisoners are to be let off for the purpose of appeasing the evil star. IV. 5. 22. तच्छुत्वा...स्मीति–It was at the instance of इरावती that the two girls were imprisoned. Now, says, विदूषक to माधविका, if the Queen taking advantage of this opportunity of wholesale release, would liberate मालविका and बकुलावलिका also, इरावती would feel greatly displeased. The Queen therefore does not want to take that odium on herself, but wants to represent that the king gave direct orders for their release, and hence she i. e. धारिणी has dispatched me to to the prison-house with this ring.' चित्तं रक्षन्त्या–With a view to spare the feelings of इरावती and keep her pleased.

IV. 6. Mere intelligence is not enough. It must have an element of deep love for the friend, to goad it on and invent the subtle means of ensuring success in a friend's undertaking. The king means that because विदूषक loves him so much, therefore he is able to work thus in a subtle matter to accomplish his purpose. अर्थदर्शनम्—Visualising of the means to promote a friend's interest. सूक्ष्मः कार्यसिद्धि-पथः–The subtle or the narrow path leading to succes in an undertaking. IV. 6. 2. समुद्रगृहकं–A summer-house built in the midst of water; an ocean-pavilion; so called from some ponds of water being attached to it, what we might call in Marathi जलमंदिर. IV. 6. 7. कुसु...हस्ता–with her hands busy in gathering flowers. IV.6.11. विदूषक puns on the name चंद्रिका of the attendant. 'Yes, we must avoid this maid-servant चंद्रिका. The moonlight (चंद्रिका) has to be avoided by thieves and lovers who have to work unseen.' IV. 6. 16. ते सखी–The king always refers to मालविका, while speaking to विदूषक, as 'Your friend.' Cf. जाने सख्यास्तव मयि मनः संभृतस्नेहं...। मे० II. 27. IV. 6. 20. प्रणम भर्तारम्–In the समुद्रगृहक was a picture of the king and his many wives. The king was portrayed as gazing at the face of इरावती, as will be clear from the later remarks. बकुला० refers to the picture; but she is purposely vague in order that she may enjoy herself a little at her friend's expense. IV. 6. 24. विप्रलंभयासि मां–you deceive me. मालविका did not notice the picture first and thought that the king had arrived. Hence her joy followed by disappointment when she could not see him at the door.

IV. 7. The पुण्डरीक or the white day-lotus blooms at sun-rise and closes its petals at sun-set. The face of मालविका also beamed with joy to hear that the king had come, but wore immediately a sad look of disappointment when she did not find him there. समवस्थे क्षणात् ऊढे–Within one moment she presented both the conditions of the lotus. IV. 7. 6. तदाहं...भर्ता–She means 'that when she met the king for the first time near the Aśoka tree, she could not satisfy herself by having a full look of him; various reasons like maidenly bashfulness, excitement of the occasion and the sudden interruption of इरावती deprived her of the pleasure of observing the king to her heart's content. But in this place she could see him in the picture uninterrupted and she feels now fully satisfied. Mr. Pandit completes the first sentence after अद्य, and reads the next sentence विभावितश्चित्रगतदर्शनो भर्ता as a separate one. न वितृष्णास्मि. My thirst for his sight was not quenched; I did not feel satisfied. IV. 7. 11. मञ्जूषा–A casket, a treasure-box. विदूषक purposely puts a different construction on this sentence to ridicule the king and remarks, ' See what मालविका says. In vain do you think yourself handsome. You did not appear to her half so charming while bodily present as you do in the picture. And yet you are proud of your personal charms which are not at all striking on the exterior. It is the pride of a casket or a box which contains the charming jewels inside. while the exterior of it is all dull and unimpressive.' IV. 7. 13. निसर्गशालीनः-modest or bashful by nature (निसर्ग). Cf. निसर्गादेवाप्रगल्भस्तपस्विकन्याजनः । शा० II. The word शालीन is generally explained as शालाप्रवेशमर्हतीति—one who is fit to enter an apartment of a house i. e. well-behaved, shy.

IV. 8. The particles च...च mean ' though...yet.' कार्त्स्न्येन...समागतानाम्. Although women desire to observe in full or completely (कार्त्स्न्येन) the features of their (lovers) whom they meet for the very first time (तत्पूर्व-

समागतानाम्-तदेव पूर्वं यस्मिन् कर्मणि यथा तथा समागतानां). न च...विलोचनानि-yet broad as their eyes are, they do not fall fully (न समग्रपातीनि) on their lovers. Their eyes are not directed full in the face but are half-averted or cast down through shyness. There is विरोधाभास between आयतलोचनानां and न समग्रपातीनि. Cf. अभिमुखे मयि संहृतमीक्षणम्। शा॰ II. 11. also विवृण्वती शैलसुतापि भावमङ्गैः स्फुरद्बालकदम्बकल्पैः। साचीकृता चारुतरेण तस्थौ मुखेन पर्यस्तविलोचनेन ॥ कुमा॰ III. 68. IV. 8. बद्धलक्ष्यः-बद्धं लक्ष्यं येन सः-who has fixed his gaze on the face. मालविका, while observing the picture minutely, gradually transformed herself into the atmosphere and the scene of the picture and has begun to think that the king with his many wives was actually present. In the picture, of course, the king would be constantly looking at इरावती. In an atmosphere of reality, however, she thought it rather strange of the king and hence her remark. We have such a devise in the शाकुंतल also, where in the VI Act the king forgets that he is observing a picture of शकुंतला and begins addressing her and the bee hovering about her. IV. 8. 11. परमार्थ-In reality, as present actually and not in a picture. क्रीडिष्यामि एतया-I'll make fun of her.

IV. 9. भ्रूभङ्गाभिन्नतिलकं (आननं)—भ्रूभङ्गैः भिन्नः तिलकः यस्मिन्-The face on which the saffron mark on the forehead was broken i. e. disfigured by the knitting of eyebrows. स्फुरिताधरोष्ठं (आननं) The face the lower lip of which was throbbing in anger. The two expressions may be taken as adverbial phrases going with परावर्तयन्त्या. कान्ता etc. Construe :—कान्ता...कुपितेषु ललिताभिनयस्य विनेतुः शिक्षा अनया संदर्शितेव। She gave an exhibition, as it were, of her teacher's lesson in graceful acting appropriate in fits of anger caused by the faults of a lover. IV. 9. 1. अनुनयः-Conciliation, propitiation. He means that the king as her lover, should step forth now to conciliate her. IV. 9. 4. आर्य...एनम्-The king has two sources of distraction One is इरावती whom she can hope to supercede and the other, this विदूषक who rarely left the king alone. She feels jealousy even for विदूषक and hence she turns in another direction pettishly. अत्रैव i. e. near the king. IV. 9. 8. प्रत्यानीयते i. e. त्यज्यते-Is left off, abandoned.

IV. 9. चित्रार्पितचेष्टया. at an action (चेष्टा) shown in a picture. किमेवमयि should be split up as किं एवं अयि. If we split it up as किं एव मयि, then the verbal form of $\sqrt{}$कुप्, which generally governs the dative, will have to be construed with the locative. अनन्यसाधारणः-Not claimed by any one else, not common (साधारण) to others, devoted to none else. IV. 10. 4. कातर्यं-Nervousness, distraction. IV. 10. 5. उदासीनः-Indifferent, apathetic, unconcerned. IV. 10. 8. अत्र...नीया-To be taken as a question. Pandit reads-अत्रभवत्यामयं तवाविश्वासः ?

IV. 11. The king explains why he has lost all faith in मालविका who plays hide and seek with him in a dream and therefore he is not sure whether he has really got her, she being so deceptive. तिरोभवति-vanishes from sight, disappears. Some read स्थित्वा स्थित्वा

in place of स्थित्वा स्वप्ने. ' Having come repeatedly.' Our reading is better. सरति–Slips away, darts off. अबला सती Though she is a weak woman. He means that मालविका a frail creature though clasped between my powerful arms slips away suddenly. मनसिज etc. Construe– मनसिजरुजा क्लिष्टस्य मे मनः एवं समागममायया इमां प्रति विश्रब्धं कथमिव स्यात् ? I am already afflicted by the pang of love; and in such a condition she plays with me with such a delusive union. How can I, therefore, repose any trust in her? समागममायया can also be taken with क्लिष्टस्य. IV. 11. 5. मम...आसीत्–She means, ' My condition is even worse and therefore more pitiable. The king is lucky enough to have at least a dream. To me, however, even the sleep is denied and therefore there is no consolation of meeting him even in a dream ' Cf. प्रजागरात् खिलीभूतस्तस्याः स्वप्ने समागमः। बाष्पस्तु न ददात्येनां द्रष्टुं चित्रगतामपि ॥ शा० VI. 22.

IV. 12. बकुलावलिका has asked her to give a reply. The king says 'why should I give a reply? I give my own self to her, and for this ceremony the fire of love stands as the witness.' In a marriage ceremony, the bride is given to the bride-groom in the presence of the sacred fire. In this, the fire of love represents this divinity. न सेव्यः सेविता रहः–' No longer am I her master. I am her humble servant who would offer her this service of love in secret.' It is a clear hint to the विदूषक and बकुलावलिका to clear off! Cf. अद्यप्रभृत्यवनताङ्गि तवास्मि दासः। कुमा० V. 86. IV. 12. 4. पल्लवानि लंघितुं–To browse upon or to crop the tender sprouts. This is a pretext to go away with बकुलावलिका, leaving the king alone with मालविका. For a similar devise which प्रियंवदा uses with a view to go away with अनसूया leaving दुष्यंत and शकुंतला to-gether, Cf. अनसूये यथैष इतोदत्तदृष्टिरुत्सुको मृगपोतको मातरमन्विष्यति । एहि संयोजयाव एनम् । शा० III. IV. 12. 7. एवम्-Even thus i. e. as you are watchful about the Aśoka tree, in the same way should you guard us. IV. 12. 8. Cf. नेदमावयोरुपदेश्यम् । I. IV. 12. 11. अप्रकाशे-In the dark, hidden from sight. IV. 12. 16. स्फटिकस्थलम्. Crystal pavement. IV. 12. 18. ससाध्वसा-Full of nervousness.

IV. 13. तव...प्रणयोन्मुखे-may either be taken with संगमसाध्वसं विसृज or with सहकारतां गते मयि. 'Leave off your nervousness of union with me who have been so eagerly yearning for your love'; For the second interpretation, see the translation. अतिमुक्तलताचरितं गृहाण-Assume the part or the behaviour of the अतिमुक्त creeper towards me who have become a mango-tree (सहकार). He asks her to embrace him closely. The अतिमुक्तलता is seen to coil itself or grasp with its tendrils the mango-tree on which it is propped up. The plant is identified with what is known in Marathi by the name of कुसरी or कस्तूरीमोगरा. For such tender associations between the mango-tree and the अतिमुक्तलता, Cf. मिथुनं परिकल्पितं त्वया सहकारः फलिनी च नन्विमौ । रघु० VIII. 6. 1. क इदानीं सहकारमन्तरेणातिमुक्तलतां पल्लवितां सहते । शा० III. IV.13.2. आत्मनोऽपि प्रियं-'Such a thing viz. embracing, which I would like so much.' It may also refer to her love for the king which her heart approves. IV. 13. 6. यो न...ननु–She means, it does not lie in the mouth of the king to tell her not to be afraid of the Queen. Just recently she had witnessed a scene in which she saw how confused and frightened the king was when इरावती surprised them. (Cf. सर्वे इरावतीं दृष्ट्वा संभ्रान्ताः) If, therefore, the king would be bold enough to accept in मालविका his beloved before the Queen, she too would have no fear in acting in response to his love. It is indeed a very nice thrust which मालविका boldly levels at the king.

IV. 14. The king explains that it was not fear of इरावती but traditional courtesy of lovers that dictated him in such a behaviour with her. He should not, therefore, be misunderstood. He loves her alone to the exclusion of all. His very life now depended on her. बैम्बिकानां–of the descendants of बिम्बक, a name of one of the forefathers of अग्निमित्र. कुलव्रतम्–A family vow or tradition of behaving with uniform politeness with ladies. 'A कुलव्रत is a family custom inherited from generation to generation and has to be observed by every member of a family even when divided.' (Pandit). त्वदाशानिबन्धनाः–तव आशा निबन्धनं येषाम्. Sustained entirely by the tie of hope of thy favour or love. IV. 14. 15. न... तारः–Descent of young women (नवाङ्गनानां) into the field or the province (विषय) of love; their first step into the atmosphere of love.

IV. 15. कम्पवती–Trembling through nervousness. रश...गुलिं हस्तं रुणाद्धि–She obstructs my hand as its fingers move about to loosen the girdle (रशनाव्यापार). Cf. नाभिदेशनिहितः सकम्पया शंकरस्य रुरुधे तया करः। कुमा० VIII. 4. पातुं etc. construe– पक्ष्मलचक्षुराननं पातुं उन्नमयतः मम साचीकरोति–she averts or turns aside (साचीकरोति) her face as I raise to sip it–her face having long eye-lashes (पक्ष्मल). For a similar idea Cf. मुहुरंगुलिसंवृत्ताधरोष्ठं प्रतिषेधाक्षरविक्लवाभिरामम् । मुखमंसविवर्ति पक्ष्मलाक्ष्याः कथमप्युन्नमितं न चुम्बितं तु ॥ शा० III. 25. साचीकरोति–Makes crooked, turns or bends aside. Cf. साचीकृता चारुतरेण तस्थौ मुखेन पर्यस्तविलोचनेन। कुमा० III. 68. व्याजेनापि–Even under the pretext of refusing to satisfy my desire. He means that मालविका showed as if she was refusing to grant me my desire of embracing her ; and yet with all her show of resistence, she has gratified me. Cf. चुम्बनेष्वधरदानवर्जितं खिन्नहस्तमदयोपगूहनम् । क्लिष्टमन्मथमपि प्रियं प्रभोर्दुर्लभप्रतिकृतं वधूरतम् ॥ कुमा० VIII. 8.

IV. 15. 4. अलिन्दः–A terrace before a house-door. While on guard on the crystal pavement, चंद्रिका seems to have observed विदूषक. She reported the matter to निपुणिका who in her turn lost no time in carrying the news to her mistress इरावती ! A similar expression occurs in विक्र० II. हंजे निपुणिके, सत्यं त्वया भणितमिदं लतागृहं प्रविशन्नार्यमाणवकसहाय आर्यपुत्रो दृष्ट इति । IV. 15.10. सविशेषम्–with something more important (विशेषं) that remains to be told. The reading सावशेषं is better. Cf. वयस्य, तिष्ठ। शृणु सावशेषं मे वचः॥शा०II. After speaking out संश...प्रेक्षितुं च–इरावती stopped in hesitation, although ordinarily she should have continued further. Hence this remark. Instead of प्रेक्षितुं Mr. Pandit reads पुच्छिदुं i. e. प्रष्टुम्–' To inquire of the king's friend about his health etc.' IV. 15. 16. अथे...नीयते–Why go to the *picture* to ask for forgiveness ? Why not approach the *king* himself when he is at hand ?

IV. 15. 19. The translation in our edition was given with the following variant reading of this sentence—यादृशश्चित्रगतो भर्ता तादृश एव अन्यसंक्रान्तहृदय आर्यपुत्रः–A husband drawn in a picture is the same as a husband who has transfersred his love to another. Here is he transferred to the picture and there transferred in mind to the woman. There is no difference between the two. Hence I select the picture. This is of course said in bitter sarcasm. Our reading of the text is however better. यादृश...आर्यपुत्रः–She means ' The picture will make it clear that when it was drawn, the king deeply loved me. He is there looking at *me* in the presence of all his wives. He has not remained the same (न तादृश) now. He loves another viz. मालविका. If I go to him now, it would be like approaching a different person and not *my* lord. Hence I select the picture. ' केवल...आरम्भः-' And I am doing it. i. e. approaching the picture to ask for forgiveness, because I spurned his prostration and I feel it was a transgression or violation (अतिक्रम) on my part of the proper decorum that should be observed by a wife towards her husband. This apology is therefore meant to wipe out or atone for (प्रमार्ष्टुं) the sin and thus satisfy my conscience. I know I do not stand to gain anything thereby.' Cf. ' न जानामि...भवतो व्रतव्यपदेशेन मुक्तरोषा प्रणिपातलंघनं प्रमाष्टुकामेति ।

विक्र० III. IV. 15. 28. तव बहुमानं वर्धयितुं-' With a view to increase that great regard in which I hold you.' धारिणी means that for herself she has no jealousy left in her mind. That time has already gone. She imprisoned मालविका apparently to spare the feelings of इरावती, or out of regard for her as her co-wife. She knows the king pretty well and therefore it is useless to thwart his wishes, however unreasonable they may be. यद्य... ग्निष्यामि-I would also intercede and request the king on your behalf if you allow. I have come to know, to my grief, of the recent happenings which have brought about an estrangement between you and the king. If you therefore permit me, I would speak to the king and request him to be reconciled with you.' IV. 15.40. विपाणिगत इव वृषभः-Like a bull in the market-place (विपाणि). The bull here referred to is the पोळ or वळु, let loose as a part of funeral obsequies. He is held sacred, feeds fat on the grain offered to him in religious charity and has the fullest liberty everywhere. He is usually found squatting lazily near some shop and dozes away without any fear of being disturbed. 'Even the Cattle Trespass Acts do not trouble him, because the people willingly put up with him. It does not seem that much change has come over the institution of these bulls since the days of कालिदास '-Pandit. IV. 15. 41. अत्याहितं-महाभीतिः-A disaster, calamity. IV. 15. 45. पापं-Evil, danger to life. IV. 15. 46. भवति मालविके -विदूषक is raving by instalments. He has said this, and falls into sound sleep again. During this interval

निपुणिका has her observation. Again he blurts out इरावती मतिक्रामन्ती भव. IV. 15. 51. कस्या...कितवः-whose son (आत्मनीनः) is this accursed rogue? By what ungrateful sire was he begotten? The translation is given with the following reading :—कस्यैष आत्मानियोगसंपादने विश्वसनीयो हताशः। सर्व...उत्स्वप्नायते-The ingratitude of the विदूषक is fully betrayed in that he feeds himself on the sweet presents of इरावती and constantly thinks of promoting the interest of her rival मालविका even in his dreams. IV. 15. 63. दर्वीकरः-A snake. दर्वी means the expanded hood of a snake. IV. 15. 72. अहं...फलितमिति-The two tooth-marks which विदूषक showed to the Queen as those of a serpent were really the pricks of the केतकी thorns. विदूषक says, 'At that time I managed to obtain these marks from the केतकी thorns and falsely represented them as the marks of the serpent's fangs. It was in a way a mockery of the snake. Observing this stick, therefore, I thought that my action of ridiculing a serpent has turned upon me and has given me the punishment I deserved(फलितम्). विदूषक refers to 'the common notion that a person who falsely pretends an evil is visited by the fates with a reality of it in retribution.' IV. 15. 73. पटाक्षेपेण-Tossing aside the curtain. When a character has to enter the stage in the hurry of excitement without previously indicating its entrance, this is the devise used. IV. 15. 79. इह...दृश्यते-बकुलावालिका has scented the arrival of इरावती on the scene, and hence this veiled hint. IV. 15. 82. दिवासंकेतः-The mid-day engagement or meeting (संकेत). IV. 15. 84. अपूर्व उपचारः-An extraordinary form of greeting. IV. 15. 86. दूत्याधिकारविषया प्रतिज्ञा– your promise (given to the king) in your capacity as a go-between. IV. 15. 89. किं तु...विस्मरति–' Does the god of rain forget the earth because frogs croak ?' She tries to flatter इरावती by comparing her to the earth. while the attempts of मालविका and बकुलावलिका to win over the king are compared to the croaking of frogs. When the rainy season is eminent, the frogs begin croaking, and thereby appealing to the god of rain as it were to send them a few showers. Now the god of rain may do so to satisfy their thirst and stop their croaking. but that can never take his mind off the earth whom he has to gratify by his fertilising showers. Similarly मालविका may try to divert the king's attention towards her by her language of love and she may succeed in it for some time. But these attempts of insignificant frog-like creatures like मालविका can never make the king forgetful of his chief love viz. इरावती, dignified and honourable as she is like the earth. The sentence can be interpreted in another way also. ' Frogs like इरावती may croak and squeal in thier pettish jealousy; will the king, however, forget his present chief beloved मालविका ?' बकुला० says thus, being touched to the quick by the ironical congratulations of इरावती on her success in the mission of a go-between, smarting, as she was, under the recent insult of imprisonment. There is another reading– किं नु...देवः पृथिवीं वर्षितुं स्मरति–Does the god remember to send his showers on the earth, *because* the frogs crook ? He does this of his own accord, without being reminded by the frogs Similarly he loves मालविका out of a spontaneous impulse of his heart, not because बकुलावलिका urges him by her suggestions. Some further read...वर्षितुं विरमति–Does Indra cease to send his showers on the earth, because frogs croak ? Will the king stop loving मालविका, because every time इरावती makes a scene by way of protesting against his love for मालविका ? IV. 15. 94. प्रसादं न गृह्णाति–you do not assume your loving friendly nature, you are not reconciled. IV. 16. अपर्वणि–When it is not the full-moon day. पर्वन् is the day of the full moon and the new moon. Here the eclipse of the moon is referred to and therefore the full moon day is meant, as the moon's eclipse is to be had only on that day. ग्रहकलुषेन्दुमण्डला–With the moon's orb obscured or clouded by the ग्रह i. e. the planet राहु who is supposed to bring about the eclipse by swallowing the moon for that period. The full-moon justifies an eclipse; so also there should be some justification for इरावती's anger. For a similar expression Cf. वद प्रदोषे स्फुटचन्द्रतारका विभावरी यद्यरुणाय कल्पते। कुमा० V. 44. IV. 16. 4. ततो......भवेयम्–'Then I should be an object of laughter or a butt of ridicule.' इरावती purposely misinterpretes the king's expression अस्थाने कोपः and means that when she is no longer being loved by the king, she has really no reason to be angry with him for loving another. She has lost all claim over him and therefore her anger would only be laughed at, instead of mending matters. IV 16. 5. अन्यथा कल्पयसि–you take it differently, you misunderstand. The presence of मालविका with me here is being misconstrued by you.

IV. 17. The king tries to account for मालविका's coming over to समुद्रगृह and meeting him. उत्सवदिवसेषु-On festive days. IV. 17. 2. दृष्टं...मयेति–' The Queen's partiality for me has been witnessed to-day.' She means ' the queen always professed an amount of love for me i. e. इरावती; very recently she said that she imprisoned मालविका for my sake. (तव खलु बहुमानं बर्धयितुं etc.). So long, however, there was no evidence for it and I am glad to say that to-day I got a very convincing proof of her love for me.' She says this in a bitter ironical manner. Some interpret it thus ' the Queen's partiality i. e. love for the king is visualised to-day. The girls were imprisoned apparently for my sake, but here they are released for the sake of the king for whom she is more solicitous.' The first interpretation is to be preferred, as it is in keeping with the sarcastic manner of her remarks, which she has maintained all along. IV. 17. 7. बन्धन...पतित: ' The house-pigeon let loose from the cage is sighted by a cat. मालविका successfully released from her confinement is immediately seen by इरावती.' It may also refer to the Queen धारिणी–' इरावती has sent the whole report of this meeting to the queen, who will surely deal with मालविका very severely now.' Some understand it as a reference to the king. 'The house-pigeon viz. the king has somehow extricated himself from the clutches of इरावती angered by him. On hearing of this report, however, the Queen धारिणी also will be enraged and the king has now to save his face with her.' The reading चिल्लायाः मुखे पतितः would mean fallen into the beak of a kite.' IV. 17. 10. यदृच्छादृष्टया-Met by chance, seen accidently. Cf. समापत्तिदृष्टेन. IV. 17. 13. उद्भिन्नः दुष्प्रयोगः-The intrigue has been evolved or planned. कामतंत्रसचिवः-A minister well-versed in the science or the manuals on love IV. 17. 17. भवति...विस्मरेयम्-'If I were to read but a single syllable of policy (नीति), I shall forget the गायत्री.' गायत्री is a sacred verse of a Ṛgvedic hymn in praise of the Sun, and is incorporated in the Sandhyā prayer of a Brahmin. The verse is as follows :— तत्सवितुर्वरेण्यं भर्गो देवस्य धीमहि । धियो यो नः प्रचोदयात्॥ R. V. III. 62. 10. विदूषक swears an oath that he has not conned a single syllable from the treatises of love and as such knows nothing of its policy ; if what he says is false, he incurs the sin of forgetting the गायत्री, the sacred treasure of a Brahmin. Another way in which it has been interpreted by some is :-' I am such a block-head and so short of memory, that it is with great difficulty that I have learnt by heart the गायत्री verse; now if I were to put an additional strain on my memory by trying to learn a single syllable of other works like the manuals on love, I am afraid I shall forget the गायत्री and therefore lose my Brahminhood" IV. 17. 25. बलवदुत्रासिता-Terribly frightened. प्रवातकिसलयमिव वेपमाना-Trembling like a tender sprout in a gust of wind. पिङ्गलवानरः-A brown monkey or the monkey of the name of पिङ्गल. IV. 17. 35. सपक्षः–'your friend, your caste-fellow.' विदूषक, for his mischievous characteristics is not only regarded by others as belonging to the fraternity of animals, chiefly monkeys, but even he himself does so in keeping with his character as a buffoon. Cf. किमिति शङ्किष्यते । आश्रमवासपरिचित एव शाखामृगः । विक्र० II. IV. 17. 43. पञ्चरात्रम्–पञ्चानां रात्रीणां समाहारः–A period of five nights. सन्नद्धः–Equipped with, covered with, pervaded with. (व्याप्तः). IV. 17. 47. सत्यप्रतिज्ञा देवी–The queen will be true to her promise of fulfilling her desires, if the Aśoka would blossom within five nights.

ACT V.

V. 0. 9. वेदिकाबन्धः उपाक्षिप्तः–An altar or a dias covered with a roof round the Aśoka tree has been laid i. e. created (उपक्षिप्तः). The सत्कारविधि or the honour done to the Aśoka refers to the kicking by मालविका. The tree very soon put forth blossoms and when it was reported to धारिणी, she gave orders for erecting this altar. V. 0. 10. अहो दैवस्य...भविष्यति–We should interpret the sentence thus :—' Oh ! After all it was Fate which took pity upon her. The other opposing forces were all rallied round her, but she could at last provoke feelings of compassion in her Fate which favoured her by getting the Aśoka to blossom. And now the queen, though so much enraged, will be certainly disposedfa to vour her. प्रसादसुमुखी–with a benign pleasing face inclined to show favour. परिजनाभ्यन्तरः-One of the servants. जतुमुद्रालांछितं चीवरबन्धम्-A package in some cloth (चीवर) marked i. e. sealed (लांछितं) with a lac (जतु) seal. V. L. चीरमंजूषा-A leather-box. चतुःशालं-A quadrangle enclosed by four buildings. कुब्जः सारसकः-A hunch-back servant by name सारसक. Generally the servants selected for the harem were dwarfs (वामनs), eunuchs (वर्षवरs), hunch-backs, or foresters (किरातs) under the command of an old chamberlain (कंचुकिन्) ! V. 0. 20. वेदपारगाणां-To (the Brahmins) well-versed in the Vedic lore. The reading विद्यापारायणं अनुतिष्ठतां-would mean ' who are performing the अनुष्ठान or the religious rite, consisting of the recital of vedic hymns for a certain number of times within a fixed period for the purpose of averting a calamity or danger. V. 0. 27. सेनापतिना-By the सेनापति i. e. पुष्पमित्र, the father of अग्निमित्र. ' He still retained his title of सेनापति of the मौर्य kings, the last of whom he had deposed,and usurping whose throne, he had put his own son अग्निमित्र on it. This is analogous to the title of पेशवा by the late rulers of the Deccan, who instead of being the Peshavas or the ministers of the descendants of Shivaji, were in reality their masters.' यज्ञतुरगः-The sacrificial horse let loose without restraint. He was permitted to roam about freely in all countries,followed by a strong escort of the king who desires to establish his supremacy over all kings. A king in whose territory the horse enters has either to submit or to give a fight with a view to try his strength. After the world-wide tour the अश्वमेध sacrifice is performed. For the description of such a horse, see उत्तररामचरित, Act IV. दक्षिणीयैः प्रतिग्राहयति-Makes the Brahmins, who are worthy of such gifts, receive the dole (दक्षिणा). V. 0. 34. मङ्गलगृहं-An apartment or a part of the palace for sacred purposes, where possibly the gods were worshipped ; like the modern देवगृह. लिपिकारः—A clerk, a scribe or a writer. V. 0. 43. महासाराणि रत्नवाहनानि-Very valuable jewelled vehicles. The word रत्नवाहन is taken by some to mean 'A vessel of gems,' while Prof. Tawney translates the word as 'waggon-loads of jewels.' शिल्पदारिकाभूयिष्ठं (परिजनं)-servants mostly consisting (भूयिष्ठ) of maidens accomplished in the arts. Cf. अभिरूपभूयिष्ठा परिषदियम् । शा० I. The compound should be solved as शिल्पदारिकाः भूयिष्ठाः or भूयिष्ठं यस्मिन् ।.

Here ends the Praveśaka which is introduced to inform the audience of the great victory won by वीरसेन over the विदर्भ king,as a consequence of which माधवसेन is set free. Out of gratitude he sends, among many presents, accomplished maids, and we are told that a sacrificial horse is let loose under the escort of prince वसुमित्र, the son of धारिणी.-V. 0. 57 धर्मासनं-The judgment seat. V. 0. 59. दण्डेनैव-By force, by the strength of the army. Among four political expedients (viz. साम Peaceful negotiation, दान gift, भेद split and दण्ड Force), the last one alone is being utilised.

V. 1. The verse means while the king is enjoying tbe spring in his gardens on the banks of विदिशा i. e. in his own capital, his armies have vanquished the king of विदर्भ on the banks of वरदा. पर...वान्-construe-पर...रेषु विदिशा...नेषु आत्तरतिः त्वं अङ्गवान् (अपि) अनङ्ग इव नयसि । आत्तरतिः- आत्ता गृहीता रतिः प्रीतिः येन-You who take delight (in the gardens); the king is compared to अनङ्ग or Cupid, the body-less, so called because god Śiva burnt his body to ashes. The word आत्तरति can be taken with (अंगवान्) अनङ्ग also, in which case it would mean 'who had taken with him his wife रति, having himself assumed a body (अंगवान्). परभृत...व्याहारेषु-(उद्यानेषु) परभृतानां कोकिलानां कलः व्याहारः येषु-Vocal with the sweet (कलं) warbling of cuckoos. Some construe it with आत्तरतिः-The king finding pleasure in the utterance (व्याहार) of the dependents i. e. bards. विदिशा.-'The river Vidiśā is in Malwa and Professor Wilson identifies it with the Bess, a small stream that joins the Betwa where the modern Bhilsa (supposed to be the same as the ancient city of the name of विदिशा) is situated.'—Pandit. उपोढ-बलस्य ते-'of you whose army (बल) is powerful.' आलानाङ्गैः-(वृक्षैः) The trees which serve as the tying posts (आलान) for the victorious elephants. The word आलान means a post to which an elephant is tied' Cf. आलाने गृह्यते हस्ती-। मृच्छ० III. It also means 'a chain or a rope and in this sense, the reading आलानाङ्कैः 'having marks of chains' would be better. It should be noted that in ancient warfare, a squadron of elephants constituted an essential part of the fighting forces. वरद-वरान् ददात्यसौ-'Oh giver of boons.' वर...वृक्षैः सहावनतौ रिपुः-It is a good illustration of the figure of speech सहोक्ति. The heads of enemies were humbled or bent down along with the tops of trees by your victorious elephants. वरदा is the modern Wurda, a tributary of गोदावरी. V. 2. Construe :--हे सुरोपम, क्रथकैशिकान् मध्येकृत्य स्थितं उभयोः चरितं सूरिभिः वीरप्रीत्या विरचितपदं (अस्ति) । दण्डानीकैः विदर्भपतेः श्रियं हृतवतः तव । परिघगुरुभिः दोर्भिः प्रसह्य रुक्मिणीं (हृतवतः) शौरेः च । The bard says, 'that the poets sing of the glorious achievements of these two heroes over the Vidarbhas ; formerly it was श्रीकृष्ण who forcibly carried away रुक्मिणी, the daughter of the विदर्भ king भीमक, and now it is you who have snatched the Vidarbha king's glory. सूरिभिः चरितं विरचितपदम्–The poets have celebrated or sung the exploits in verse. विरचितानि पदानि–पद्यानि–यस्मिन् तत् । Mr. Pandit observes 'It appears that in the time of कालिदास, there were extant, written by learned scholars, memoirs (चरितs) of king अग्निमित्र, in which his victory over the Vidarbhas was celebrated. These memoirs would appear to be other and older than the accounts found in the Purānas, because सूरि is a modest term, and is not applied to the authors of the Purānas which pretend to have been composed by the Rishi Vyāsa.' सुरोपम–God-like. क्रथकैशिकान् मध्येकृत्य -Putting the क्रथकैशिकs in the middle, while on both the sides were the two heroes श्रीकृष्ण and अग्निमित्र, i. e. the क्रथकैशिकs were the common enemy of both over whom victory was obtained; and even in songs the common or the middle factor was the क्रथकैशिकs for the exploits of both श्रीकृष्ण and अग्निमित्र. क्रथकैशिकs are the same as विदर्भs. दण्डानीकैः–By means of your armies (अनीकं). परिघगुरुभिः दोर्भिः–With arms as powerful and long as an iron bar of a gate (परिघ). Cf. एकः कृत्स्नां नगरपरिघप्रांशुबाहुर्भुनक्ति । शा० II. 15.

प्रसह्य-हठात् or बलात्-Forcibly. शौरि is an epithet of कृष्ण who was the grand-son of the यादव king शूर by name. The story of the kidnapping of रुक्मिणी is well-known. She was first betrothed to शिशुपाल against her will. She however, loved कृष्ण and secretly sent him a message requesting him to carry her away. कृष्ण successfully took her away just on the wedding day, after a severe fight with her brother रुक्मि and the forces of शिशुपाल. V. 2. 4. मुखालिन्दतोरणं-The arch (तोरण) of the main (मुख) terrace.

V. 3. सुलभेतरसंप्रयोगां- सुलभेतरः संप्रयोगः यस्याः-Whose union is not easy (सुलभेतर-other than easy) to secure. दुःखायते-Feels grieved or sorry, Denom. of दुःख. The king says that the joy he feels at the news of his victory is not unalloyed, but is mingled with a feeling of sadness at the thought that मालविका appears to be still unattainable. His heart, full of such contrary feelings, he compares to a lotus in the hot sun being sprinkled with cooling showers. सुखमश्नुते-Enjoys happiness. च-च has the sense of simultaneous action of two things. V. 3. 2. एकान्तसुखितः-Absolutely or perfectly happy without the slightest distress on account of मालविका. V. 3. 9. वैदर्भविवाहनेपथ्यम्-The wedding-dress which it is customary for the women in the विदर्भ country to wear. Perhaps it is a speciality of the विदर्भ people. तत्रभवती......मनोरथम्-विदूषक means, ' it is not with any idle curiosity that मालविका is thus attired in the wedding-costume. The queen intends possibly to celebrate your marriage with मालविका.'

V. 3. 22. मद......मेतत्-What you say is not impossible judging from her former actions (पूर्वचरितैः), since she is known to adapt herself or conform to my expectations which she has never thwarted. The queen did not object to my marriage with इरावती, on a former occasion. She is thus free from jealousy (निवृत्तेर्ष्या), and is always willing to surrender and subordinate her wishes to mine. मदपेक्षानुवृत्त्या-मदपेक्षाणां अनुवृत्तिः-तया or as a बहुव्रीहि compound मदपेक्षायाः अनुवृत्तिः यस्याः सा-तस्याः । The word may thus be looked upon as Instr. Sing or Gen. Sing. V. 3. 21. मालविकापुरोगेण परिजनेन-With her retinue of which मालविका is the foremost (पुरोगा-पुरो गच्छति सा.). It is not without any suggestion that this detail is mentioned by the प्रतीहारी who knows full well the king's maid and knows also that the king is sure to hasten to the place on hearing this.

V. 4. अग्रे In front of us, on the outer side of the tree. विकीर्ण...सहकारं (यौवनं)—विकीर्णानि कुरबकानि, फलजालैश्च विभिद्यमानाः सहकाराः यस्मिन्-In which the कुरबक flowers were scattered (in front of us), and the mango-trees were bursting with the net-work of fruit. There too are the indications of the advanced state (परिणाम) of spring. The reading फलजालविभुज्यमान...would mean, bending under the load of fruit etc.' चेत उत्सुकयति-Fills the mind with eagerness, at the thought that the spring coming to a close,the days of enjoyment will be very soon over. V. 4.5. यद...उद्वहति-Unlike others, Aśoka was late in blossoming and therefore now when all others have lost the glory of their blossoms, this Aśoka with its Dohada satisfied, has burst into an uncommon or extraordinary splendour of its blossoms.

V. 5. सूचितवसन्तविभवानां--The other Aśoka trees which exhibited the wealth or glory of spring. Some read मुकुलानि 'buds' instead of कुसुमानि. V. 5. 2. विश्रब्धो ...मन्यते--विदूषक means that the present behaviour of धारिणी who allows मालविका to be with her even though the king is approaching, offers a contrast to her behaviour on earlier occasions when she made a special effort to keep her out of his sight. Does it not indicate that धारिणी has reconciled herself to your love of मालविका and would no longer put any obstacle in the way of your winning मालविका ?

V. 6. The Queen is imagined to be the earth (वसुमती) while मालविका by her side is compared to लक्ष्मी The Goddess of wealth bereft of a lotus in her hand. Laxmi is always represented as having her seat on a lotus and also a lotus in her hand. The poet fancies, however, that on this occasion it appears as if she has forgotten to equip herself with it (विस्मृतहस्तकमलया). There is another reading विनयादनूत्थिता प्रियया. 'My beloved who rose immediately after the Queen'. This reading is also good, and it cannot be argued that this action of मालविका is contrary to her position as a maid. Possibly धारिणी saw the king coming first and when she rose from her seat, मालविका noticed the king and she also immediately left her seat. For विस्मृत some read विस्तृत meaning ' with an expanded lotus in her hand.' This reading would require मालविका also to have a lotus. For this association of a lotus with लक्ष्मी, Cf. छायामण्डललक्ष्येण तमदृश्य किल स्वयम्। पद्मा पद्मातपत्रेण भेजे साम्राज्यदीक्षितम् ॥ रघु० IV 5.

V. 4. जानामि निमित्तं etc. I know the reason of this festive decoration (कौतुकालंकार). The निमित्त was, of course, the festive occasion that was being celebrated by the queen, because the Aśoka had put forth blossoms. It cannot be, as some imagine, the prospective marriage of मालविका with the king. The Queen will never willingly consent to it, unless forced to do so. She argues, therefore, that the reason is such as has nothing to do with me personally. And yet (तथापि) my heart flutters and my left (दक्षिणेतरत्) eye twitches often, a good omen indicating the fruition of my desire viz. union with my lord. Throbbing of the left eye is considered a good sign, suggestive of a prospective union with the person loved. The opposite is the case with men.

V. 7. अन...सिनी-Wearing a silk garment (दुकूल) not hanging too far (अनतिलंबि). लघुभिः आभरणैः—with a few ornaments. लघुभिः should also be construed with उडुगणैः ' with a few clusters of stars.' उदयोन्मुखचन्द्रिका-उदयोन्मुखा चंद्रिका यस्याः सा-(चैत्रविभावरी)-The Caitra night with the moon-light imminent. The first quarter of the night is indicated. गतहिमैः-free from the (enveloping) mist. The ornaments correspond to the stars while the light which the rising moon spreads beforehand beautifully represents the pale-coloured silk dress. V. 7. 5. अभिमतसिद्धिरस्तु– Note the blessing of परिव्राजिका who thereby hints at the prospective union of the two lovers. V.7.8. संकेतगृहं काल्पितः –This tree is fixed as a trysting bower or a rendezvous where lovers should meet by appointment. It is the very tree which was the scene of the first meeting of the king and मालविका. The Queen knows this and therefore she clearly indicates thereby that far from resenting the king's latest adventure, she is in a mood to favour their union and thus reconcile herself with the king. V. 7. 9. आराधितोऽसि–' You have been propitiated or won over. The Queen is trying to make amends and win your favour.'

V. 8. नायं etc. Construe—अयं अशोकः ईदृशानां सत्काराणां भाजनत्वं न नेयः (इति) न। (अपि तु नेयः एव). This अशोक tree *must* be made the recipient of such honours of favours, like the construction of the altar etc. माधवश्रीनियोगे सावज्ञः– Who treated with contempt the injunction of the goddess of vernal beauty (माधवश्री), i. e. who did not flower at a time when spring demanded it, but waited for your efforts in the matter. The king means that since the tree showed so much regard for you by putting forth blossoms when *you* favoured him, he deserves to be honoured by you. V. 8. 1. विश्रब्धो etc. A similar devise like the one used by बकुलावलिका (III. 14. 16) is used here by विदूषक, who uses vague language so that this remark may refer to मालविका as also अशोकशोभा. And when confronted by धारिणी as to whom he means, he replies with his ready wit that he referred to अशोकशोभा ! V. 8. 6, संनिधिविप्रयोग:-Separation in the very presence of the person whom you love. Though the beloved is near, the presence of other people makes it difficult to take any liberty of even touch or talk with her, and therefore for all practical purposes. it amounts to separation. Compare the varieties of वियोग in the drama भावबंधन of of the Marathi dramatist Gadkari.

V. 9. रथाङ्गनामा-रथाङ्गस्य चक्रस्य नाम यस्य सः-The चक्रवाक bird who is named after a part of the chariot i. e. the wheel. The convention about this bird with Sanskrit poets is that the male is separated from its mate at sunset to be reunited when the day begins. The distance between the two may not be more than that of a leaf. It imagines however, that it is far away and cries piteously for the whole night. Their love for each other is proverbial. Kālidāsa has used this convention so often in his works. Cf. रथांगनाम्नोरिव भावबन्धनं बभूव यत्प्रेम परस्पराश्रयम् । रघु० III. 24. चक्रवाकवधूः, आमंत्रयस्व सहचरम् । उपस्थिता रजनी । शा० III. निनाय सात्यंतहिमोत्किरानिलाः सहस्यरात्रीरुदवासतत्पराः । परस्पराक्रंदिनि चक्रवाकयोः पुरोवियुक्ते मिथुने कृपावती ॥ कुमा० V. 26. रथांगनामन् वियुतो रथांगश्रोणिबिंबया । अयं त्वां पृच्छति रथी मनोरथशतैर्वृतः ॥ विक्र० IV. Similarly here the queen धारिणी, who represents the night has practically brought about a separation of these two lovers though they are very near each other, since she would not permit their mutual contact (अननुज्ञातसंपर्का) V. 9. 3. मार्ग...शरीरे-With their persons languid (अलस) owing to the fatigue of the journey. V. 9. 11. प्रसीदति...आत्मा-My inner self feels delighted.

V. 9. 14. आगामि...करोति-The approaching happiness or misery strengthens the heart accordingly. The heart gets fortified beforehand to receive the shock of calamity or joy. समर्थीकरोति-Strengthens, is fortified, having for its subject सुखं वा दुःखं वा. It can also be taken in another way 'the heart indicates or foretells the coming happiness or misery.' समर्थीकरोति however has not the sense of indicating and hence the first interpretation is to be preferred. Here it is an agreeable indication and therefore some delightful event is to happen. V.9.24. अभियोग:-Application, special study, proficiency. V. 9. 25 अभ्यन्तरे-well-versed, proficient. Cf. अनभ्यन्तरे आवां मदनगतस्य वृत्तान्तस्य । शा० III. V. 9. 43. चन्दनं...दूषितं-She means that मालविका, a Princess, was treated by her as an ordinary maid. A sandal wood which ought to be better used for sacred purposes, was defiled (दूषितं) by her, being used (परिभोग) as a slipper (पादुका). V. 9. 58. स्वरसंयोगः-Voice, lit. a combination of sounds. V. 9. 61. दुःखेन विभाव्यते-Is recognised with difficulty (दुःखेन). V. 9. 71. तथागतभ्रातृकां-तथागतः भ्राता यस्याः सा-whose brother माधवसेन was reduced to such a plight viz. imprisonment at the hands of the विदर्भ king. पथिकसार्थ-A group of travellers, a caravan. V. 10. The main sentence is- प्रतिरोधकानां अनीकं आविरभूत्, while the other compounds go to qualify अनीकं. तूणीर...रालं-तूणीरपट्टैः परिणद्धानि भुजान्तरालानि यस्मिन्-whose chests (lit. the intervening space between two arms) were encircled with the quiver-straps (तूणीरपट्ट). आ...धारि आपार्ष्णि लंबिनं शिखिनां बर्हकलापं धारयति तत्–wearing tufts of peacock feathers (शिखिबर्ह), reaching down up to the heels कोदण्डपाणि–कोदण्डा पाणिषु यस्मिन्–with bows held in hands, armed with bows. निनदत्-Shouting, yelling, प्रतिरोधकानां अनीकं a host of highway-man or bandits आपातदुष्प्रसहम्–आपातः (attack, our laught) दुष्प्रसहः (Irresistible, hard to stand or endure) यस्य. V. 10. 1. मालविका भयं रूपयति–मालविका, in her timidity of heart, feels as if the incident of which the memory is fresh,is happening at this very time and hence her fright which she gesticulates. Compare a similar situation in the उत्तररामचरित, where in the first Act, सीता also is filled with fear as she observes the various pictures in the Picture-gallery. V. 10. 5. पराङ्मुखीकृताः–Were turned back or routed.

V. 11. दुर्जातेः परीप्सुः–Desirous of rescuing her from the ruffians or barbarians. दुर्जातिः–A wicked tribe. V. L. दुर्जाते–'In this disaster.' असुभिः आनृण्यं गतः–Paid back the debt with his life, i. e. was killed in the scuffle. V. 11. 5. ईदृशी लोकयात्रा Such is the lot, lit. the way of life, of those who have a body or mortals (तनुभृतां) Cf. मरणं प्रकृतिः शरीरिणां । रघु० VIII. 87. सफलीकृतभर्तृपिण्डः–Who made the food (पिंड) he had eaten of his master yield a fruit, i. e. who proved true to the salt he had eaten. V. 11. 7. संज्ञा–consciousness. V. 11. 9. कृच्छ्रं–Distress,misery V.11. 10. पुनर्नवीकृतवैधव्यदुःखया–Whose sorrow of widowhood (वैधव्य) was revived. The death of my brother renewed my grief for the loss of my husband, which so long I had managed to suppress, but which now revived with greater intensity, as I felt forlorn. काषाये गृहीते-I took to these yellowish-brown garments i. e. I renounced the world and turned an ascetic woman. It may not necessarily refer to the Buddhist order of nuns. Even Brahmanic Sanyāsins used to wear these coloured garments. Cf. नाहं काषायं वृत्तिहेतोः प्रपन्नः। स्वप्न० when यौगंधरायण taking to these robes is certainly not a Buddhist monk. We may, therefore, look upon परिव्राजिका, not as a Buddhist nun, but an ascetic woman of the Brahmanic order. V. 11. 13. आटविकः-A forest-dweller ; a derivative noun from अटवि. अवसानं-End V. 11. 15. किं...भणति-" The force of ' now ' is that मालविका is afraid lest the king should refuse to marry her, because she was without protection during the time that she passed from the wild men to Vīrasena, and from the latter to the Queen "—Pandit. A similar situation we get in the शाकुंतल as well. The message of काश्यप has been given and शाङ्गंधर requests the king to accept शकुंतला his legal wife. At this शकुंतला remarks to herself. ' किं नु खल्वार्यपुत्रो भणति । शा० V. V. 11. 17 परिभवोपहारिणः विनिपाताः-calamities (विनिपात) which bring on indignities or humiliation (परिभव).

V. 12. प्रेष्यभाव-The position of a servant who could be ordered about (प्रेष्य). स्नानीयवस्त्रक्रियया उपयुज्यते-is used to serve as a bath-towel. पत्रोर्णम्-wove-silk, a silken garment. No man of some sense would use a silken cloth as a bathing towel. Similarly a Princess, worth the title of a queen (देवीशब्दक्षमा) should not have been treated as a maid servant. V. 12. 3. असांप्रतं-अयोग्यं--improper V. 12. 5. नैभृत्यं-Abstract noun from निभृत-Secrecy. V. 12. 8. देवयात्रागतेन-who had come in the course of an idol-procession. देवयात्रा--A procession in honour of a deity going from place to place, just like the आषाढी यात्रा going from Alandi to Pandharpur. V. L. लोकयात्रागतेन 'who had come down to the state of a mortal.' सिद्धादेशेन-whose prophecy (आदेश) was infallible. तमेनं......पश्यामि-When I saw that the sure prophecy was proving true, (परिणमन्तं) as she was here serving at your feet as a maid, I thought I had better bide the (कालप्रतीक्षा) time and I think I did well acting accordingly. V. 12. 13. उपेक्षा-waiting. Some take it to mean 'Respect for prophecy.' V.12.14. कथांतरेणांतरितं-Put off or side-tracked by another episode or matter. The stage-direction प्रविश्य appears to be unnecessary, as the chamberlian was all along on the stage. V. 12. 17. द्वैराज्यं-Doube rule,joint kingship.

V. 13. शिष्टाम्-Let the two brothers rule. Inperative II Dual of √शास्. 'to govern.' V. 13. 1. अमात्यपरिषद-The council of ministers the cabinet. V.13.9. कल्याणी बुद्धिः Benevolent, generous mind. दर्शनम्-View, opinion. V. V. 14. संग्रहीतुः-of the charioteer ; it should be construed with ते,'of you.then controller or chastisér.' The two brothers यज्ञसेन and माधवसेन,with no one to put them up, were fighting. Now under your control,they will be peaceful. परस्परावग्रहनिर्विकारौ-unaffected or undistracted (निर्विकारौ) by mutual squabbles. V. 14. 5. सप्राभृतकः-Accompanied with a present (प्राभृत). उद्वेष्टयति-loosens, opens. V. 14. 11. ततो-

मुखम्—Turned in that directions. अतिभारे-In a great burden, in a heavy responsibility. V. L. अधिकारे 'in a responsible post.' V. 14. 14. स्वस्ति-A letter in Sanskrit always begins with this word. यज्ञशरणात्-From the sacrificial compound, noting the place whence the letter was dispatched. राजसूयदीक्षितेन-Consecrated for the राजसूज sacrifice. It is a great sacrifice performed by a universal monarch (in which the tributary princes also took part), generally at the time of his coronation as a mark of his undisputed sovereignty. दीक्षित-दीक्षा संजाता अस्य-Who has performed the consecration ceremony for making himself fit for performing the sacrifice. संवत्सरोपावर्तनयिः-which was to be brought back after a year. निरर्गलः-without restrain or check. रोधसि-On the bank. अश्वानीकेन प्रार्थितः-was claimed i. e. seized by the cavalry. संमर्दः-struggle, conflict. V. 15.3. अंशुमतेव सगरः-Like सगर whose horse was brought back by अंशुमान्. The horse of king Sagara was carried away by इंद्र to the nether world, where the sixty thousand sons of सगर traced him in the territory of कपिल. They attacked the sage who enraged burnt them all to ashes. The horse was later brought back by his grandson अंशुमान्. While भगीरथ brought the heavenly गङ्गा to the earth and thence to the पाताल to purify his ancestors. अकालहीनं- Without any delay or loss of time. विगतरोषचेतसा- With a mind free from anger. Various views have been given about the causes that laid to the strained relations between the father and the son. Mr. Pandit conjectures that 'अग्निमित्र had disapproved of his father having sent out the boy वसुमित्र as champion of the courser.' This is not probable, however, as the क्षत्रिय kings instead of resenting did always exult in such adventures. "The real ground for anger seems to be due to the religious opinions of the two. अग्निमित्र was indulgent towards the Buddhists while पुष्पमित्र tried to uproot it out of India."

V. 16. परिव्राजिका says that by her marriage with अग्निमित्र, the queen धारिणी has already been the foremost वीरपत्नी; and now by such a valiant son, she is to get the title of a वीरमाता. वीरसू:-वीरं सुते सा-Onewho gives birth to a hero. V. 16. 3. कलभ-A young elephant. Some rightly put this sentence in the mouth of परिव्राजिका; the king could not have referred to himself in a such boastful Language. यूथपतिः-The leader of a herd of elephants.

V. 17. वीर-विज़ृंभितेन-By such an unfolding of valour, such heroic display. यस्य त्वमप्रधृष्यः उच्चैः प्रभवः-Whose source i. e. father (प्रभवः) you are, unassailable (अप्रधृष्यः) and lofty (उच्चैः--उन्नतः). The कंचुकिन् means 'with you as his father, it is no wonder that he has displayed such heroism. What else is to be expected?' अपां दग्धुः वह्नेः ऊरुजन्मा--Like the thigh-born sage Aurva who is the generator of the subterranean fire that consumes the oceanic waters. The legend about the sage और्व is as follows:—The कार्तवीर्यs or the sons of कृतवीर्य destroyed all the descen dants of भृगु, for the purpose of appropriating their rich treasures, and they even went to the length of killing children in the womb of their mothers. One of the women concealed her embryo in her thigh, and the son who was thus born came therefore to be called और्व (Thigh-born). To have his revenge, he produced a fire-flame which blinded all the कार्तवीर्यs and proved a great menace to the whole world. He was therefore, induced to cast the flame into the ocean, where it lies hidden with the face of a mare (hence called वडवानल). It is believed to be responsible for keeping the ocean within its fixed limits, the additional annual supply of water being consumed by this fire. V. 17. 1. उररीकृत्य– Including (the brother-in-law of यज्ञसेन, the same as मौर्यसचिव referred to in Act I.). V. 17. 11. मम वचनेन... व्येति–' Entreat her on my behalf that I should not be forced to fail in keeping my promise.' The Queen had given her word of honour to मालविका, before she was asked to fulfil the longing of Aśoka. The time has now come when she must gratify मालविकाs desire of uniting her in marriage with the king. And in that, no objection should be raised on the score of her low birth because it has been amply proved now that मालविका is a Princess. इरावती therefore is to be requested not to oppose the queen in fulfilling her promise given to मालविका–viz. अभिलाषपूरयितृकं प्रसादं ते दास्यामि ।. V. 17. 17. अविभक्तपरितोषाणां– whose joy is undivided i. e. equal to your joy. रत्नमंजूषा संवृत्ता–She means that she has received so many ornaments as presents from the ladies for having told them the glad news, that she has become a veritable casket or box of jewels. V. 17. 22. सदृशं...मिति इरावती means that was highly worthy of the Queen to have given such a promise before; she is all powerful, being the chief Queen; and now, therefore, it should not be retracted. Note that she first gets a formal consent of इरावती before proceeding to celebrate the union of the two lovers. Mr. Pandit observes, 'Irāvatī's message is not altogether cordial. She is a little bitter as shown by प्रभवन्त्या (which is equivalent to : 'what is the use of consulting me ? You are so powerful that you will do what you wish') and प्रथमसंकाल्पितं (which means : 'what is the use of asking me now ? You have already arranged it'.) V. 17. 26. प्रथमसंभावितां-Already destined before. V. 11. 30. प्रियनिवेदनानुरूपं पारितोषिकं-A reward highly befitting the good news regarding वसुमित्र's victory. No other prize would be so fitting as this मालविका. V.17. 3?. जोषमास्ते-sits silent (जोषं). V. 17. 33. किं...पुत्रः-The Queen knew full well that the king will never refuse such a reward. Jokingly, therefore, she asks him this question. अवधीरयति-Despises, ignores. V. 17. 36. लोकव्यवहारः-a common custom of the world. V. 17. 40. कृतदेवीशब्दां-who has been honoured by the title of Queen. He would not like her to be treated as an ordinary wife, but on equal footing with the Queen धारिणी not only by reason of his marriage with her but by her high birth as well. Kings possibly had two classes of wives ; one class recruited from lower grades of society, inferior to the king in rank and nobility of birth, while the other class was recruited from royal families.

V. 18. आकरसमुत्पन्ना–Sprung from a mine (आकरः). असंस्कृता–unpolished. जातरूपं–gold. परिव्राजिका means that मालविका though born in a royal family must first be dubbed a queen before she is married to the king. मालविका represents a jewel while the king is the gold. V. 18. 4. कौशेयपत्रोर्ण–A silken veil. ' धारिणी means that in the joy of the news she forgot to dress मालविका as a princess, to honour her with a महावस्त्र as a princess ought to be. V. 18. 9. त्वच्छास...वयम्–The king shows as if he is reluctantly accepting मालविका, simply because such are his Queen's orders. V. 18. 10. हन्त–A particle expressive of joy. She is delighted that the ambition so long cherished has been fulfilled, and her attempts have borne fruit. V. 19. 12. धारिणी looks up towards the servants indicating to them that they should now greet their new queen with a customary salutation. V. 19. 14. When the formal greeting is offered to मालविका, धारिणी looks at परिव्राजिका to see what view she takes of her action.

V. 19. प्रातिपक्षणोपि–Even by creating a rival for themselves. She means, in their deep love for their husbands, they are prepared for any sacrifice ; even at the risk of having a rival for them, they would willingly consent to a marriage of their husband to another woman, simply out of consideration for the pleasure and happiness of their lord. The case of the big rivers which carry along with them many smaller rivers illustrates the point very well. समुद्रगा–समुद्रं गच्छति सा–A river. V. 19. 6. प्रसादमात्रेण–Only reconciliation and pardon. इरावती means that the provocation given by her should now be forgotten by the king since he has secured what he desired most, and that he should at least show her a favourable disposition devoid of any ill-feeling, although all expectation of love is at an end now. V. 19 8. अवश्यं...ज्ञास्यति–He will certainly see his way (ज्ञास्यति) to conform to her request. The reading अनुज्ञास्यति would mean ' will grant her request. ' V. I9. 12. चरितार्थम्–कृतार्थ–चरितः अर्थः यस्य सः–Who has accomplished his purpose; Cf. –वत्से, चरितार्थासि । शा० VII. सभाजयितुं– To pay my respects Cf. स्नेहात् सभाजयितुमेत्य दिनान्यमूनि । नीत्वोत्सवेन जनकोऽद्य गतो विदेहान् ॥ उत्तर० I.; also ऋषयो देवं सभाजयितुमागताः । शा० V. सभाजनाक्षराणि–Complementary words. He means that परिव्राजिका need not personally go to congratulate him; her compliments will be conveyed to माधवसेन by the king in his own letters. भरतवाक्यम्–The verse in a drama, a sort of benediction, said to be in honour of भरत, the founder of the dramatic science. The remark तथापीदमस्तु भरतवाक्यम् generally occurs at the end of every play.

V. 20. त्वं...हेतोः–The king means, ' Angry as you are, you should always be disposed to favour me by reconciliation. In the interest of your rival, this is what I beg of you.' The request looks raher strange. The king would not like to impose any restrictions on himself in matters of love; his wife, however, should have a conciliating attitude always, though there might be fits of anger and jealousy. She should always look with a favourable eye on his amorous activities in which he would have no restraint! ईतिविगमप्रभृति आशास्यं-A blessing such as the removal of national calamities (ईतिs); they are, excessive rain, drought, locusts, rats' birds and foreign raids. गोप्तरि अग्निमित्रे न खलु न संपत्स्यते-So long as king अग्निमित्र is their protector, these blessings will surely be secured for the subjeets.

This भरतवाक्य should really have been pronounced by an actor as an actor and not as king अग्निमित्र. Here, however, the king speaks it. According to the commentator काटयवेम only the last two lines of the verse constitutes the भरतवाक्य. Cf. इतः परं (i. e. after the first two lines) भरतवाक्यम् ।...सत्यत्र नाटकान्ते भरतेन सर्वकालसाधारण्येनाशंसावचने कर्तव्ये अत्र प्रजानां आशास्यसिद्धिं प्रति गोप्तुरग्निमित्रस्य कथनं तत्कालराजोपलक्षणामिति मन्तव्यम् ॥

APPENDIX A.

श्लोकसूची.

APPENDIX B—METRICAL TABLE

Number of Syllables	Name of the Metre	Where employed	Total	Measure.
8	अनुष्टुप्	I. 10, 14, 15, 19 ; II. 7, 9 ; IV. 4, 6, 12, 14; V. 9, 11, 12, 13, 15, 16, 18.	17	पञ्चमं लघु सर्वत्र सप्तमं द्विचतुर्थयोः । गुरु षष्ठं च पादानां चतुर्णां स्यादनुष्टुभि ॥
11	इन्द्रवज्रा	V. 17.	1	स्यादिन्द्रवज्रा यदि तौ जगौ गः ।
”	उपजाति	I. 2, 16, 17 ; III. 10; IV. 8; V. 14.	6	स्यादिन्द्रवज्रा यदि तौ जगौ गः । उपेन्द्रवज्रा प्रथमे लघौ सा । } इत्यनयोरुपजातिः ।
”	शालिनी	III. 14, 21 ; V. 8.	3	मात्तौ गौ चेच्छालिनी वेदलोकैः ।
12	द्रुतविलम्बित	III. 6; IV. 13; V. 7.	3	द्रुतविलम्बितमाह नभौ भरौ ।
”	वंशस्थ	III. 15.	1	जतौ तु वंशस्थमुदीरितं जरौ ।
13	प्रहर्षिणी	I. 21.	1	म्नौ ज्रौ गस्त्रिदशयतिः प्रहर्षिणीयम् ।
”	रुचिरा	IV. 16.	1	जभौ सजौ गिति रुचिरा चतुर्ग्रहैः ।
14	वसन्ततिलका	I. 12 ; IV. 9 ; V. 3, 10, 20.	5	उक्ता वसन्ततिलका तभजा जगौ गः ।
15	मालिनी	II. 5 ; III. 12	2	ननमयययुतेयं मालिनी भोगिलोकैः ।

17	पृथ्वी	III. 17.	1	जसौ जसयला वसुग्रहयतिश्च पृथ्वी गुरुः ।
”	मन्दाक्रान्ता	II. 6, 8 ; III. 4 ; IV. 1.	4	मन्दाक्रान्ताम्बुधिरसनगैर्मो भनौ तौ गयुग्मम् ।
”	शिखरिणी	III. 1.	1	रसै रुद्रैश्छिन्ना यमनसभला गः शिखरिणी ।
”	हरिणी	IV. 11 ; V. 1, 2.	3	नसमरसला गः षड्वेदैर्हयैर्हरिणी मता ।
19	शार्दूलविक्रीडित	I. 4 ; II. 3 , III. 5 ; IV. 15.	4	सुर्याश्वैर्यदि मः सजौ सततगाः शार्दूलविक्रीडितम् ।
21	स्रग्धरा	I. 1 ; II. 12.	2	म्रभ्नैर्यानां त्रयेण त्रिमुनियतियुता स्रग्धरा कीर्तितेयम् ।
10/11	वैतालीय (वियोगिनी)	III. 2.	1	विषमे ससजा गुरुः समे सभरा लोऽथ गुरुर्वियोगिनी ।
11/12	अपरवक्त्र	III. 20.	1	अयुजि ननरला गुरुः समे तदपरवक्त्रमिदं नजौ जरौ ।
”	औपच्छन्दसिक	III. 3, 11.	2	पर्यन्ते यौ तथैव (वैतालीये इव) शेषमौपच्छन्दसिकं सुधीभिरुक्तम् ।
12/13	पुष्पिताग्रा	I. 11.	1	अयुजि नयुगरेफतो यकारो युजि तु नजौ जरगाश्च पुष्पिताग्रा।
	आर्या	I. 3, 5, 6, 7, 8, 9, 13, 18, 20, 22 ; II. 1, 2, 10, 11, 13, 14 ; III. 7, 8, 9 ; 13, 16, 18, 19, 22, 23 ; IV. 2, 3, 5, 7, 10, 17 ; V. 4, 5, 6, 19.	35	यस्याः प्रथमे पादे द्वादश मात्रास्तथा तृतीयेऽपि । अष्टादश द्वितीये चतुर्थके पञ्चदश सार्या ॥